RELENTLESS

A RACE THROUGH TIME

Patsy McGonagle

WITH CHRIS MCNULTY

HEROBOOKS

HEROBOOKS

Published by Hero Books
1 Woodville Green
Lucan, Co. Dublin
Ireland
www.herobooks.ie
Hero Books is an imprint of Umbrella Publishing

First published 2019

A CIP record for this book is available from the British Library

ISBN 9781910827079

Cover Design and formatting: Jessica Maile

Ebook formatting: www.ebooklaunch.com

Cover photograph: Donna El Assaad.
Inside photographs: Kate Slevin Photography and the McGonagle family collection

For Rosaleen and my family who stayed the pace
and jumped every hurdle with me.

Acknowledgements

'HAVE I REALLY got a story do you think, Chris?'

This is an early recollection of a conversation on a quiet Saturday, as I met Chris McNulty at Letterkenny IT to discuss a book.

'Ah sir, every man has a story,' came the reply. There and then, as we walked through the IT, this book began.

I was hard work and, I've got to say, Chris was patient with me. He captured my thoughts, and expressed them so well. My good friend, Pierce O'Callaghan and my family also pushed me on each occasion when my focus waned.

We were so fortunate that Liam Hayes came in behind the project, an absolute gentleman from Hero Books; our publisher, adviser, our editor who was a delight to work with and so encouraging. I will be forever grateful that Liam, like Chris, saw that I had a story worth telling.

Pierce pretty much insulted, praised and tortured me for 18 months to get me over the line.

Thank you, lads.

On this journey, my thoughts go back to the lawn at St Columb's College on Bishop Street in Derry and to a teacher, Cathal Logue who provided me with the opportunity to run – and I ran from that day, and continued running for 55 years. I will always be grateful for that first chance to run.

In acknowledging people, my wife Rosaleen tops the list, simply for putting up with me. Both of us set out in life together in our teens - not an easy task as I wasn't your normal settled family man. I was someone driven by dreams that I was determined to achieve.

I am so proud of my children, my sons, Brendan, Conor and Niall, and the two girls, Aine and Aoife. I have so much love for my grandchildren, Maebh,

Brenus, Caitlin, Conor, Aibhe, Michael, Scarlett, Luke, Danann, Rosie and the list wouldn't be complete without Finn, my youngest grandchild.

To my extended family, who have solidly supported me, I'm sure you wondered at times but never, ever admitted it. Like me, I'm sure you had no doubts. I say that in jest.

An added 'family' for me was Finn Valley AC.

Many thousands came, went or stayed. There were always going to be stand-out people who through their actions in many instances impacted with great dedication and loyalty.

I think of great people like Neil Martin, Peader McGranaghan, Kieran Carlin, Patsy McGinley, Noreen Bonner, Paul and Susan Doherty, Patsy and Bridgeen Doherty, Mark Connolly, Dermot McGranaghan, Sean Carlin, Michael McGranaghan, Bernie Alcorn, Ted McGarrigle, Francie Irwin and my son, Conor with whom I spent endless late nights planning and ultimately delivering the Finn Valley Centre.

I had a special bond with the army officer cadre regular and FCA that I gained so much from. I made many friends at LYIT and in the world of Gaelic Games, my county football managers, PJ McGowan and Brian McEniff were a privilege to work with

On my retirement as Irish team manager, many athletes and management sent me good wishes – I really appreciated your kind words. You all joined me on a journey that had mighty days and some days not so good, but I was so blessed to be in your space and appreciate your ambitions and attitude on behalf of Ireland.

Important moments were awards of recognition, important not just for me, but the profile of the sport. The Freedom of Donegal, the Rehab Donegal Person of the Year and Donegal Person of the Year are among the many.

Those groups, like me, are proud to be from Donegal.

I began in the media world, blasting out the athletics story thanks to the late Sean Curran and Charlie Collins. I feel you did this sport of mine a great service giving me a platform to tell the story.

My mentor, the great Olympian, Maeve Kyle, gave me such encouragement along the way,

And, finally, my parents, Patsy, an army officer, and Kathleen, the local chemist, I hope you would be pleased that I managed and impacted as well as I did - and how I will continue in the years that I may still have left to run this race.

I'll be forever grateful to you.

Patsy McGonagle,
May 2019

✦ ✦ ✦ ✦

THE DAY AFTER PATSY McGonagle announced that he had stepped down as the Irish Athletics team manager, I received a rather to-the-point message from Pierce O'Callaghan.

"Have u any interest in writing Patsy's memoirs/story?"

That was Saturday, October 27, 2017, just 24 hours after Patsy brought the curtain down on a 25-year spell as Irish manager that spanned four Olympic Games.

After considering the question for about 30 seconds, I rang Pierce. It was my first time to speak with him, and I have been in almost daily contact with Pierce since.

Pierce's value to me and Patsy in writing this book should not be underestimated. For long periods, he was a driving force. There are times when I feel as if Pierce should have a by-line on the book, such was his input.

Patsy and I have had a strong relationship going back to my early days as a sports writer with the *Finn Valley Voice*. It never mattered whether Patsy was in Ballybofey or Beijing, Stranorlar or Sydney, he made time to give a local angle to an international story. Patsy's recall, his detail and his honesty were crucial to the success of this book.

To say that it was an honour to work with Patsy on his life story would be an understatement. The journey hasn't always been easy, but it has been enjoyable every step of the way.

The McGonagle family, especially Rosaleen, opened their door and allowed me through the keyhole and into their lives. The endless supplies of tea, soup and scones certainly helped the productivity.

There were immense contributions from others in recalling Patsy's life and times. To Rosaleen McGonagle and Aoife Mailey, who also read and proofed some of the early drafts, I am forever grateful.

The time given by former Irish athletes, Sonia O'Sullivan, Rob Heffernan, David Gillick, Jamie Costin, Breda Dennehy and David Matthews gave a real feel of what Patsy was like on the international stage.

At Finn Valley, Catriona McGranaghan and Kay Byrne provided a cracking insight to their magical journey through the years under Patsy's watch.

My colleague and good friend Alan Foley gave a much-needed critical overview at times. Without the encouragement and confidence of my editor at *Donegal Daily/Donegal Sport Hub*, Stephen Maguire it would not have been possible to do this. My thanks, too, to all of my colleagues for their unwavering support. Donna El Assaad's cover photo and the images inside – obtained from Inpho and the McGonagle family collection – help to illustrate the man and the story.

Liam Hayes was no mean sportsman himself and his professionalism, advice and, most of all, his faith in this project were absolutely key, as was the input from his team at Hero Books.

The staff of the Donegal Central Library in Letterkenny and their research facilities were priceless throughout all phases of the writing.

My mother, Anne supported – and funded! – my love of sport from a young age. Growing up in St Johnston, it wasn't easy to follow the various teams and sportspeople, but she made sure I managed to do just that.

My girlfriend, Alice was a constant source of encouragement from the moment I first opened a notebook for this book. At times when the going got tough or the inspiration was lacking, her words of wisdom kept the flame burning. Maybe now you might get the kitchen table back!

Chris McNulty,
May 2019

Foreword

By Sebastian Coe

President of World Athletics IAAF
Chairman of London 2012 Olympic Games
Two-time Olympic 1500m Champion

THERE COMES A stage in everyone's life when you look back at key decisions and people, moments which although seemed trivial at the time, ultimately shaped the next 50 years of your life.

For me, that moment was when I joined my local athletics club, Hallamshire Harriers at the ripe old age of 12. As a young boy, the club was a haven from the insecurities of life in the 1970s North of England.

With the help of my father and club coaches, I learned many crucial life lessons in the club, including how to set targets, how good it felt to be a scoring member of my local cross-country team, and the fun and camaraderie we always enjoyed at club training.

As I read the story and adventures of Patsy McGonagle's life and service to our sport, I am transported back to my own days in my club and wonder how different my life would have been but for people like Patsy in the North of England.

I also realise that there are not too many people like Patsy McGonagle on the planet.

They say the best committee is a committee of one, and while Patsy has always led from the front, he has walked the delicate tightrope to bring so many in his local community of Ballybofey and Stranorlar along with him.

Undoubtedly, he is a force of nature, a one-man driving movement of energy and passion who combines the rare skills of leadership, integrity and empathy, and who presents a vision and moves all hurdles in his way until he achieves that dream.

The story of his local club, Finn Valley Athletics Club, the birth of which coincided with my own running career in the 1970s, has long been an interest of mine.

Developing as it has, from small rural beginnings of a field for athletes to run around in training, to the world-class track, clubhouse, indoor facilities and swimming pool, is a great testament to the vision and hard work of Patsy and the many volunteers within Finn Valley without whom athletics could not exist.

The roll of honour of the club says it all about how to bring success to a community, and the legacy of all those athletes who passed through Patsy's hands will sustain the sport in Donegal and afar in the years to come.

Patsy's achievements and awards are far too numerous to list in this foreword, but what is clear is even though he managed the Irish team at four Olympic Games and six IAAF World Championships, I can see his heart and mind were never too far from Finn Valley Athletics Club back in Donegal.

I was aware that the IAAF World Championships in London in 2017 marked the final chapter in the 68-cap management career for Patsy and I will always treasure the laughs we shared in the London Olympic Stadium, as we invariably did whenever we met.

Of course, it helped greatly that he came from good stock - a driven ambitious mother in Lena and an Olympian father, Patrick who represented Ireland in football at the 1948 Olympic Games in London.

He was also most fortunate in choosing a strong life partner in Rosaleen to support him so staunchly in the background, and his five children, Brendan, Niall, Conor, Aoife and Áine all played a central role in Patsy's career.

I will always have fond memories of meeting Patsy, always armed with a smile and the look of a man on a mission during the major championships he attended with the Irish team under his wing.

His unwavering passion for athletics is a source of inspiration to everyone who has ever had the pleasure of meeting him and it is very fitting that the track at Finn Valley has been named in his honour.

I wish Patsy the best of luck and success for the next chapters in his life, which I'm sure will not include retirement in any shape or form.

I am sure you will enjoy this book as much as I have

Sebastian Coe
May 2019

Prologue

THERE ARE 112,000 people gasping for breath as Sonia O'Sullivan comes around the bend and goes for gold. Gabriela Szabo, the reigning World champion, is holding on.

But Sonia, the Sonia of old, is battling for dear life.

The night of September 25, 2000, will be regarded as the greatest night in the history of athletics, but we don't realise that as we watch Sonia and wait for Sonia all at once.

We are consumed in the moment and lost in the Sydney night.

It is one of the great Olympic nights and nobody inside Stadium Australia can take their eyes off the epic battle on the track. People in those days didn't view history unfolding through the lens of a mobile phone.

With 300 metres to go in the women's 5,000 metres final, Sonia goes for it. Four years earlier, she had a disaster in Atlanta. Sonia didn't finish the 5,000 metres final and failed to qualify from the heats of the 1500 metres.

But now Sonia is back. Her name has been dishonoured in the Australian media and we wondered how it would all impact on her.

It is very clear that Sonia is in the zone.

She's going to win this.

I GREW UP in rural Donegal. My dream was to coach an athlete who would get to the Olympic Games and win a gold medal.

Here I am, now, on this night of nights, at the finish line in Sydney, thinking it is going to happen. I'm not coaching, but I'm managing and being associated with this sensation of Irish athletics.

Sonia has a couple of goes, but she just can't get up to Szabo.

I know all about the Romanian. In my early days as Irish team manager, Szabo won gold in the 3,000 metres at the 1994 World Junior Championships in Lisbon. I was never a man for looking at splits or lap times. People shout all this information at various intervals, but I just watch the person, see where that person is and what the whole landscape looks like at a particular moment in time.

Two Ethiopians, Gete Wami and Ayelech Worku are arguing amongst themselves as the race hots up. Their plan was to have the pace at such a height that Sonia would get lost.

Faster, faster, faster!

WAMI IS ON the trail of glory.

Worku fancies her own chances.

They are flat out by now but, soon, the battle for gold is down to two... it's Sonia versus Szabo. It's a frenetic fight to the finish.

Szabo goes first.

Sonia responds and, as they're heading for home... neck and neck.

'GO ON... SONIA!'

SONIA'S ON HER shoulder, but Szabo finds a little something... again.

I'm waiting for Sonia to burst past Szabo, but... it doesn't happen. Sonia is out of time... out of track. Szabo has nicked it.

Twenty-three hundredths of a second.

One stride.

So close.

So far.

Fuck...

FUCK IT.

MY FIRST MEETING with Sonia O'Sullivan was before the 1994 European Cup, the first of 17 times I managed Ireland at the European Cup.

The fact Sonia was even turning out for this was a big deal. She was big business and not all athletes treated the European Cup too seriously. This one was in Dublin, which helped, but it was still a big thing to have Sonia with us.

Before the event started, I piled all the athletes into a tiny little room in the Skylon Hotel on the north side of the city, declining the option of a big room for a reason: I wanted proximity.

I didn't want distance between me and the team.

I had to get them psyched.

I asked Fr Liam Kelleher from Cork to say a Mass in the middle of the 'meeting', but I got him to shunt the Mass in a direction of a team talk. At the end of it all, I was at the 'altar' – a table, with some sort of Holy-looking cloth around it – beside Fr Liam and we got the team so up for it, they were ready to burst out the door from Mass.

Sonia was one of the last to arrive that day.

The seats were all taken and you could see her train of thought.

Where am I going to sit?

I had never met Sonia O'Sullivan before.

I looked over at the ground beside the wall.

'There you are... over there.'

Part of me was worried that she was such a big star that she'd kick up a fuss but, no, Sonia hunched down on the ground and didn't bat an eyelid.

Sonia was a gem.

She was part of a very good European Cross-Country team that I had in Edinburgh in 2003. She won silver with Catherina McKiernan, Rosemary Ryan and Anne Keenan-Buckley. Of all the athletes I ever managed, Sonia was the best, without question.

I managed John Treacy at the World Cross-Country Championships in Mallusk, but he was coming near the end of his career at that stage. I was in Limerick when Treacy won the World Cross-Country title in 1979, at the Greenpark Racecourse. I was a coach with the Northern Ireland team that year. It was an absolute privilege to be there, amongst 30,000 people, in awe, witnessing an Irishman win the race.

They had to throw an army blanket around John after the race in the jockeys' weighing room. It was pre-African dominance in distance running, but John, a tough, hardy boy from west Waterford was the best in the world at the time.

I remembered seeing him as a 15 year-old running for Munster in an under-16 race on the banks of the Mourne river in Strabane, on a day when Moira O'Boyle from Glenties won the girls race. Maeve Kyle was in charge of the Northern Irish women's team and it was a time when Finn Valley were dominant, so she brought me along.

That was the start of a long association and friendship with Maeve. She was recognised as a world-class coach and was a world-class sportsperson herself. A special lady, she was at three Olympic Games as an athlete and one as a coach.

But '79 in Limerick was my first time involved at an International Cross-Country Championships. I loved that event. I was back to watch Northern Ireland again in 1980 at Longchamp Racecourse. I took a group from the Regional Technical College in Letterkenny, where I was working, to Paris on what I had to call 'an educational tour'. We went to an art gallery one afternoon to justify the tag.

The World Cross was a special event for me. The heart beat a little faster to see five of our athletes from Finn Valley – Sinead McGranaghan, the Harron sisters, Camilla, Noelle and Rosemary, and Kay McGowan – compete in the event during the 1980s.

Any Cross-Country Championship is brilliant to manage. There is the team element to begin with, and you have a group of athletes who are just so excited to be there. The whole mix is different from Track and Field. I loved that team aspect of it.

The 2002 World Cross was in Leopardstown and the Irish people turned out in their thousands. It was just brilliant. We needed to come in mentally built and I developed that environment for six months. There was no point turning up one day and going, 'We're there next week'.

It had to be the end of the world.

The team won a bronze, with Sonia seventh. Anne Keenan-Buckley was tenth and Rosemary Ryan and Maria McCambridge also scored. Medalling at home felt a little bit extra special.

SONIA WAS MAGIC, but the 1996 Olympic Games in Atlanta was a nadir for her. Ireland expected gold.

Sonia expected gold.

She came through the heats and the semi-final, but with two laps to go in the women's 5,000 metres final, Sonia dropped out of the race. There was a question over where Sonia would go after '96. The country adored Sonia and nobody wanted Atlanta to have been the end.

Sonia studied at Villanova in the late 1980s and early 90s and developed shin splints, which kept her out for a year. She struggled, but she came out the other side and showed incredible resilience to do that. If a silver medal at the World Indoors in 1997 hinted that Sonia would be back, Marrakesh in western Morocco and the World Cross-Country Championships in 1998 was the confirmation.

She went to Marrakesh with the intention of running in one race. She got dropped off at the wrong hotel, lost her bag and her phone, but went to stay with Tina Ryan from Nike. Sonia was annoyed that she might be scratched from the second race, but she handled it so, so well.

It was the first year that there was an eight kilometres race for the women and the first year there were two different races.

Sonia went for a run around the course the night before the race and was prepared for the gap in the fence the participants had to go through to get to the finish line.

It was set up for a sprint finish. Sonia had that knowledge from the previous night and Paula Radcliffe admitted afterwards that she was just going to stop at the fence and not go through the gap. Radcliffe's hesitation and Sonia's knowledge meant that there was only going to be one winner.

That evening run made it for Sonia. She came out and nailed the second race too.

The heat was wicked because the race was at midday, but Sonia just took Marrakesh in her stride. Her confidence was back, and, with it, the stardust also returned. She was just awesome at that time, a true icon.

Sonia, the oldest runner in the race, won silver in the Olympics in Sydney, but there was a certain disappointment. She ran a new personal best time, and her 14 minutes and 41.02 seconds was a new national record too.

There was a feeling around the midway point that the race was gone from her. She drifted back to 12th and the fear was that she wouldn't claw it back. But Sonia did.

Szabo put her two arms out and got over the line for her moment. Sonia looked to the Sydney sky as we waited for the reaction. She looked over and smiled.

Once I saw the satisfaction written on Sonia's face, my mind, scrambled as she crossed the line, changed. She got her medal, becoming the first Irish woman to medal in athletics at the Olympics, and did a lap of honour just as Cathy Freeman, Australia's heroine and by now Sonia's arch nemesis, was being paraded as the 400 metres champion.

Sonia darted down the home straight, draped in the Irish Tricolour and accepting the adulation of the Irish supporters. Her father, John was anxious to get to her. Nic Bideau, her coach and partner, and their daughter, Ciara came over. So too Fr Liam Kelleher, who saw her briefly.

They met under a street light, with Sonia in the Olympic zone and they in a spectator area. The smiles from each side of the fence told the story. We had to get Sonia out of there.

There was a demand for a press conference, but we didn't do one. We only got out of the place after midnight. Sonia had the 10,000 metres to do as well, and our minds quickly turned to that. She went away into the night with an Olympic silver medal around her neck and a furry wombat under her arm.

THERE I WAS, all the way from the sticks in Donegal, at the finish line in a packed Olympic Stadium, watching it all unfold.

The Olympic Games fulfilled me.

I came out of nothing, out of an environment I helped create in Donegal, and I was there because of myself.

I had journeyed from zero to the Olympic Games.

I piled all the athletes into a tiny little room in the Skylon Hotel in Dublin before the 1994 European Cup, declining the option of a big room for a reason: I wanted proximity to the athletes.

IN A ROOM of the Samyoung Hotel in Seoul, the beads of sweat began to drip.

The 1992 World Junior Championships offered me a first taste of managing an Irish team. I had left Dublin with no instruction, no advice. And no cheque book.

When you arrive at a Championship, it's customary to settle the visiting team's account with the local organising committee. However, nobody had given me any indication of this, never mind a few bob, before we flew to Korea.

I joined a queue, listening away to what was going on at the various tables at the top of the room.

'You owe us x thousands.'

'You owe us y thousands.'

The administrator advised the sum owed and, one-by-one, each delegation from the different countries settled their bills.

The Ethiopians went up. Senegal were there.

The Japanese boys slid up and moved away again.

The United States, all bravado as usual, got the business done.

The queue was getting shorter and my mind was in overdrive. I wasn't long off the plane after a 13-hour flight, via London.

They're going to throw us out of this Championship.

It was a scary thought. I genuinely hadn't a clue what to expect.

Next up... Ireland.

'You owe us...' But my mind was doing loops and I didn't actually hear the figure that was announced. I began to tell the young lady behind the table a long story about it being my first Championship, but I did not get very far with my sobbing.

'Ireland...

'Typical!'

But her face had brightened, and then broke into a smile. I knew then we'd be okay. I was excited about Seoul and took my appointment as team manager in my stride. Of course, I was excited. I was privileged. And I was honoured.

I also had an unbelievable belief in what I was doing and in my approach to everything. I had managed teams abroad with Finn Valley during the 1980s and was with Northern Ireland consistently as a coach for Cross-Country Championships. Belief was something I never lacked.

Belief in myself and belief in my teams.

In 1978, I coached Northern Ireland for a trip to Wales and the team included Margaret Gallen and Kay McGowan from Finn Valley. It was the first time for Northern Ireland to field a senior ladies squad.

The papers nailed my thoughts.

"The major significance of this is that Patsy McGonagle believes that his team can get in behind England in the intermediate race, with the senior ladies to beat Wales," one newspaper reported boldly.

I CARRIED THAT unwavering confidence all through my career.

In 1991, I was elected to the management committee of Bord Lúthchleas na hÉireann (BLE), the precursor to Athletics Ireland, and at one of the first meetings I attended the job of team manager for Seoul came up.

'Aww sure that's me.'

'I'll manage that.'

'I can do that.'

'I want to be there.'

People put themselves forward there and then. I also put my hand up, without talking to anyone.

'Aye, I want to go,' I announced.

Sean Naughton was a highly regarded coach from Nenagh and he also went forward. Sean's daughter, Patricia was on the team as a hurdler. He must have been seriously disappointed, but he didn't show it. He was very respectful. I became very friendly with him years later and had him in the coaching team for the 2000 Olympics.

I ALWAYS EMBRACED changing technology, which was a big strength over the years. But I was left to curse technology in Seoul. Deirdre Gallagher from Ballina was with us for the 5,000 metres and she took 14 seconds off her personal best in Seoul.

I faxed the result through to the BLE offices in Dublin and they passed it on to the media in Ireland.

The *Irish Independent* led with the news.

"Ballina athlete Deirdre Gallagher made history in becoming the first Irish athlete to win a medal at the World Junior Athletics Championships in Seoul, collecting a bronze in the 5,000m walk."

There was one problem. Deirdre, in fact, hadn't won a bronze medal. The first page of the fax to Dublin got lost and Deirdre was listed third on the second page. Lo and behold, everyone in Ireland thought she had won the bronze.

Her father, Danny who hailed from Glenties, was driving home from the All-Ireland football final – which Donegal had won, famously beating Dublin – when he heard the news on RTE Radio. The poor man nearly crashed the car.

BLE had to issue a clarification.

Again, the *Independent* delivered the news.

"BLE have announced that Deirdre Gallagher of Ballina has not in fact won a medal in the Junior World Athletics Championships in Seoul. It was announced that she had finished third in the 5,000m walk, but the information from South Korea has now proved to be incorrect. BLE have apologised for any embarrassment caused."

I didn't have a press accreditation in Seoul, so even getting the results proved a difficult assignment. I ended up, through a very helpful Korean official, befriending an Irish Columban priest, Fr Kennedy. He aided me in getting the essential information I needed.

I knew of the influence of the Columban priests through news back home of Fr PJ McGlinchey, a Letterkenny man who was based on Jeju Island, an island in the Korea Strait, for over 60 years and whose work will be remembered for generations.

Jeju's people, when he arrived in 1952, were among the poorest in their land. Fr McGlinchey – a brother of the Letterkenny-based Senator, Bernard McGlinchey – set up a textile factory, helped form a credit union and aided in improving the farming practices and yields on the island.

The food in Seoul was a challenge. Everything was chicken or beef. But my abiding memory, even now, was the evening when we went to a Korean restaurant with the priest.

We were served a bowl of stuff, with meat in it that the party of Irish people just convinced themselves wasn't a dog. The waiter came out and cracked a raw egg into a bowl.

You wouldn't have fed it to the dogs.

'Aye, that's gorgeous.'

We couldn't have our hosts disappointed.

SEOUL WAS THE first time I was in a city where the problem with traffic was so prevalent. The place was bumper-to-bumper 24/7.

Language was also a problem at times. We had a small team at those Championships with just four athletes – Deirdre, Antoine Burke, David Matthews and David Cullinan. We went exploring in Seoul one evening for a look around and we hit trouble when it was time to go home.

I went to get a taxi.

'The Hotel Samyoung, sir'

Your man looked at me as if I had 10 heads. The next taxi man was the same. And the next! Eventually, a US military police officer spotted that a bunch of Irish athletes were in a bit of a jam. At the same time, I learned that there were thousands of US soldiers stationed in South Korea, a knock-on from the Korean War.

'Hey Paddy, where d'yall need to go?'

He didn't have a clue either, but he radioed his base.

'Ah...the Samyoung Hotel'.

I'm still baffled by the Koreans on that one.

Trying to explain the name wasn't helped by our descriptions, of course. 'It's a golden kind of place,' we repeatedly pleaded to the deaf ears on the taxi rank, but eventually we got back to base.

Back with a valuable lesson banked. From that day on, we carried a card from the hotel so we could just show the driver.

David Matthews had arrived late into Seoul, getting in just 48 hours before his heat. David was fancied to get to the final in the 800 metres, but he was fourth in his heat, despite being knocked on the way by a Spanish athlete, José Manuel Cerezo.

It was hard for the athletes to acclimatise and the 13-hour flight took a toll. Antoine Burke from Limerick reached the high jump final and set a new Irish senior record of 2.13 metres. He just failed to clear 2.16 metres.

SEOUL OFFERED ME a first connection to the Chinese athletes who would become world leaders in the sport. They were the same athletes who would become a big part of Sonia O'Sullvian's story in years to come.

'Ma's Army', in reference to the coach, Ma Junren, who looked after 18 athletes in the Liaoning Province, which borders North Korea and the Yellow Sea, was certainly different. The regime banned girls from having long hair. They weren't allowed to wear cosmetics and boyfriends were a no-no.

And then there was the food. Their diet was based on a concoction of caterpillar fungus, soft-cell turtle soup and powdered seahorse.

The Chinese success was unnatural.

Liu Dong won 1,500 metres gold in the World Junior Championships in Seoul and also beat Sonia to gold at the 1993 World Championships in Stuttgart. Zhang Lirong was third in the 3,000 metres in Seoul and edged Sonia to a podium place in the 3,000 a year later. The 10,000 metres gold medallist in Seoul, Wang Junxia took gold four years later in Atlanta on that fateful night when Sonia dropped out in the Olympic 5,000 metres final.

At the 1993 Chinese National Games, the 3,000 metres world record, which had stood for 10 years, was bettered by five Chinese runners. The seven fastest 3,000 metres of all time were set at that one meet.

You couldn't but be suspicious.

Sure enough, in 1997, six of the seven athletes being coached by Ma failed drug tests and were banned from the Sydney Olympics. Within a year, the seventh also failed a blood test. Ma was sacked from his role, but he has denied any wrongdoing ever since.

In February, 2016 a letter emerged, allegedly signed by 10 athletes, claiming that they had been forced to take 'large doses of illegal drugs'.

You never know, Sonia may yet get a gold medal from Stuttgart.

The Chinese used to do training sessions in the days prior to their events, which I thought a strange practice. I felt they were going too hard and assumed they were just inexperienced and didn't know what they were at. The theory with us was that you rested up in the days prior, but the Chinese were hammering it out on the track. It was part of their training that they ran a full marathon every day, at high altitude in Tibet.

Their psychology was all about keeping the mind strong, active and competitive. I took that back to Ireland.

In the early days of my own career, we always rested pre-competition but, after Seoul, my athletes always went for a run. It might have been a subdued run or just a couple of strides, but it helped to calm their minds.

I was learning at speed.

I didn't take everything from the Chinese, mind you. A chain-smoker, Ma was a former solider in the People's Liberation Army and was extremely sore on his athletes. There were allegations that he threw a brick at one runner who had disappointed him. It was known that he had some of them running behind a motorcycle, which they were tied to with a rope.

And they sometimes thought I was harsh with them at Finn Valley…

Others impacted at those Championships in Seoul, and would become familiar later on, too. A certain Gabriela Szabo won silver in the 3,000 metres, and Gete Wami was the silver medallist in the 10,000 metres.

The men's podium in Seoul had the likes of Haile Gebrselassie, Ato Boldon and Darren Campbell, who went on to impact seriously at World Championships and Olympic Games over the next decade and more.

THERE HADN'T BEEN much fuss in Donegal about me going to Seoul with the Irish team but, then again, there were bigger fish to fry in the county in the autumn of 1992.

Donegal were in the All-Ireland football final for the first time. The place went daft for a month and more, lost in the giddiness of All-Ireland mania.

Before I left for Seoul, I went to Dublin with my son, Conor who was a photographer for the *Donegal Democrat*, and who was dispatched to take pictures of Dublin – Donegal's opponents in the final – training at Parnell Park.

I visited Justin Brady, who was heavily involved in the Sean MacCumhaill GAA club in Ballybofey, in hospital the evening before I left for Seoul, conscious of the buzz and excitement building for the All-Ireland.

Late in the night of September 20, 1992, I dialled home to my father, steadily popping 10 Korean Won coins into the phone in the hotel lobby. My father thought he'd lead me on a merry dance for a while.

'What?

'Who is it?

'Hello…'

I was at the other end, screaming by this stage.

'Daddy… who won the fucking match?'

The whole hotel seemed to just stop in its tracks to watch this mad Irishman, firing his rapidly diminishing stack of coins into the phone and shouting like a mad man. Just before the last coin, he told me they'd won it. Donegal had beaten Dublin by 0-18 to 0-14 and were All-Ireland champions for the first time.

I ran up the stairs to tell everyone else.

Nobody so much as batted an eyelid.

When we arrived back in Dublin the following day the signs that greeted us were a nice lesson in how not to get ahead of oneself.

DUBLIN ALL-IRELAND CHAMPIONS 1992.

Dublin were the raging hot favourites and everyone, including themselves, thought it was only a matter of turning up and sending Donegal back home empty handed. They had their merchandise at the ready, their posters prepared. Manus Boyle kicked nine points and Donegal was ready for a few weeks of endless bank holidays.

I smiled, chuckled and headed on the long four hour journey back to Ballybofey, and to whatever the next mission at Finn Valley was.

AFTER SEOUL, I believed that I should manage every team that left the country. I put myself into the position of a leader.

The BLE was a completely voluntary organisation, controlled by a board, which was referred to as the management committee. You were at the whim of the board, but I was retained as manager for the 1994 World Juniors in Portugal.

I was a lot wiser than I was in Seoul and I felt more in control.

Antoine Burke was with me again in Lisbon. I already had a good relationship with him. Antoine finished 19th overall in Seoul and had high hopes coming into Lisbon.

The Estádio da Luz, the home ground of Benfica, is an intimidating venue.

It seemed even more imposing when, one day before the start of the Championships, Antoine picked up a leg injury. We were warming up on the warm-up area in the shadows of the stadium when Antoine went down.

'Fuck!'

Antoine handled it unbelievably well. He was a medal hope and he knew it. He defied his injury scare to go out and win a silver medal, clearing 2.20 metres, just missing gold. An Australian, Jagan Hames, who was later a Commonwealth Games gold medallist, pipped him in the end.

I was back from Lisbon with my first medal as a manager.

I was on a roll.

IT WAS COMMON for me during the 1990s to head off to international meets with certain athletes.

There'd be no coach; just me and whatever athletes were competing. We could be in Slovakia, Latvia, Russia, Slovenia, wherever really. It was all to taste the experience of international competition. Always a great opportunity for Irish athletes.

I was in Japan at the Chiba Ekiden Relay in 1995 with Pauline Curley, Cathy Shum, Teresa Duffy and Elaine Fitzgerald. That was a cracking team, and what an event to go to. Thousands of people lined the streets to watch the race, which is essentially a marathon broken into varying distances for the athletes to run.

The challenges you faced at the big events paled into insignificance with some of the corners you could be in at the more remote athletics outposts. In 1998, I took a team to Moscow for an international meet, which was just a small, one-day event. I got on a plane in Dublin with seven or eight athletes in tow and I was all business, bound for the Olympic Stadium in Moscow. Or, so I thought.

I arrived at the airport in Moscow, but quickly sensed there was something not right.

Nobody knew a thing about this competition we had arrived for. I had the likes of Derval O'Rourke, Paul Brizzel and Antoine Burke with me. We anticipated that someone would meet us at the airport and take us to the stadium.

Instead, we got lost in Moscow.

I piled the whole team into a taxi, but hadn't a clue where I was going. I had a basic mobile phone and managed to make contact with someone in Dublin. We ended up, all of us, in a little athletics office in Moscow – the Olympic committee's headquarters - attempting to find answers from the broken English of the staff.

We left there and checked into a hotel, still none the wiser about this international meet we were in town for. The hotel was knee-deep in prostitutes and not exactly the perfect place for a team of athletes. For some reason, I decided to go back to the airport the following morning, and it was a good thing I did.

I found out that the meeting was actually taking place in Tula, a town 200 kilometres south of Moscow. Eventually, we got shoved into what felt like an old Russian military bus and we were off to Tula. It was the journey from hell on a cement road initially built for army tanks and through what seemed like an endless forest.

Finally, we arrived in Tula and found our competition.

Vyacheslav Voronin, a Russian who was on his way to becoming a World champion, competed in the high jump. Voronin was in 2.35 metres territory. Antoine, doing well, was around the 2.15 metres mark.

So, Antoine jumped and was out quickly.

Though he didn't appear too bothered as he ambled over to me.

'Patsy, would you mind if I get a train to Moscow? I'll meet you in the airport?'.

'Batter away, sir!' I told him.

We had a joke about it later. I used to often tell Antoine that he was probably back in Moscow before the high jump was over.

Tula was an eye-opener. You could see all the Russian medics wearing their long white coats. It was all very different coming from Ireland to see these people operating in their own environment.

The Irish team had been changed late for Russia. Derval was a late addition, taking the place of John Davis, a coach from Kildare who withdrew.

Only when we were in Copenhagen on the way home did we realise that Derval had travelled the whole way to Moscow and half of the way home with a plane ticket in the name of John Davis. She got into Copenhagen, on to Moscow and back to Copenhagen on the ticket.

In the queue in Copenhagen, I started to panic.

This isn't John!

I had to think on my feet. I was good at that, dealing with any and every eventuality. Derval and I ended up at a little Scandinavian Airlines desk and they were probably expecting a sob story. A little earlier, in a long queue at Moscow Airport's departures, I was thinking we'd never get away with it. In truth, I was scared.

We were a bit closer to home in Copenhagen and, for some reason, I told them the truth.

'I can't believe we got her this far!' I volunteered.

We got her another ticket and away we went, Derval and the rest of the team gobsmacked.

BY THE TIME the 1999 World Championships in Seville came around I was, in many ways, doubling as a coach.

I was in the ear and the head of certain athletes. I was aware of creating a final run-in for the athlete. I wasn't just a manager who sat back. I was joint manager with Michael Quinlan for Seville and those Championships were my first major at senior level.

Seville was good for us. Mark Carroll reached the 5,000 metres final, Ciaran McDonagh was in the long jump final, Brendan Reilly got through to the high jump final, and Jeff Cassin – who competed for Finn Valley - was 28th in the 50 kilometres walk.

My abiding memory from Seville was Marion Jones getting injured in the 200 metres semi-final and being carried off on a stretcher. Her husband, the shot put champion CJ Hunter, sprinted from the stands and onto the track as they carried her off.

I saw all of this developing and ran into the stadium. I was in there as they carried Marion in on the stretcher, taking in who was saying and doing what, making some mental notes.

I knew I'd be back on the big stage with Ireland again.

2

An early picture of me (left) with my brother,
Charlie and sister, Susan.

PATRICK McGONAGLE SENIOR, my father, was at the 1948 Olympic Games in London as part of the Irish football squad.

He was one of very few Donegal men playing League of Ireland soccer at the time. He played for Bohemians and an indication of how much they valued him was that they put on a taxi to take him all the way from Dunree Fort – deep in the Inishowen peninsula, where he was stationed in the army – and back for games in Dublin.

I wasn't even a year old when he went to the Olympics in '48. The Olympics was never something that was talked about when I was young. I was aware of the meaning and that he had been in London – but it was never a topic of conversation.

When I was going to boarding school at St Columb's College in Derry, I needed a jersey, so my mother took the Irish badge off of his Olympic top and gave it to me. Imagine! His Irish jersey that he'd worn to the Olympic Games. That's how much regard an Olympic jersey had.

I still have the badge but, unfortunately, not the jersey. I kept his competitor's medal from the Olympics and it's something I treasure deeply.

My father had real standing because of his football career and his job in the army. He joined the army during World War Two and was stationed in The Curragh when he got an order from a Colonel to join Bohemians Football Club.

He was walking along the quays in Dublin one day when a staff car pulled up alongside him. The Colonel stepped out of the car and just told my father, a Second Lieutenant who was on the books of Shelbourne at the time, that he was going to Bohemians.

There was no discussion, argument or debate about it. It was, simply, an order that he had to adhere to.

His league career ended in the early 1950s. Distillery beat Derry City in the cup in 1951 and he retired. Though he still played and was regularly on the Summer Cup circuit around Donegal. It was always a big deal if he was going to play for Ballybofey. If he was coming back for the weekend, having been posted to Mullingar, the Ballybofey boys would have him tortured to play.

We were all over Donegal. In Swilly Park, Raphoe, Killybegs, anywhere there was a tournament of note. Summer Cups were a massive part of the soccer landscape in Donegal.

Killybegs had a very strong team and Kildrum Tigers, who were managed by Bobby Toland, a famous goalkeeper and a legendary figure in Donegal soccer, were another team that was always competitive in those cup competitions.

I never actually watched games; I just ran about like wee fellas do at football matches. My father was always running late so he always drove like mad to get there. Nothing ever started on time, so we were never late.

Married men versus single men matches were all the rage at the time and always drew a crowd. It was at one of these fixtures at Finn Park that my father's football career finally ended.

The town sewer, an actual open sewer, ran alongside one of the touchlines at Finn Park. My father, who was at the end of his tether, was getting a beating by this young fella on the wing, so he did what he had to do. He got your man off balance and nudged him into the sewer.

The match had to be abandoned and that was the end of my father and football. From the Olympic Games in London, playing in the League of Ireland and the Irish League to the threshold of the sewer in Ballybofey. It was some comedown, in fairness.

I WAS BORN in Ballybofey in 1947, the eldest of six children.

Charlie, Mary, Susan, John and Eamon would follow, but I was the first.

Ballybofey was a very simple place in the 1940s.

We lived in a typical Irish thatched cottage, alongside the Donegal railway line, just beside where Jackson's Hotel now stands. When I was six, my parents moved us around the corner, to Donegal Street, where they built a two-storey house on land owned by the Byrne family. The good thing about our new home was there was room to play outside.

We had a 'football pitch' out the back.

We had turf and my father got the lend of a horse and cart the day we moved. He allowed me to sit on top of the turf and I was like the king of the castle waving away at everyone going up Donegal Street. It was only 100 yards away, but it felt like a long procession as I waved off the cart to the people on the street below.

My father was an army officer, stationed in Mullingar, Dunree, Athlone and, finally, Rockhill. My mother, Kathleen or Lena, as she was known to most people, was the chemist in Ballybofey. When she finished her studies in UCD, she got a job filling in as a locum for a Mr Farren, the chemist in Ballybofey who became ill. My mother came for only a short period and stayed with a family in Ballybofey before she took over the shop. She was in Ballybofey for life.

On time off from school, we'd be taken in to fill tablet boxes, polish glass. 'Keep the children busy,' was a mantra she lived by. My mother was like a doctor and a chemist rolled into one. People didn't go to the doctor the way they do now. So, people would drop into her for advice.

She also had an interest in veterinary medicine and would throw out tablets and mixtures to the farmers, too. Over the years, my mother developed a very strong advisory relationship with people in Ballybofey and the surrounding areas.

My mother was well regarded in Ballybofey.

She told it as it was. She had a strong personality and called a spade a spade. She just told customers out straight what the problem was. It wouldn't have been nice sometimes, but it was pure black and white. That's something I've certainly taken from her.

People could come to the door any time looking for medicine and it would never be a bother. She'd put on her dressing-gown and bedroom slippers, leave whoever came for medicine looking after the children and pop down to open the chemist.

She was available 24/7, as the shop was only 200 metres away.

I remember a story of a man walking all the way from Convoy - a village 11 miles away – to Donegal Street to get medicine for a child who was bad with croup who could have died. Many people have related to me their stories of my mother helping them out. Money was scarce, but her local awareness allowed her to develop a strong sense as to who needed the medicine, money or not.

My mother, as always, wiped the sleep from her eyes, shook her head clear and went away down the street to get the man his medicine.

I WAS COMING up the street one day and I knew we had just got a television because I could see a fella putting an aerial up on the house. This was the most exciting thing ever.

My mother put the new TV in the sitting room, but the excitement soon died when she locked the door. We were only allowed in to see whatever she wanted us to watch: *This Is Your Life* with Eamon Andrews, the *Black and White Minstrel Show, Sunday Night at the Palladium* were the regulars.

We did get around the problem at certain times. My mother always worked to nine o'clock on a Saturday night, so we'd climb in the sitting room window, watch some TV and get out before she got back.

MY PARENTS' GENERATION were slow to show any evident emotion and I'm cut from the same cloth.

My sister, Mary was going to join the Poor Clare nuns in the 1970s. The Poor Clare Nuns is a closed order. Basically, you don't get out at all and you never see your people again. Obviously, it was a big deal that Mary was going away. She went to school at the Convent in Buncrana and left to go to the Poor Clare Nuns in England.

The car came to take her away and the abiding memory of that moment is that my father didn't even say goodbye.

I went back in.

'Daddy... are you not going to say goodbye to Mary?'

'You might never see her again.'

'Ah for Heaven's sake,' he replied. 'The Poor Clare Nuns? She'll be home before Christmas'.

She wasn't home before Christmas, but a year later her health broke down and she got out. Mary died in July, 2014. She taught in a public school in Rugby, a town in Warwickshire, after leaving the nuns because of the hardship. The poor woman just wasn't able for it.

MY FATHER WAS a pioneer, a non-drinker, which was unusual for an army man, but my mother took a drink occasionally. There was really no element of drink in our house. There was a drinks cabinet in the house that was only for visitors – army officers, priests, or other people of standing.

Women didn't go to the pub at all in those days. They may have gone into the snug in the pub, but it was an unusual occurrence and I remember being struck when I saw a woman coming out of Tobias McLaughlin's pub.

There must be something wrong with those people!

Different times, indeed.

THE DAY HARRY McNulty's takeaway opened was a seismic day in Ballybofey.

Harry started to make chips in his shop at the bottom of the Donegal Road. He only opened at the back of the grocery shop on a Saturday night. Harry used to hand out a portion of mushy peas with them.

This was at a time when there weren't even biscuits in most houses so you can imagine the excitement of the chip shop and the mushy peas. Milk was delivered to houses by horse and cart by the Reid family, who went around and filled the milk jugs. At weekends, we would jump onto the back of the wagon and went around 'helping' the milkman. I'm sure we were more of a hindrance, but that was just children finding a way to pass the time.

I'll never forget the day I got my first ice cream. My grandfather bought me one after Mass in Clonmany one Sunday. It came in a block, you just cut it off and put it between two wafers. I got so excited about the ice cream I gulped it down and gave myself a throbbing headache.

IT SEEMED TO snow every winter when I was a child. We looked forward to the snow and we made the most of it. Bonner's Forge on Donegal Street made this timber sleigh with rollers on it. There could be 15 of us on it at any time, with some fella up front to 'drive' it.

Away we'd go up to the top of Ard McCarron, at the time a newly constructed housing estate just outside the town. Traffic couldn't move and the whole town would be out. There might be the odd car, but the shout would go up... 'CAR COMINGGGGGGGGG!'

We could get to the bridge. We could go right down through Ballybofey's main street and it felt like the whole town was involved in this exercise. The council would come and wreck the fun by throwing grit on the snow. We'd be firing snowballs at them thinking it would scare them off, but it never worked.

I had no interest in school and I wasn't any good at it anyway. If I could hide behind someone at a desk, I did that. We got slapped and it was accepted that you got slapped. You didn't dare go home and talk about getting slapped. If you did that, you'd be slapped again for having been out of order at school. My mother would slap me, but my father would rarely do it.

She did it on the spot.

BANG!

She dolled out the punishment, but that was just normal. She had a rod, which was in all the houses. You'd get a good skelping, and that was the end of the story.

It was my mother who walked me from the house to the bridge below Sessiaghoneill school on my first day at school.

Nowadays, going to school is a great big hullaballoo. My mother met someone who was also going to school and sent me up with them. There was no such thing as, 'How was school?' or 'How did school go?'

We walked the mile and a half to school every day. In the evening after school, you didn't just come straight home. We'd mess about in the fields and we'd come home through the fields. The guards would often visit the school to check attendances. On an odd occasion, the guard might arrive in with some fella who hadn't been in for a while.

I remember a boy who lived up on the hills landed in with the excuse that there were cows on the road, which meant that he couldn't get in.

Paddy Heaney was my teacher in Sessiaghoneill and his mantra was always: 'Love thy neighbour'. He repeated it so, so often and put real emphasis on it. His whole religious teaching was about being neighbourly and charitable.

One summer's day Master Heaney sat us down on the grass and ran a race around and around this circle of probably 150 metres. It was between Frankie McFeely, who later played midfield for Donegal, and John Doherty. There wasn't five yards in it from start to the finish. There wasn't room to run the two beside each other and the race finished how it started.

My first race experience.

MY YOUNG WORLD changed completely one Saturday in 1956.

I was lying in my bed when the wailing started. My mother was roaring and crying uncontrollably.

My grandfather, Charlie McLaughlin died of a heart attack out in the byre feeding cattle at their home in Inishowen.

He was known as 'Charlie The Gasúr Man'. In the family generation before him, there were a lot of boys, so the family nickname stuck. Family names like that are regular around the Inishowen area of Donegal especially, with particular emphasis on Dohertys, McLaughlins and McGonagles.

It was tradition in those days when someone died that the radio wasn't turned on for a year. There was a cover, usually a towel, a pillowcase or something similar, thrown over it and it remained untouched for a full year.

But I wanted to listen to the radio one particular evening in 1957.

Ronnie Delaney was running in a race at White City in London and I got so agitated wanting to listen to the radio. I tortured them so much they made an exception. I have no idea why I wanted to listen to the race so badly. I had no particular knowledge of athletics at the time and how I even knew he was running or that the race was relevant in any way is a mystery.

They relented and let me listen to the race. My granny cried, but when the race was over, the radio was turned off and put back under cover.

Ronnie won the half-mile title and there were 23,000 people at it. Little did I realise then, but a decade later I would be at White City competing myself.

Before I knew it, I was sent down to keep my grandmother company and to help out on the farm. It was a world of going to the bog, of horses and carts, of no electricity and of the neighbours visiting night after night, céilidhin as it was referred to. I sat as a young boy listening to the chat - nobody drinking I should add – and it went on until the small hours.

Later, I would be in the bed right beside the open blazing turf hearth fire as the conversation continued under the thatched roof.

My uncle lived across the river and there was no road into his house. The only access at times was on horseback. Depending on the tide, we had some scary moments. I was up early every morning to go out to feed the sheep, most memorably in the winter. I felt this was great being given a responsibility all on my own. It was such a change from living in a town and I loved it.

There was no running water, so we carried it in buckets. My grandmother baked bread in the open hearth. There was a bed beside the fire and the curtains around it were pulled during the day. That was normal in Irish houses.

There was another room in the house that was freezing cold. An open-hearth fire was the only source of heat in the house. There always seemed to be a kettle on the boil on the hearth. Half the heat went up the chimney, and the lamp had to be readied for the impending darkness.

For some reason, though, we never dwelled on the fact that we were cold. Maybe you might have heard 'There's a wild draft', but that was the height of it.

In the summer evenings, crowds of people used to meet at the crossroads at the bottom of the Giblin Road and just talk into the night.

MY NEW SCHOOL in Rasheney was fine to begin with. I loved the teacher, who was also new to the school. The problems started when the new term came around.

Master Sweeney originally hailed from west Donegal. He never seemed in the best of form. We got it tight from Master Sweeney. He slapped a lot.

Slapping was a regular occurrence, but he was over the top. It's still a topic of conversation in that part of the world and he's been dead over 40 years.

I was completely scared out of my wits.

One day, I could take no more and cried to my mother about how bad it was. I was back in Ballybofey during a school holiday. She was making the beds in the house and I just started bawling.

Youngsters were always just told what to do. They were never given a say in things, but it must have been so obvious how I was being affected.

My mother took me straight back to Sessiaghoneill school again. Though I still spent summers in Rasheney. I loved the experience of being on the farm and being given responsibility. I had to bring a big horse over to the forge to get shod. I had to walk about three miles and I stopped every now and again to see if anyone was watching me. I just couldn't believe that I was allowed to actually do that job. I gathered spuds, pulled lint, carried water – everything an Irish farm in the 1950s engaged in. I used to look forward to the travelling shop coming around and watch my grandmother bartering away with the guy in the shop. She'd have eggs to give him and there'd be all sorts of trading going on.

She missed my grandfather, though, and was never the same without him.

I was left in the house the day of his funeral. He was buried in Carndonagh and during the funeral a group of local women came in and gathered up all of his belongings. By the time people came back from the funeral there wasn't a trace of him left in the place.

WITH MY FATHER'S football career over, he took to playing golf. He was quite good as it happened. He was a scratch golfer and I caddied for him all over the country. He was one of the leading golfers in the army, winning the Army Championships, which he played in annually. He also competed in the Irish Close Championship and the West of Ireland Championship.

When I was 11, I played in an Open men's competition in Ballybofey & Stranorlar Golf Club.

I was nervous as hell standing on the tee. I was playing against men and didn't know if this ball would go two yards or 100 yards. I survived it. I was going brilliant and was on par, but my focus fell apart.

The men who were playing had to be thinking, *Who does this wee fucker think he is?* There was no tolerance for youngsters in those days.

We spent summer holidays on the golf course at Ballyliffin and I played 36 holes a day. It was a simple timetable. Wake up, eat breakfast, play 18 holes, eat lunch, play another 18 holes. A lot of the time, you played against yourself or against the par of the course.

Myself and my younger brother, Charlie helped out a lot when the Ballybofey & Stranorlar Golf Club was being built in 1955 and 1956. We went around and lifted up the stones. We spent endless hours and days just gathering them up. Jesus, that was tight going. We put the stones into buckets and carried them away. The golf club, which opened in January 1957, was a new dimension to the town.

My parents were very much Inishowen people, but they became an integral part of Ballybofey.

My mother was one of the people who started the Credit Union and she was regularly reaching out to those who were less well-off. There were a couple of families living in bag tents on the Donegal Road in the 1950s. There was one child in particular, wrapped in a shawl, whom my mother would bring in to have dinner with us. Families were big, and some might have 15 or 16 children. Times were tough, but nobody died of hunger.

The McGurn family was huge and their house had only two rooms in it. The story at the time went that if a youngster in the McGurn house was crying you'd have to open two or three drawers to see who it was.

The McGurns all emigrated to Coventry, but a week later they were all back. It was a Saturday evening and I can still see Mrs McGurn walking up Ballybofey Main Street and all the children filing up behind her.

They eventually returned to England.

WE SWAM IN the river. We learned to swim at Sharp's Pool, a bend in the river just out the Glenfin Road. It was a miracle that nobody was drowned. There was a rock out in the middle of it and I thought one day I'd swim out to the rock.

Before I got anywhere near the rock, down I went.

Someone went in and pulled me onto the rock.

I was a better swimmer from that day on.

SPORT WAS A different landscape back then. Guys who played Gaelic football weren't allowed to play soccer. We'd play 15 or 20-a-side matches in a field where Finn Park is now. It was simply called 'the soccer field'.

We wouldn't have dreamed of playing soccer in the GAA field. Your name could have been read from the altar for that. Parochial sports were a big thing in Ireland then. It was something that you prepared for because the schools were involved.

In Ballybofey, the sports were held in Mick Martin's field out the Dreenan Road. Years later, I held the Ulster Cross Country Championships in the same field. The winners that day in the Under-9 race, the first Ulster Cross Country that we hosted at Finn Valley, were Donal Reid – who won an All-Ireland with Donegal in 1992 – and Kay McGowan, who later went on to compete internationally, as Kay Byrne.

The parochial sports day was the only 'day out' for athletics. Sessiaghoneill Sports was very well established. It was a big deal, and you had everything from athletics, boxing, football, cycling, tug of war, Irish dancing and singing. The day kicked off right after Mass and you'd have had thousands of people turning up.

There was always a boxing ring set up on the grass and that was very popular. There was a boxing club in Ballybofey, upstairs where Heaney's pub is now on Navenny Street, and you would always hear talk about the Anderson family.

Brian and Peter Anderson, two brothers, were very good boxers. They made a real name for themselves and, even now, are regarded in high esteem for what they achieved in the ring. I remember walking over towards the bridge and being almost star-struck when I met Brian Anderson, who boxed at the 1964 Olympic Games in Tokyo.

That particular day he was wearing his Olympic blazer and I didn't have the courage to even speak to him. That moment stood out for me for the rest of my life.

3

With Sonia O'Sullivan at the 2000 Olympic Games in Sydney.

SYDNEY 2000 WAS my first Olympic Games and it should have been an enjoyable experience. Being named as the Irish athletics team manager in August, 1999 was a dream come true. Unfortunately, the experience between being named as manager and actually getting to the Olympic Games was anything but enjoyable.

The run-in to Sydney was seriously stressful.

Clothing had become an issue at the 1996 Olympics in Atlanta, where one of the more infamous images was of Sonia O'Sullivan having to take off her Reebok strip and change into Asics gear.

At the time, Reebok had a deal with the Olympic Council of Ireland and Asics had a deal with BLE. Both thought their deal covered the Olympic Games and there was a civil war of sorts.

I let it be known I'd be going with the contract as it was, even though I knew it would put me offside with BLE.

The BLE ceased to exist in 1999. The NACA, the National Athletics and

Cultural Association, had merged with the BLE in November,1999.

Jimmy McDaid, the Minister for Sport, had said that after 2001 funding would only be available for one athletics body. That ultimatum forced the two bodies together. The BLE meeting to disband lasted 75 minutes, whereas the NACA meeting went on for seven hours.

There was an opportunity at this time to form a unified grouping to organise athletics on the island of Ireland. At one meeting in the Ashling Hotel, in Dublin, I felt I was the only person in the room who strongly fought for such a solution.

Athletics, like cycling on this island, could and should have been unified. There was an opportunity to do the right thing, but it was allowed to pass.

ULTIMATELY, THERE WAS a total breakdown between me and Athletics Ireland. Athletics Ireland traditionally nominated the coaches for the Olympic Games, but, for Sydney 2000 I had to nominate and appoint the coaches.

Out of loyalty to Athletics Ireland, there was a point prior to this where I was almost at the stage of giving up the chance of going to the Olympics. That would have been stupid, but I wasn't thinking too clearly. I had delayed on signing my OCI contract.

Sean McGarrigle was in doing a bit of work for me in the house at the time. I was ranting and raving to him about my difficulty. Sean had done a bit of coaching with Finn Valley in his time, but he hadn't a clue about the bureaucracy of it all.

There was something he just threw out that day that stuck with me.

'Why wouldn't you just sign the contract?' I decided there and then I'd sign it. I actually just needed someone to tell me what to do.

Little did I know, but my troubles were only just beginning.

WE HAD A final selection meeting for the Irish team at Morton Stadium in Santry in August of 2000. It was the final night of the National Championships and discussions were hot and heavy, tight going from start to finish.

The team was flying out at 6.30am the next day.

I came out of the meeting and was so stressed that I went to the boot of the car on the Clonliffe Road and just started to cry.

The weeks and months in the approach to this point had been seriously stressful. What should have been an exciting period became more complicated day after day. I was at a low ebb. My head was in an absolute spin as we were leaving Dublin and heading to the other side of the world.

The trip of a lifetime, indeed.

I WAS JUST relieved to get away. Far, far away.

In the weeks leading up to the Games, we based ourselves in Newcastle, a city around 100 miles from Sydney. I had flown to Australia to check it out just before Christmas in 1999. But even that choice of base was not satisfactory. Athletics Ireland was keen to set us up a separate training camp in Wollongong

Around every corner, I could foresee a problem.

When we got settled into Newcastle, everything was brilliant and, finally, the focus was 100 per cent on athletics again. Not for long, though.

I was handed a letter from Athletics Ireland, basically saying that they had already picked the relay teams back in Dublin.

To hell with that.

We had definite form leaving Ireland and you could have said, 'That's the team', but a lot can change in six weeks. I met the athletes and told them we were going to have a trial. We had to find out who was focussed and on form. The athletes all agreed that was the right approach. There was no point picking a team six weeks out.

I was totally exasperated by the letter, but it got worse before it got better. Athletics Ireland took a bloody case to the High Court in Dublin, in a challenge related to the selection of the men's 4x100 metres and 4x400 metres relay squads. We had a squad of six in each.

All of them were in Sydney... with me!

The trip of a lifetime?

Yeah... right!

Athletics Ireland lost their case in the High Court in Dublin. But I still had trials to run in Sydney.

I tossed and turned the whole night.

All the athletes turned up for the trials, but Gordon Kennedy, a 400 metres runner, got badly screwed. When we left Ireland, he was the number one, but he didn't make the final four. He lost his focus, I felt. His dream was over. He never got to compete at the Olympics.

I was annoyed that he didn't make it because he was from Tullamore, a great, country club and it felt personal to me. I have flashes to this day about those trials, with so much on the line a week away from competing in the Olympics.

THE COACHES I appointed for Sydney were all over 70 years of age and the selection certainly raised eyebrows. Maeve Kyle, Dr Zbigniew Orywal and Sean Naughton, however, were all brilliant. They had massive experience.

Maeve had been to three Games as an athlete and had been Ireland's first female Olympian. Sean developed that indoor arena in Nenagh and came from a very vibrant club. Dr Orywal, meanwhile, had been to the 1960 Olympic Games in Rome. He had previously been the head coach with the NACA for years. I had outstanding pairs of hands at work with me.

Little did I know, but Maeve's needle-and-thread handiwork would also come in handy.

We had another issue with gear. It wasn't quite Atlanta all over, but it was an episode that just outlined how unprofessional things could be at times. Some gear worked, but some didn't. Getting a proper kit for Sonia became a massive issue.

There was an ample amount of gear allocation to the team by Adidas, but it wasn't distributed properly. For Sonia's 5,000 metres heat in Sydney, she was left wearing an old floppy singlet, cut off at the bottom.

Maeve had to do a bit of a job on it.

It was unbelievable to think that Sonia O'Sullivan was away to run in the Olympic Games and only had something to wear because of the sewing skills of Maeve Kyle.

The OCI had distributed Olympic pins, but they weren't too generous in giving them out. They kept them in this little safe that was locked with a password.

In this environment, seemingly small things can become pretty important. We were in a bubble. And we all wanted pins.

One day in the Olympic Village I came up with a plan to raid the safe and get our pins.

Phoning home was expensive from Sydney, but in that OCI office there was also a phone. I came up with another plan, one that usually involved hoisting an athlete up to the window, and quickly enough having the OCI door opened up for us.

We'd go in and everyone would phone home. One of the boys was left on guard watch, to alert us if the officials were on their way back. It was silly carry-on, but it was good fun, and valuable in terms of a bit of craic, simple amusement for our athletes. And me too.

But, the OCI were getting on my nerves. My first Olympics should have been a massive experience but the reality was that I was worried sick about nonsense, trivial things that should never even have been issues.

THE GAMES, OF course, were not about me. They were mostly all about Sonia O'Sullivan.

Sonia was the key lady, but she wasn't staying in the village. Instead, she stayed at a house in Mortdale, out in the suburbs of Sydney.

Before the Games, Sonia had spent time on an island, Couran Cove, and took a boat into the Gold Coast. Gabriela Szabo had exactly the same plan.

Sonia was our big deal and we just knew she'd be pushing for gold.

She had failed badly in Atlanta four years earlier and moved to Australia, but the fact that we were in Sydney made Sonia's situation tricky. Between Atlanta and Sydney, Sonia had moved in with Nic Bideau, a coach, who was the partner to Cathy Freeman, Australia's national treasure.

Sonia joined them in the house. At the end of his relationship with Freeman, they began dating. There were all sorts of tabloid stories flying about, most of them pitching Freeman as the victim. When we arrived in Sydney, there was a two-page spread in one Australian paper about Sonia.

It was very clear that Sonia was being portrayed unfairly by a great number of Australian journalists as the baddie. By that stage, Cathy Freeman was back in business and she was unbelievable.

Freeman carried the stress and the pressure of an entire nation in 2000. She lit the Olympic flame, and she was in demand everywhere. She still had to run and win the 400 metres – and she did exactly that.

The night she won the 400, she lay down on the track, about 30 yards from where I was standing, in a stadium with almost 120,000 people watching. It was one of those iconic moments that just seizes you.

I'll never see the likes of this again… nobody will.

Freeman had won the 400 metres, Haile Gebreselassie and Paul Tergat were head-to-head with nothing between them in the 10,000 metres, beating the heads off each other, side-by-side in an epic battle going up the straight.

It was a mighty night.

A night still referred to as "Magic Monday". It was the greatest night of athletics ever.

It was also the night Michael Johnson won the 400 metres, Jonathan Edwards won the triple jump, and Colin Jackson failed to medal in his third successive Olympic 110 metres hurdles final.

THE OLYMPIC VILLAGE, a modern housing estate adjacent to the stadium, was deserted in the early evening of September 25, 2000. It was a sell-out night next door and it felt as if everyone had gone to the stadium… bar me and Sonia O'Sullivan.

I had tea with Sonia the weekend before the race and she had made it clear that she wasn't going to do any media interviews. There were to be no distractions. Her focus was solely on racing. Her character and her mentality were just something else.

When Sonia was in the zone, she was just a machine.

Sonia had her preparation down to a tee. Just before she left the Gold Coast to come to Sydney, she took part in a low-key meet at the aptly named Runaway Bay. Three other Irish athletes – Eugene Farrell, Gary Ryan and Emily Maher – were in action there, too, trying to make the 'A' standard to qualify. None of them managed to make it, but Gary was most unfortunate, his block slipping at the start of the 200 metres and his chance of going to the Games slipping away with it.

Sonia was third in the 800 metres in Runaway Bay and came with a late charge in windy conditions to win the 1,500 metres race.

In the days prior to her first race in Sydney, people had sent cards, prayers, all sorts of good luck messages, many of them from schoolchildren. They were all left in her room for Sonia.

I actually wasn't certain that she knew the impact she was having in Ireland. Ireland had stopped to watch her too, just like Australia stopped for Cathy Freeman.

'You know what you'll do now, Sonia,' I advised her. 'Go in there... say a few prayers and read those cards.'

She was in the room for ages.

Then, it was time.

We had to get a bus to the stadium. I was nervous as hell, but I was clear about how I was going to handle the night. I didn't want her and Freeman to have any interaction. There was no way they could come face-to-face.

Great Britain had two physio places in the warm-up area in the stadium and I needed one of them for Sonia, so I pulled the GB stuff down and claimed one of them the day before the final.

We small-talked our way to the track, but she was querying the situation about the 10,000 metres – which was just a couple of days away - and questioning if we had left her entry in. We quickly moved on from that conversation.

She was reading a book, *Winning Attitudes* by Herb Elliott.

All she had was the book and a backpack.

'Lie down there and read that book.'

I kissed her on the cheek.

'I'll be back for you when it's time to warm up'.

I took complete control of her. She was biddable. Sonia had this ritual of lying down with her legs in the air. It seemed to be a relaxation thing. She was there... just her, her legs high up above her head and her book. It was as if there was nothing else in the world, let alone in the heaving cauldron of noise and excitement just outside the door.

I went out to watch Freeman and one of the Olympic Games' most famous moments. Freeman headed down the tunnel and the moment had arrived.

'Right, Sonia... it's time'.

ONE OF THE things I was able to do in Sydney was sneak people into the stadium. It was a question of being able to basically bullshit the right people at the right times. Myself and Sean Naughton would be up talking to people at the kiosk, blathering away and these Irish lads filing in behind us. They had their own accreditation cards printed and they all got in.

Pat Hickey, the OCI President, had such influence that he was able to get all of his Olympic Council people accredited to be in the village.

But I had my own ways and means.

The night Sonia won silver I will never forget the scene in the mixed zone. Kieran Carlin and Ricky Simms from Finn Valley AC sneaked in. There I was, in a top security area with Sonia O'Sullivan, who had just won a silver medal in the Olympic Games, and these two boys were in there in the middle of the whole joyous world with us. I was so glad they were in and a part of it.

That was quite something. The lads from home. Sharing it all.

Pierce O'Callaghan had qualified for the Games, but he over-trained and ended up neither able to race or train. Instead, he coached Jamie Costin. When they got to Sydney, I was able to hand Pierce an accreditation. One of our athletes had his name misspelt on his original one and had to get a new one.

Thinking quick, I stuck the erroneous one in my pocket. Pierce was able to get 50 Irish supporters into the stadium every single night on the back of that one accreditation.

AFTER THE RACE, there was obvious euphoria... we had a silver medal!

The phone started ringing and I was doing as many interviews as I could. My first port of call was always *Highland Radio*.

I never got carried away to the point where I'd go to RTÉ first. I always had to get *Highland* done. I needed them to tell the local athletics story at the weekends back at home, so I wanted to make it as good as I could for them. I was also doing a weekly column for the *Donegal Democrat*, ghosted by a journalist, Ciaran O'Donnell.

That was important too because people in my home county could relate to me and feel as if they were keeping in touch. I could tell them about everything I did, and everyone I saw.

I nearly bumped into Muhammad Ali in the canteen one afternoon. There were several of the world's best athletes standing back, in awe of him. The

Greatest, indeed, had this aura about him. It was evident you were in the presence of sporting royalty.

But it was great to meet and great people from all over. I got talking to the Costa Rican swimmer, Claudia Poll one afternoon. She won a bronze medal and was telling me about the seven 50-metre swimming pools in Costa Rica. She couldn't believe we didn't even have one in Ireland.

The look of bewilderment said it all.

At the end of Sydney, I felt good. Sonia, obviously, was the highlight, but our three relay teams all broke Irish records. I felt justified by that, and learned a lesson to stand by my guns in the future.

Overall, though, the team wasn't doing well. I was being interviewed regularly and was setting down a marker about what needed to be done in Irish athletics. Everything was being done voluntarily. I was beating the drum about needing a performance manager.

Tom O'Riordan, a veteran journalist who was also a former Olympian, asked me, 'Do you feel under pressure, Patsy?'

Of course, I felt under pressure. Everyone knew I was under pressure. There were a dozen journalists in front of me when Tom posed the question.

'Pressure?' I replied.

'You want to be in the changing rooms in Clones at half-time... and you're three points down to Down... with Manus Boyle firing water bottles at you.

'That's fucking pressure'.

BREDA DENNEHY-WILLIS came off a women's 10,000 metres heat, threw her arms around me and cried inconsolably in the mixed zone. She felt as if she had let everyone down. That moment showed how hard and harsh this sport could be.

Breda was someone I spent a lot of time helping. When I was appointed team manager for Sydney, she was on the road racing circuit in America. I knew how good she was and knew she could be an Olympian. She was in Florida and was difficult to get hold of.

But I persisted.

'You have to try for the Olympics,' I told her. 'You can't let this chance pass you by.'

I got Breda back to Ireland to compete in the Irish Cross-Country Championships in 1999, but she took some persuading. She was unhappy from 1996 when Katie McCandless – a Finn Valley athlete, as it happened - was picked for the Atlanta Olympics ahead of her.

She had a fear of never making it – and that took her to Sydney.

Breda insisted that she had to run the national championships a few weeks out from Sydney. I could hardly watch. This was a month before the Olympics. I turned around for the last 600 metres of the race, but Breda came through it, thank God.

Breda had doubts. A lot of them.

Her questions were the same.

'Is it worth it?'

In the two years prior to Sydney, my mantra was also the same.

'It doesn't matter a damn, if you're standing in the Olympic Stadium with not a penny to your name,' I'd tell her. 'You'll always be an Olympian. If you're standing representing Ireland at the Olympic Games, nothing else matters.'

She earned her spot… big time.

Nine days before her race in Sydney, disaster struck, and the wheels came off. Breda contracted the flu. She had been flying. The day before she began to feel unwell, she ran a mile in 4:34. Twenty minutes later, she repeated the trick.

She knew it wasn't going to happen and the race panned out much as we had expected.

Five weeks beforehand, she was in Dublin and didn't get a flu jab because it was too close to the race. How unfortunate and unlucky can you be?

Sydney was the last we saw of Breda. She was never seen in an Irish singlet again.

EVERYONE THOUGHT, COMING away from Sydney, that I was looking for the High-Performance job which would be up for grabs within Athletics Ireland, but I made it clear I didn't want it. I had a big blast on the performance and professionalism issue just before we left Sydney.

All the media picked up on my quotes.

'It's not an athlete-friendly situation. Athletes will say that about Athletics Ireland, the contact there is not athlete-friendly.

'There's a job for somebody out there. Sorting it out. I should have been a tightrope walker. I was either going to fall on the Olympic Council side or the athletics side, and I was going to be eaten alive either way. And there was no crowd cheering for me.'

WHEN WE ARRIVED back at Heathrow Airport in London, I could see all the officials huddled around the papers. The shit would soon hit me on that front.

I used to drive officials mad in meetings.

They'd be digging into me, about 15 of them around a table. I'd just get up, walk over and make a cup of tea, lift a biscuit. They were fit to be tied around the table.

After Sydney, I had to do a report for Athletics Ireland, but because I didn't screw the OCI and, in fact, gave some credit the OCI in the report, I was told to do it again.

There was a massive reception for me at Finn Valley, which was good for me but, when the dust settled, I promised Rosaleen that it was over.

'I won't be doing the Olympics again,' I promised her.

'I won't be going near it!'

DEEP DOWN, I never had any intentions of giving up athletics after Sydney.

I was going through a tough time with my own health and wellbeing around the time of the 2000 Olympics, so I told people what they wanted to hear. What they heard and what I did were entirely two different things, of course.

I didn't need Athletics Ireland to go to the World Student Games in 2001 so I put myself forward and was appointed team manager. It was an exciting time in Irish athletics. Derval O'Rourke and Deirdre Ryan were beginning to emerge as prospects and Sonia's Olympic silver was still shining bright.

I had 13 athletes in Beijing for those Games. I had no coach and no athletics administrators, so I did it all myself. I was quite happy for it to be like that.

My support staff were all university people.

Mickey Whelan was one of those with me. Mickey had played senior Gaelic football for Dublin and was held in high regard on the university circuit. I came up against him when he managed the Bolton Street soccer team. He was an adversary of mine in those days, but he was Chef de Mission in Beijing and was seriously supportive. He was and is one of the people in Irish sport that I have real, genuine regard for.

I actually enjoyed Beijing and Gareth Turnbull won a silver medal in the 1,500 metres. One night, with a couple of beers on board, Gareth and I decided it would be a good idea to do an interview with the BBC.

The interview went alright, but it was a balancing act that we managed to get right. I was lucky that didn't go the wrong way for me.

BY THE TIME of Vaasa and the European Cup in 2001, the 'trouble' with Athletics Ireland had simmered. And Sonia was still big business by the time the European Championships arrived in Munich in 2002.

The heavens opened for the women's 10,000 metres. The rain was actually bouncing up from the track, but Paula Radcliffe ran an amazing race. It was one of those performances that define an athlete. Nobody could have lived with her. It was a spectacular performance.

She splashed and squelched around the Olympiastadion in 30 minutes and 1.09 seconds. Sonia won a silver medal and set a new Irish record of 30.47.59 which still stands to this day. But she was still 46 seconds behind Radcliffe. Talk about mixed emotions.

Radcliffe didn't want to run in heats for the 5,000 metres, so I pushed for heats and lodged an objection.

The rules suggested that there should have been heats once 25 athletes had declared. The British were influential and TV companies always had a big say in such final decisions. They just wanted a straight final. But I created such a stir about it, and Radcliffe withdrew from the start list.

Fernanda Robeiro from Portugal also pulled out and the technical delegate decided to allow 24 athletes into the final. Sonia was enraged. I lodged an appeal on the grounds that the rules state where between 20 and 38 athletes enter, there must be two heats.

We argued the case, but I lost the appeal and it was a straight final.
Radcliffe is gone... brilliant!
Sonia will win gold here.

Sonia was the reigning 5,000 metres champion. In the previous two Europeans, she won gold in Helsinki in 1994 over 3,000 metres and in Budapest in 1998 over 5,000 metres and 10,000 metres.

Radcliffe was away home. Szabo was concentrating on the 1,500 metres and world champion Olga Yegorova hadn't appeared in Munich. The race went according to plan until the final turn.

Sonia took the lead coming into the straight and could see the line.

We have this…

She's done it again.

Just when we were about to toast, a Spaniard, Marta Dominguez, came up on the inside and Sonia left town with another silver – by nine-hundredths of a second. Yelena Zadorozhnaya from Russia was third, and I felt sorry for her. She had a wee child back home in Russia and would get absolutely no acknowledgement for winning a bronze medal.

The talk was all about Paula and Sonia. Then Dominguez and Sonia. The poor Russian was instantly forgotten. If you asked even athletics people the following morning who won bronze in the women's 5,000 metres, I would safely wager most wouldn't have a clue.

That was the way of it sometimes.

I saw people get Olympic medals and a year or two later, they mightn't have had shoes on their feet. I remember gathering money one time in South Africa for a Kenyan who got third in the 400 metres hurdles in Barcelona. I gave him some Irish kit; the boys gave him some runners and a few bits and pieces.

This poor fella was an Olympic medallist and couldn't get a pair of shoes.

I used that to get at some of our athletes.

'You lot would want to start appreciating things. If that were any of ye… you'd be away off opening supermarkets!'

In Ireland, if we came home with a medal it would be perceived that we had a great Championships. People never look beyond the medal. On occasions like that, you were carrying one athlete. If one athlete medalled, the others were actually forgotten about and that's something that still annoys me.

Munich was decent for us, though.

I had a good men's 4x400 metres relay team in Munich. Robert Daly, Paul McKee, Antoine Burke and David McCarthy worked well, and they broke an

Irish record, finishing fifth in the final.

I was relevant again in the grand scheme of things, but I didn't consider going for the team manager's role for the 2004 Olympics in Athens. Nobody had ever done more than one Olympics. It was an understanding that if you did one you wouldn't do another.

Michael Quinlan was appointed manager for the 2004 Olympics in Athens. We got on very well and I managed the training camp before the 2004 Olympics in Cyprus. We had been at a Board meeting of Athletics Ireland in Glasnevin.

Michael got up to go to the toilet and I went too.

'You're all set here?' I asked him.

'Aye.'

'You know what, sir,' I proposed. 'I'll do the training camp.'

That deal was done, there and then at the urinal. It was a two-second conversation. I was excited to be a part of the Games. I knew I had a contribution to make and it was presumed that I knew what it was about anyway. I had recovered from my fight with Athletics Ireland in 2000 and had seriously good support again. I was in a strong position.

Overall, Athens was a disaster of a Games for Ireland. There was nothing positive to talk about and poor Sonia finished last in the 5,000 metres. It was no way for an icon to bow out, but sport doesn't have sentiment.

I watched the 2004 Olympics from home in Ballybofey, having headed east when the last of our athletes trooped into Athens from the training camp in Cyprus. But a big story broke across the globe when the former priest, Neil Horan, ran out in front of the Brazil's Vanderlei de Lima, costing him the gold medal in the men's marathon.

The local journalists as usual were still thinking if something big is going down in the athletics world, that I'd be the man there.

Highland Radio rang me up, and I chatted away about the priest.

Whatever way the first question was phrased, I couldn't go back and tell Shaun Doherty that I wasn't actually in Athens.

I just rolled with the story.

I had to bluff the odd time, too.

Me (right) after a St Columb's College 400 metres race I won – my first race win.

"Well, as Kavanagh said, we have lived
In important places. The lonely scarp
Of St Columb's College, where I billeted
For six years, overlooked your Bogside.
I gazed into new worlds: the inflamed throat
Of Brandywell, its floodlit dogtrack,
The throttle of the hare. In the first week
I was so homesick I couldn't even eat
The biscuits left to sweeten my exile.
I threw them over the fence one night
In September 1951
When the lights of houses in the Lecky Road
Were amber in the fog. It was an act
Of stealth."

– The Ministry of Fear, Seamus Heaney

I BECAME AN athlete without having any prior ambition to become an athlete.

A spring afternoon on the lawn of St Columb's College in Derry in 1964 changed my life.

I was in Fourth Year as a boarder at St Columb's, the legendary institution on Bishop Street that housed some of Derry's most famous names: John Hume, Eamonn McCann, Bishop Daly, and Seamus Heaney among them.

Tucked just outside the city's ancient walls, overlooking the Foyle to the front and the Bogside to the rear, St Columb's was a daunting place in the early 1960s.

The onset of sport was a chance and an opportunity all at once.

Fr Cathal Logue announced that he was having a trial race.

The lawn at the front of the school is on a steep slope and, up on that embankment we ran a 100 metres race. In that moment, across that incline in front of St Columb's, I may as well have been in Tokyo – where that year's Olympic Games were held.

I was barefooted, but I won the race.

I was an athlete from that day forward. My confidence was never higher. I do believe that day was the making of me. Anything that went on in the environment of the college like that was a big talking point.

'Patsy won the race'.

It went right to the core of St Columb's. It gave a standing to be talked about like that.

The summer term was all geared towards the sports day, held at Brandywell Stadium.

I wasn't brilliant, but I was the best there was and I actually held the school record over 440 yards for a while. We got out early from study to train on semester evenings and had to stick to the concrete walks around the perimeter of the school.

That all changed when Fr Logue started cross-country and we'd run away up to Termonbacca, up on a hill way above the city of Derry. Termonbacca was better known as St Joseph's Home, run by nuns, and is now a religious retreat centre. At that time, all I knew were the gruelling runs that took us high into the Derry skyline.

Until then, boarders generally weren't allowed outside the gates of St Columb's, bar the odd exceptions. Now, we were permitted into the real world.

Away I'd go, up the Lecky Road, past Celtic Park and on out the Letterkenny Road. It was a case, literally of just run like hell, take a breather and get back again.

The County Donegal Railway bus, known as the CDR bus, from Ballybofey always drove past. I used to slow down to a jog and look for someone I knew. All the passengers saw was this mad young fella out running with hardly any clothes on him.

I had this madness to get to Monellan or Killea, to just cross the border back into Donegal.

That was massive for me, mentally.

I never got the length, though.

I *always* ran out of time.

THE TAILTEANN GAMES were held at Croke Park in Dublin and I wanted to compete. I was desperate to compete and I had myself convinced that I'd make it.

All I need to do is get there... and I'll win them.

I read about the Tailteann Games in *The Irish Press* and I went as far as writing a letter trying to get entered, but it didn't matter a jot. I never made it. I did get to the Brandywell, though.

My father got me a pair of second-hand spikes at Finner Camp, where he was stationed in the army, from Paddy Prendergast, an All-Ireland winner with Mayo in 1951 – the last Mayo team to win the Sam Maguire Cup.

I had a pair of spikes and I thought I was complete.

To win in the Brandywell was a big deal. These were proper races, and a stage like the Brandywell just heightened the experience and the achievement. All the priests from the college were there in a VIP area, sitting on what seemed to me like fancy seats.

Athletics was becoming quite serious in St Columb's and Fr Logue brought in purple and blue vests for the school athletes to wear. Soon, I was the first ever St Columb's athletics captain. We ran against Foyle College in a one-on-one that was an experience of a different kind. We went down the

Buncrana Road and ended up nearly to our necks in water. The conditions were so bad that I lost my shoes and had to run the rest of the race barefoot.

I was picking stones out of my feet for ages. If I'd stopped, I'd have been perceived as being weak. Stopping, therefore, wasn't an option.

I'd worked too hard from that day on the lawn. I just *had* to keep going.

That day I ran across the front lawn of St Columb's was in my second-last year in the place – but it saved the day. It made boarding school bearable.

I FIRST ROCKED up to St Columb's in 1960, an innocent wee fella from rural Donegal.

My parents drove me in the gates and into the grounds, which felt eerie in so many ways.

Even the doves that look over the gates to St Columb's felt haunting. The chapel, peeking out as the centrepiece of the building, was a reminder of the religious values of the place.

History wasn't far away either on the former "Windmill Hill". To the right of the building stood – and stands even now – a 17th century windmill from the days of the Siege of Derry in 1689.

The site was the stage for some of the city's most fierce battles during the 'Siege', yet the windmill and the adjoining ice-house survived in remarkable condition. I was just wide-eyed at the whole place.

It was like landing on the moon.

What do I do now?

I just followed the crowd.

St Columb's was very regimental. Close your eyes and the clink of the hobnail boots made you feel like you were in an army camp. The thick smell of chalk was a reminder otherwise, however.

You went to the refectory at specific times and you studied at specific times. Daily life consisted of getting up at seven o'clock and going to Mass every morning. You were in big trouble if you didn't go to Mass.

Getting to secondary school was a unique enough opportunity in those times and I was fortunate to get the chance. There might have been a certain snobbery to it. It was probably expected of me because my family was perceived to be well off, my mother being a chemist and my father an army officer.

The only other outlet in our area, in Ballybofey, was the Finn College on the Main Street, which was a small private college. Youngsters had no say what happened in those days. It was a different Ireland and a different world. My mother just told me that I was going to St Columb's and there was no discussion. That was that.

The boarders in St Columb's were mainly lads from south Derry with a few from Donegal, who lived in the Derry diocese. There was an exception made for me, though. I lived in the Raphoe diocese. My mother was influential and was friendly with a sister of Bishop McFeely, the President of the College. Ireland in those days was all about connections. Her connections ensured I was off to St Columb's.

The primary purpose of St Columb's at a time was to provide vocations for the priesthood – not something that was ever on the cards for me, I might add.

St COLUMB'S WAS founded in 1879 and the student population stood at 800 by the time I got my blazer in 1960. The crest was emblazoned on the front with the motto… *Quaerite primum regnum Dei*.

"Seek ye first the kingdom of God".

After a week, they cut the study short and all the first years got out. There was to be an induction. Or, as it was known, a 'ducking'.

We knew very little about it, but it didn't take us long to figure it out. The senior boys put us under the water taps that were dotted around the perimeter of the school. There was a lot of pushing and shoving. I was, as they'd say in Ballybofey, only a 'wee green caddy' – basically, an innocent young fella - and there I was under a tap outside St Columb's, the boys holding me, with nowhere to go and the water just gushing down.

I was scared stiff.

Crying.

I didn't know where or how it was going to end.

The priest just walked past, staring down at his brevery, seemingly oblivious to the happenings under the faucets.

It's important to note that this experience wasn't exclusive to me. This was done to every young fella who came in the gate. Not that knowing that made it any easier, mind you.

Homesickness was always there. Maybe I was just a soft young fella but, when study ended around half-nine or ten, I went to bed and cried. You were there, isolated and confined, for eight weeks at a time with no such thing as a mid-term break.

I had a calendar on my wall. I marked every single day off. Away ahead of me, I had marked in the day I'd get home or a day when my mother would be visiting. The only contact with home were letters and they weren't all that regular. My mother came once a month with a food parcel but, otherwise, contact with the outside world was non-existent.

The only way of getting out was if you had to go to the dentist.

The place was so bad you even looked forward to the dentist. I was so desperate at one stage, I stole appointment cards from the dentist and used to write my own appointments.

My uncle Sean was a notorious Irish teacher in St Columb's, whose reputation – he was nicknamed 'The Nipper' – certainly went before him. He lived on Carlisle Road and at times I used to go down to his wife, Evelyn who would make me some dinner. A proper dinner!

I didn't care if I was spotted because I had my release papers - the appointment card. If I'd gone to the dentist that often, I wouldn't have had a tooth left in my head.

We were allowed to see a film once a month in the school. Here you had a couple of hundred boys watching a black and white television away down in the corner. You could hardly see the TV itself, never mind whatever it was showing. The only one I remember is *Mise Éire*.

We did get to watch the 1964 Olympics in Tokyo - my first Olympic memory. I was standing on the chair at the back of a crowd, watching John Lawlor, a hammer thrower from Dublin, who had finished fourth at the 1960 Games in Rome.

IN THIRD YEAR, I got the balls to jump the Wall. I was getting braver and hatched a plan.

There was a swimming pool on William Street where we were allowed to go. Away we'd go, towel under the arm, past the wee houses on the Lecky Road... and into the pictures.

Everyone thought we were at the swimming pool, but we were at the pictures. There was the Rialto, the William Street and another at the bottom of Shipquay Street so you weren't stuck for choices.

We were there, almost with the cinema to ourselves, but we never saw the end of the film because we had to be back in St Columb's for five o'clock. Three quarters of the way through the film, we knew you had to get out.

'Another wee minute.'

Then, we ran like mad to get back for five o'clock. If a priest saw you on the walls, you were in bother. You'd be up there hiding as if a sniper was out to get you. I don't believe I saw the end of those films until about 10 years later.

The only constant were the walks around the perimeter of the school grounds.

Denis Bradley, a former priest who later became Chairman of the Northern Ireland Policing Board, was a regular partner of mine. Pascal Harkin, later a teacher in Carndonagh, was another. We met at every break and just walked and walked, around and around, for hours.

Weekends were long days with nothing to do on a Sunday, save for Mass in the morning. Mass was always held in Latin and the priest had his back to the congregation. The day – the world – just passed us by.

ONE OF THE big thrills of the weekend was when Derry City were playing at the Brandywell, which was at least half-a-mile away.

The College grounds were surrounded by this great big wire fence. We had faces pressed against it trying to make out a football match away in the distance. From 200 yards away, I got so good I could nearly tell who was on the ball.

That vantage point from St Columb's gave a neat panorama of a setting made famous by Phil Coulter, another St Columb's alumnus, in *The Town I Loved So Well*... 'the Creggan, the Moor and the Bog'. There was no sporting outlet at the time and Derry City Football Club was the banner for the city.

One of the real highlights was Derry City winning the Cup in 1964.

I had an affinity to City anyway given that my father had played for the club and was well received in the city. The goalkeeper was Eddie Mahon. Billy Cathcart was at full-back. The captain was Frankie Campbell. Johnny McKenzie was in from Scotland. What a team that was. That Derry City team was ingrained in my mind.

They had a big parade down through the city and we were peering over the wall, looking out at the players going past on a lorry. Willie Ross was the manager. He managed them on three different occasions. He managed when my father was there. I hadn't been to the Brandywell since I was nine, but I watched all the home games while I was in St Columb's.

Sport only came into my life in my last two years at St Columb's.

The Gaelic football team started and that was an outlet. It was a chance to be part of a group. Of a school of 800, only 20 were going to be involved in the Gaelic. There was no tolerance of soccer, and yet we always played soccer in our free time.

At the weekends, the Donegal lads would play the rest of the students. The game went on for hours. The score could be 20-18 and we just played on and on. We broke for lunch and went back again with the score still the same.

Fr McQuillan was very influential in the advent of Gaelic football in the school. He had captained Fermanagh to a Junior All-Ireland in 1959, and he would become President of the college. Priests weren't allowed to play so he captained Fermanagh under the pseudonym Sean Maguire.

I wanted to play and was part of the panel. I thought I was good enough, but I wasn't.

THE BIGGEST SPORTING event, in a global sense, that we keyed into were world heavyweight boxing fights and Floyd Patterson v Sonny Liston in 1962 was massive.

We got a thing called a crystal set. You could scrape the radiator, put the wires in to get an earth off the heater and put the little plug in your ear. We could get the BBC on it!

This would be at four o'clock in the morning and, of course, the Dean knew the fight was on, so he wandered around trying to catch us out. Floyd got defeated and that was a big disappointment. It was portrayed to us that he was this nice, black man. He was a good man and he might even have been a Catholic. Better again.

IN MY EARLY days, the only form of sport we experienced were the jostles to get in for food. The bell went to signal the end of study time and we ran like hell. It was important to be prominent in the queue, amid the punching, pushing and shoving, waiting for these two great big doors to open.

I could never figure out the rush.

The food in St Columb's was so bad. We were never hungry, and it was vile stuff. I actually led a mutiny about the food one day.

There it was, a bowl of the wateriest soup I ever saw. I can still see it now. It wasn't soup. It was just water with the faintest colour in it.

'No, we're not taking this'.

That was me spouting up.

I don't know where that came out of. It was my first sign of leadership and it was a bad move. The priest was at the edge of the table, just standing staring at us. He asked us what was going on.

'This is crap. We're not taking this'.

Me again!

He said nothing.

We got called in. Another hammering.

The food hall was a lesson in itself. There were a dozen or so around big wooden tables and the potatoes were fired out on two trays. If you didn't have a potato in your pocket by the time "Grace Before Meals" was said… well, you'd have none when you sat down.

The day boys – the students who lived at home in the city and went home every day – had their uses. We sent them out for food and they used to throw it over the wall to us.

There was tension between the boarders and the day boys, too.

They were the enemy.

They were 'different'.

They came in all spruced up, all fresh every day. We probably resented the fact that they were outside and we were inside.

They had the comforts of home. We had a basin down a cold corridor and got a shower once a fortnight.

For the boarders, school was about rules, prayer, study, poor food and walking.

And punishment.

Always punishment.

The worst thing was, you knew it was coming. Punishment was just part of the fabric of life at St Columb's. The Foyle flowed, the world spun and you were lashed by the priests. You could almost guess how many times you'd be lashed. Every teacher had his own leather strap. It came with a grip just to make sure it had the desired effect.

Heaney, one of two Nobel Prize winners from St Columb's (the other was John Hume) put the experience neatly in his poem, *'The Ministry Of Fear'*:

"On my first day, the leather strap
Went epileptic in the Big Study,
Its echoes plashing over our bowed heads,
But I still wrote home that a boarder's life
Was not so bad, shying as usual"

I BECAME A Mass clerk, which meant getting up very early in the morning, but I got breakfast for my troubles. An actual breakfast of bacon and egg.

It wasn't about the Mass, but about the food.

There was a retreat every year that lasted for three days and you weren't allowed to speak. You had to be 'in prayer', but at the end of it you got food. It was amazing how big of a deal an egg was. You wouldn't get one until the retreat the next year.

Also as a Mass clerk you got 'across the road'.

About 20 feet across Bishop Street was Nazareth House. I never could figure out what Nazareth House was. The only girls you ever saw were the maids in the school.

The priests would go over and say Mass for the nuns. We never saw the women or children and weren't aware anyway of what might be going on there.

And, besides, I was only in for the feed.

MY EXAM RESULTS weren't brilliant at St Columb's, but that was no surprise. I wasn't seen as being intelligent or smart. I was in the worst class in the school and couldn't pass a maths exam if you were going to shoot me in the head. I got through it and that was an achievement in itself.

On my final day, I was ready to get out. Before I sat my final exam I already had my stuff sent home. I handed up the paper and, finally, it was over.

I walked out the gate and kept walking.

Free at last.

Down Bishop Street and along a road that mirrored the meandering waters of the Foyle.

To Nixon's Corner and the left turn, to Molennan.

I ran these roads many times just to get a glimpse of Donegal but, in those days, I had to turn.

Now, I could keep walking.

Every step was taking me closer to Ballybofey.

I walked all the way through the sleepy villages of Carrigans and St Johnston.

I was nearing Raphoe, a market town midway between Ballybofey and Derry, when the CDR bus drove alongside me.

It was as if I had forgotten about the bus when I bid a quick farewell to St Columb's. I hopped on and made for Ballybofey.

Freedom.

My life sentence was over.

5

I've watched Ricky Simms grow from being a young athlete at Finn Valley to reaching the forefront of the athletics world, working as the agent for some of the sport's biggest stars, including sprint sensation Usain Bolt.

GATE 71.

I WILL never forget that number in Tokyo Haneda Airport.

For the 2008 Olympic Games, we flew to Beijing via Tokyo, which became an ordeal and a panic that I have rarely found myself in.

Usually, I'm really in control when the shit hits the fan, but in Tokyo there was no mention of Patsy McGonagle on the roster to board the flight to Beijing. Someone had messed up the booking.

Well, someone had messed up my booking. The athletes were okay and got on board the China Airways flight.

I, however, needed a plan B.

What the fuck am I going to do here?

There was a Japan Airlines flight leaving from another terminal, but it was leaving… now. Time wasn't even tight, it was nonexistent. I had to board a bus to another terminal.

Right… what gate?

I can still see that number 71 yet.

The seconds ticked and tocked. I almost had to chase the plane down the runway. Rarely have I felt relief as when I buckled the seat belt.

I HAD A vision of Beijing being the biggest kip I'd ever be going to, having formed that opinion on a pre-Olympic visit with the OCI for a reccie of the location.

The big issue for Beijing was smog. There seems to be something for the media to focus on before every Olympic Games and in Beijing it was the smog. For me, also, the problem was people. The whole city was completely overcrowded.

We stayed in a six-star hotel and you couldn't get from A to B without it becoming a whole ordeal. Bicycles are a standout feature in Beijing. So, you'd get to a set of traffic lights and there'd be nothing but hundreds of bicycles waiting for the green light.

Once you went out from the city, it was like a different world altogether.

We went to look at a place for a possible training camp. It was poor and extremely backward. It wasn't too far away from Beijing, but it was just a completely dispirited place. When you went out from Beijing to a place like it, a taxi was just a bicycle with a board on the back of it.

We looked at the rowing centre and, we thought, if a rower falls in, we'll never see that person again. This was reality. The place seemed to be devoid of any health and safety measures.

It was also heaving. Everything was just so polluted. The dirt was so prevalent. And the famous Birds Nest – the 91,000-seater stadium they built to hold the Olympic Games – was still under construction when we did the pre-visit in late 2007.

A fella could fall from the roof, and he'd be thrown into the back of a van and never seen again. Our thoughts!

I have to emphasise how they turned it around from our initial visit and they built an absolutely outstanding venue. They did brilliantly. I walked past the stadium one night and where the long-term parking would be there were just hundreds of soldiers lying in ready for action if it was necessary.

WE HAD THREE athletes carrying injuries in the lead-up to Beijing.

It's difficult for an athlete to be injured at any stage, given the individual nature of the sport, but coming up to an Olympic Games it is a nightmare scenario. Some athletes might only have one shot at ever becoming an Olympian.

Derval O'Rourke, Eileen O'Keefe and Joanne Cuddihy were in big trouble before Beijing, and I knew it.

Joanne, for instance, could only do aqua sessions.

Journalists would often ask, 'Should you have allowed them to compete?'

These guys began their athletics careers at eight or nine years of age. They weren't going to perform, but I wasn't going to take the Olympic experience away from them. They had worked their whole lives for that moment. They had done nothing else bar athletics and they had dreamed *the dream* for years. Those athletes had to be regarded as Olympians.

I would do the same again.

Joanne was struggling for months. We had to have her paced over 300 metres at full pelt by 800 metres athlete, Thomas Chamney. That's how we decided if Joanne would go to the start line. Watching this was worse than watching an actual Olympic race. This was going to define if she would be an Olympian or not.

This was a lifetime's work, literally, on the line.

There was nothing only the sound of silence as Joanne bent down on the start line. Just as we were about to set her off, my phone rang. It was Brendan Mooney from *The Irish Examiner* enquiring after Joanne's fitness. I always had a good relationship with journalists. I knew that they had a job to do and appreciated giving my sport their time. Where others would have told Brendan where to go with himself, I took the opposite view.

'Hold on a minute, sir,' I asked him.

Joanne attacked the sprint, maintained momentum and held it together. She did the business.

'She's in one piece, Brendan,' I happily informed him.

'She'll start the race.'

We knew she wouldn't impact but that she was able to run.

Eileen picked up an injury in the camp, when she overtrained.

Eileen had started throwing the hammer out the back of her house in Kilkenny. She was self-taught and there were attempts to engage her with leading coaches. But she liked to do her own thing. She had unbelievable ability.

She had been a finalist at the 2007 World Championships in Osaka and had potential to medal in Beijing. She was a 70 metres-plus thrower, but she couldn't be held back in camp and she wasn't prepared to listen.

Eileen just kept going. The result was she came to Beijing slightly injured and, worse, her confidence was badly dented.

There was a need for sports psychology. The OCI had a psychologist there, but as I made the argument one time at a seminar, sports psychology is a long and involved process. The athlete needs a relationship; not just land there and hit it off with a stranger That can't possibly work.

WITH DERVAL, THERE was never a question; just a presumption.

I took the heat when people were questioning her participation. Not once did I ever have a conversation with her about not going.

Derval was the World Indoor champion just two years earlier. Of course, she wanted to go to the Olympic Games!

We needed Derval to run over the eight hurdles aggressively.

Twice.

We had to get her to do that to satisfy herself and those of us anxiously watching.

I didn't get too involved with Derval. It was just a case of making sure she was where she had to be, when she had to be. I stayed in the background. I just stood back and supported Derval and her coaches, the husband and wife team of Sean Cahill and Terri Horgan.

There was no room for anyone else.

It was unexpected for an Irish sprint hurdler to run and win in a global race. Derval was different. She was special. She began at about nine in the Community Games. She had a great story and it was all to do with her mentality and her work ethic. She was a natural winner.

Mentally, she was so strong, and you could never doubt her. Ever. You looked at Derval before a race and you sensed something that very few athletes have. She just had that magical thing we simply refer to as… it.

My mind always flicks back to Bydgoszcz and the 2000 European Team Championships when I think of Derval.

I had a girl, Susan Smith, who finished ninth in the 400 metres hurdles at the 1996 Olympics in Atlanta and who was a brilliant athlete. Susan always did the short hurdles and the long hurdles. I dropped her to put Derval into the short hurdles. That took a lot of balls on my part.

We were driving from Warsaw to Bydgoszcz and stopped at a roadside cafe.

I walked Derval up the road and told her what was happening. Ordinarily, an athlete would be over the moon with the news. Not Derval. She didn't show emotion at any stage. She would have felt that it was her place.

Her right. Susan didn't feel the same.

Derval failed to qualify out of the first round in Beijing, finishing sixth in her heat. The questions came flying. People said it reflected poorly on the team.

But Derval O'Rourke was our lead athlete. A true leader. Nobody was going to tell Derval O'Rourke that she wasn't competing in Beijing. Because of her mentality, some people found Derval difficult, but I always had a very good relationship with her. We always knew where we stood. She trusted me. She was very much her own person. Pre-race, she was just zeroed into the job.

She chased medals.

She got medals.

She missed medals.

And she was cheated out of medals.

Nevin Yanit from Turkey, I remember as being a slim, slight, girl. In Barcelona at the 2010 European Championships, I looked at Yanit and instantly went... *Holy fuck!*

Her physique, all of a sudden, was akin to that of a nightclub bouncer. Yanit won gold in Barcelona, but Derval was always sceptical.

Derval *knew.*

Three years later, Yanit tested positive for stanozolol, but it didn't impact on the colour of Derval's medal. Derval was seriously focussed and in control of her environment. When she arrived at the Championships ready to bite, you knew she was in the zone.

In 2006, in Gothenburg at the European Championships, we had to fight to get Derval a silver medal in the 100 metres hurdles. She shared the same time – an Irish record of 12.72 seconds – with a German, Kirsten Bolm. Derval got the silver.

While we were in Gothenburg, a group of six swimmers - including Henry O'Donnell, Ryan Ward and Ann-Marie Ward from Donegal – were doing a relay around Ireland. It took them four weeks and 1,300 kilometres, but they managed it.

They made contact with me from a boat off Galway one night during the Championships. It was perfect for me and I used it in a team talk with the athletes.

'These people are 30 miles off the coast and they're touching base with us!' That underlined the importance of what we were doing and the impact we were having.

ALISTAIR CRAGG WAS my kind of guy.

There was no bullshit with Alistair. I related to him purely on that basis. Alistair got unreal results at college and was a success story. His spell in America was very impressive and he was one of the key athletes in the world at the time. He won the 3,000 metres at the 2005 European Indoors in Madrid, but had to drop out of the 2006 European Championships in Gothenburg.

He had constant Achilles trouble and it came back to haunt him again in Beijing. He was one of the athletes the Irish media always focussed on because he was a potential performer.

Immediately after his heat in the 5,000 metres, without realising he had actually qualified for the final, he gave a very raw interview.

'Prominent names in this sport are sitting in Ireland and are talking about how we are not great like they used to be,' he stated. 'But they forget that in the seventies they never had 13 Kenyans under 13 minutes.'

I loved that about him. There was no claptrap from Alistair. At each Championship you just hoped that it would be the one to click for him. I really wanted him to do well and before the heat in Beijing I told him, 'You've been down too many tunnels'.

He seemed in control in the warm-up.

When you go to the check in, you feel almost as if you're going to be shot with the tension in the air.

'It's a race just like any other... get in there and engage.'

I took a lot of interest in him and got close to him.

He was one of only two white men in the final, along with Spaniard Jesus Espana, but it didn't happen for him that night in the Bird's Nest, either. The Achilles went on him and he dropped out. He needed someone to put an arm around him to settle him and I actually invited him to live in Ballybofey at one stage. I just felt he needed a change of scenery and surroundings.

IN ATTEMPTING TO qualify for Athens in 2004, Paul Hession ran the 200 metres in 20.61 seconds. The 'A' standard was 20.59 seconds. The OCI made no exceptions and he had to sit at home in Galway and watch the Games on TV.

Paul had a great run through the rounds in Beijing in 2008. He actually won his heat and finished fifth in the semi-final. He was ranked ninth after the semi-finals and only eight qualified.

Paul was nicknamed 'the fastest white man in the world'.

A white sprinter from the west of Ireland getting to that level was phenomenal. The list for the final bore that point out: Usain Bolt, Shawn Crawford, Walter Dix, Brian Dzingai, Christian Malcolm, Kim Collins, Churandy Martina and Wallace Spearmon.

We were disappointed that he didn't make the final, but in the cold light of day we began to accept that performance for what it was.

Paul is now a doctor.

He'll be a success on every road he walks down life.

6

*In November, 1967, Rosaleen and I got married in London. Here we are with
Michael Logue, Dympna McGarrigle and Fr Cunningham.*

THERE WAS NO plan when I left St Columb's.

Or, at least, I had no plan. My mother did the thinking in our house. That
was the way it was in most houses in Ireland in the 1960s.

My mother always seemed to have a plan. The roadmap for me was that
I was going to be an army officer, so the Cadet School was to be the port of
call. I was an ideal candidate, having been in the FCA since 13 (you had to be
17, really, but I could fire a .303 rifle so I was in!), the fact that my father was
an army officer and I had fluent Irish. I loved Irish, having visited Rannafast
regularly, spending a lot of time in the Rosses area of west Donegal.

But I didn't get accepted into the army and that was a setback. My mother
never sat about for too long and, that autumn, she had me on the plane to
Birmingham.

Growing up in the 60s, there were no such thing as family holidays, so
going away like that was a daunting experience. There was a means of getting
into teaching in England, by becoming a monitor in a school for a year. That's
where Birmingham came in for me.

I was 18 years-old and on a plane for the first time in my life.

I arrived in Birmingham and was met at the airport by Mrs McCusker, nee Herron, who was originally from Glenfin and was friendly with my mother at school. She brought me to her house, on Selly Oak and I was then moved to lodgings at Minstead Road – where the Garvelly Hill Interchange, or 'Spaghetti Junction' is now located.

That was a soft landing, but I was seriously homesick in Birmingham.

In a little box room of a B&B, I felt detached from the rest of the world. I was so detached that I even resisted the want to go and join the Birchfield Harriers, a top athletics club who were, literally, just down the road from me.

Alexander Stadium was close by, too.

I went as far as the gate so many times, but never crossed the threshold. Athletics didn't exist for me in Birmingham, where I had two outlets… Mass and Aston Villa.

I wouldn't have missed Mass for all the money in China. It felt like all the Irish people in the whole of Britain were sandwiched inside of St Chad's Cathedral. It felt homely; just what I needed.

I was a regular at Villa Park. Tony Hateley was the main man, banging in the goals for Villa. I used to be on the Holte End, bouncing away as Hateley netted again, and again.

THE LIGHTS AT Villa Park were something else. I never experienced anything like that at home; the closest I came was peering in at the Brandywell from the grounds at St Columb's College over the previous few years.

I had to learn quickly at St Chad's National School, working under a teacher, who would escape away and leave me with them, 35 mad 10-year-olds. Some of them were hardy boys. I'll never forget Redmond, a sturdy wee lad originally from Dublin. He pushed me as hard as you could push anyone. I stayed close to the door. Before he got to the door, I got a slap at him. He still went on. He went down a bit, but he kept going. I was afraid to go to school the next day.

All these Dublin boys are going to land.

They never arrived and Redmond didn't come back for a week or so.

Punishment had been a big thing for me in St Columb's, but now I was the one in possession of the wooden ruler dishing out the punishing. My basic job was to keep them quiet and I couldn't let the other teacher down. If the noise got up, someone was going to come and notice that something or somebody was amiss.

I put a few sums on the board, told a few stories or at times urge the children to tell a few. I might get them out for a while to play around outside. Basically, it was a case of just punching the day in.

I was on nine pounds a week, good money in those days.

IN THE DIGS I was staying, the man of the house was an absolute religious fanatic and was in the Legion of Mary. Seeing as I wasn't running and Aston Villa and Mass weren't as regular as I'd have liked, what'd I do... but join the Legion of Mary. There I was, off at Legion of Mary meetings on a Sunday evening. I was so lonely that it felt like a good idea. I expect I was just chasing some company and longing for a link with some people on a long weekend.

I was coaxed into going around doing a survey one week.

'Are you a Catholic?'

'Do you go to Mass?'

I had to do it, just to get out of the house, but I soon copped myself on.

At night, there was Irish dancing in the school hall. I wandered along, but never had the bravery to ask any woman out to dance. I was still very shy at that stage of my life.

After Christmas, Danny Breen from Convoy came to Birmingham with me and we got a room on Hagley Road from a Mrs Bradley, whose family used to own a pub on Navenny Street in Ballybofey. Connections again.

Danny had been to Scotland to do hairdressing, but he went on to become a teacher. The Bradleys, who were into construction and plumbing as trades, took us out to work at times and we'd help them out.

One Saturday – July 30, 1966 – stands out. There wasn't a person in Birmingham moving. Not one sinner.

England were playing in the World Cup final and the country literally shut down.

We watched it in the house on a black and white TV. I had no interest in the game and approached it from an 'Anyone but England' point of view.

I GOT A big break when I was in St Chad's.

The principal, Mr Wells was very highly thought of in Catholic education. St Mary's College in Strawberry Hill, down in London was a Catholic-ethos College. Strawberry Hill and Loughborough were the two top PE colleges in England. Mr Wells lined me up to go down to St Mary's for an interview.

I arrived in London and I hadn't a clue where to go next. I stood like a dummy and listened as different boys said where they were going. I had been given instructions. Once I heard 'Waterloo' I was away after the fella. I did the same until I got to Richmond and I got lost.

There was a colours match on at Twickenham that day between Cambridge and Oxford universities so it was busy but, eventually, I got to St Mary's. I was interviewed – the only person being interviewed – by a priest and a layman in this big drawing room in Waldegrave House. Fr Joe Sweeney was originally from Dungloe in west Donegal, and was the bursar for St Mary's College.

His brother was Major General Joe Sweeney... now there was an interesting man. He was elected as a Sinn Féin MP at just 21, but he didn't take his seat. He was elected as a TD in the first Dáil and remains the second-youngest ever TD. He fought in the Easter Rising at the GPO and was an IRA commander in west Donegal. He was a Major General in the Free State Army during the Irish Civil War.

Their sister lived 50 yards from our home house in Ballybofey, married to Willie Tom McMenamin, a solicitor. Connections in Irish life in those days were so important and that is something that stands true to the present day.

If I had gone in, lay on the ground and started to shout at them, I think I would still have got a thumbs up. Sure enough, a couple of weeks later, I got a call to say I was accepted into St Mary's.

It wasn't even part of the plan, but yet the plan was, somehow, working. Again, like all plans at this time, it was being instigated, I suspect, by my mother, with not a word spoken to me.

Strawberry Hill opened up a whole learning process for me.

First of all, there was athletics. Actual, serious athletics. There was a programme and there was tradition, history and acceptance. The lecturers were interested in athletics and I was being introduced to all the sporting activities.

I had to do a physical trial. They put me in a hall with gymnastics equipment. They got me to run and attempt to clear the box, a horse they called it. It nearly killed me stone dead. I jumped up and hadn't a clue where I was going to go after that. I came down and nearly broke my back.

I studied PE and sociology, but I hadn't a clue what sociology was. After a year, I stopped going to the sociology lectures.

At that time, no-one was doing PE in Ireland apart from the Church of Ireland teacher training college in Dublin. PE just wasn't relevant. The only PE we got at St Columb's was a thing called 'drill', which was basically just exercises. You'd have had maybe 50 of us out doing the same movements at the one time. What they actually were, were just old army drills with Mr Day.

There was good emphasis on the practical side of the education in Strawberry Hill.

In the years ahead, a lot of people doing sports-related courses in Ireland were to rely too much on theory. People had theory coming out of their ears, but they didn't have the practicality to deliver. That was to the obvious disadvantage of the students.

ST MARY'S COLLEGE, nestling in a residential area of south west London at Twickenham, was a great opportunity and a great experience. I could run when I wanted. I enjoyed study at that stage. I had no distractions. There was no social life. The social life was playing rebel songs in my room on a record player. We'd be battering the songs out; a crowd of us Irish lads belting them all out.

The *Boys of the Old Brigade*... "Oh, father why are you so sad...On this bright Easter morn..."

Sean South... "Twas on a dreary New Year's Eve when the shades of night fell down.

"A lorry load of volunteers approached a border town..."

It was all about the volume.

I GOT A part-time job at the weekend in a bakery owned by a Pakistani family, none of whom had a word of English.

I had difficulty with the language barrier, but I copped on to what I had to do. I was just glad of the work at that stage and I was making decent money on the nightshifts.

I grew up in an Ireland where there was no lorry load of pastries thrown at you. You were doing rightly if you got jam on your bread. I went into the bakery on my first night there. I saw all these pastries and buns.

This is some job.

Nobody in Ireland would ever buy you pastries, but I couldn't resist. I fell to the pastries and ate the cream by the hand-load. I was sick at about three o'clock in the morning and for about two days after it.

I WAS PART of the athletics team at St Mary's and I became a good team man in cross country. I got to know all the main venues, these iconic places you read about... Hyde Park, Richmond Park, Crystal Palace, White City, Bushy Park and Parliament Hill.

They weren't iconic. They were just iconic in your own mind.

At White City in 1970, I was an extra in the film *The Games*, which starred Michael Crawford, Charles Aznavour, Stanley Baker and, very briefly, Patsy McGonagle! I was part of a large group of runners who took part in a big race for the film.

We got a few quid for it and got fed, which was a bonus.

At St Mary's we had a weights' rooms when athletes didn't do weights and we had the hockey pitch to do speed work. The track wasn't great. It was just like running the road. There were no top-notch facilities and we did a lot of the running on cinder. At that point, even in Ireland, Santry was still a cinder track and Billy Morton was holding big meets.

The environment and the opportunity were the big things.

On occasion, I ran for the National Athletic and Cycling Association (NACA) – an Irish organisation – and we worked the training out ourselves. Yes, we experimented, but we trained hard. We had an unbelievable training background in Richmond Park.

Sunday morning was a 20-mile run. I ran out the door, into Richmond Park and had 20 miles done by the time I came back. I raced on Saturday, and Sunday was the easy run – those 20 miles. That was the full Sunday morning taken care of.

David Bedford came along and that just heightened interest in the whole thing.

He became the world record holder at 10,000 metres (27:30.80), had a brilliant personal best for 5,000 metres (13:17.21) and later was to become the Director of the London marathon, a position he held for almost 20 years.

British athletics was in the doldrums when I started off in London and nobody was going to the meets. Then along came Bedford. He predicted he would win and he won. He was a superstar and he highlighted athletics.

In London, athletics was held at the White City Stadium, on a cinder track. Bedford packed it.

We moved to Crystal Palace and he packed it too.

Bedford packed everywhere he went because of his personality. Everyone wanted to know about him. At that stage, the African influence on global athletics was only North African – Morocco, Algeria and so on - and South Africa. That was the way the world was then. No Ethiopians or Kenyans existed in athletics. So, Europeans actually won these races.

Bedford was just a star. It was thrilling to be in his company. I was a member of the team and that was a massive learning experience. We had Jim Hogan, who ran at the 1964 Olympics for Ireland and became European marathon champion in 1966 for Great Britain. He was just a real down-to-earth man from Limerick. Jim had a great personality; tough and always funny.

It was probably the world's elite group and I was blessed to be in it. I also ran a few races with London Irish. We had extensive parklands - Richmond Park and Bushy Park – with deer running about. It was beautiful. There was the path down the Thames to Kingston. It was an ideal location for an athlete. I was in such a unique, privileged running environment.

I went to Glebe Farm in Birmingham – back there again! – and won a British Novice Cross-Country title. Glebe Farm was also the venue for the GAA in the English Midlands at the time.

I LIVED IN a very modern building and was very fortunate that everything was hunky dory – but I knew nobody. I lived in the apartment with Michael Logue, who later became the principal at St Bernadette's school in Letterkenny.

I was able to lead my own life. I went to the swimming pool in the evenings and I ran a lot. We were all over London racing. I then veered towards looking to play Gaelic football with a view to staying on for the summer. I played briefly for Tir Chonaill Gaels. In all honesty, I probably wasn't good enough, but I was part of a history-making squad in 1971.

We beat St Anthony's, 1-8 to 1-6 in the London Intermediate Championship final. Tir Chonaill Gaels were heading to senior football for the first time since their foundation in 1964. Jackie Greene and Adrian Cannon (Dungloe), Charlie Tully (Dunkineely), Jim Cunningham (Kilcar), Mick Glynn (Glenties), Hughie Haughey (Ardara), Joe Kelly and Eddie Gallagher (Glenswilly), Anthony Gallagher (Letterkenny) and Jim McCready (Lettermacaward) were among my teammates and we had a Derryman, Charlie O'Donnell, starring for us.

I later signed for Cú Chulainns, who had no home, so the games were fixed for wherever they could get playing. We played a lot of games at New Elthom and out at a field near Croydon Airport. Ruislip, where London GAA has its base now, didn't exist.

We played on Sundays and we often played down near Wormwood Scrubs, the jail, with the playing fields right next to the perimeter wall.

I FIRST MET Rosaleen Houston in the Butt Hall in Ballybofey at a dance.

I didn't have the courage to ask her out to dance. Later that night, Rosaleen was walking up Donegal Street and I got up ahead of her. There were no street lights and the rain was hammering down. I was with a friend, Sean Quinn, just wandering up the street, when I said to him:

'I'm going after this woman.'

Rosaleen had an umbrella.

'You're going to get wet! Do you want me to hold your umbrella?'

Those were my first words to her.

Sometime later, I tried to track her down and she was going with another fella from Convoy, who was interested in her big time. Donegal were beginning to do well in Gaelic football and for one big game, I thought I'd get the Donegal supporters bus at Duncan's Cafe.

Rosaleen's father organised the bus.

She's bound to be on it!

She wasn't on it.

As we were coming back home, I looked out the window as we were going over the bridge in Ballybofey. There she was, walking with this other fella.

My world's over… this is a waste of time.

It wasn't long before we did get together.

One summer's night in 1967, I suggested to Rosaleen, as we walked through Drumboe Woods, that she come with me to London. My marriage proposal to Rosaleen, that evening as we strode through the towering trees on the banks of the Finn was more of a statement than a question.

'Sure, we better get married.'

That sentence to Rosaleen Houston – who was working in Donegal County Council – was one of my best ever. Rosaleen and I have been married for almost 52 years now and have raised a loving and beautiful family. She has been a consistent bedrock of support ever since she said 'yes' by the spruce trees of Drumboe.

MAKING A PHONE call in those days wasn't easy and people just wrote letters.

I used to phone home on a Saturday evening – but it was far from a straight forward process. You had to go through the Irish service in Liverpool, and they put you through to Ballybofey, where someone else connected you. Jesus, that was torture.

Rosaleen came over to live with me in England and got a job, but she was really homesick.

My parents were upset with me for a while when they were told that Rosaleen was pregnant and that we were getting married. In hindsight, I realised they would simply have been concerned about how my studies were going to be affected. Theirs was a natural parents' reaction.

The wedding was in Richmond. Fr Cunningham, a lovely man who worked in the college, married us on the 25th of November, 1967.

Rosaleen got a loan of a dress for the day, and Eamon Logue from Milford was my Best Man. Rosaleen's cousins, originally from Strabane, but living in London, came along and a few others. The Kerrs from Fanad were there.

But it was all very low key.

Not one person belonging to me was at the wedding.

THE NIGHT AFTER our wedding, most of our guests – most of them were Irish students – went for an Indian meal. We couldn't afford to go, so we just said we'd stay in. All the students had to get a bus from the wedding to the party. There's a picture with about 30 of them standing waiting to get the bus.

We had a close bond of Irish people in London and that was so important to help us struggle through.

The way we passed our time was playing cards and drinking tea. Alcohol was never brought into the place. It was never even in the discussion. Even the day of the wedding, there was no drink. That's hard to believe, isn't it?

Within a month of getting married, the priests in the college allowed me to rent a caravan and pull it into the side of the house they lived in. I'll never forget them for it. We used the facilities in the house and the priests were very good and very understanding towards us. When Rosaleen gave birth to Brendan, that support was invaluable to us.

I was trying to keep up my training, go to lectures and look after a baby.

Brendan was born at Middlesex Hospital on April 29, 1968. I was at college when he was born.

I dashed out and got to a payphone to check in with the hospital. All I heard was... Rosaleen had given birth to a 'baby boy'... mother and baby were 'doing fine'.

I was excited. But I was nervous. And worried.

I was concerned as to how I was going to handle everything. That was all going through my head. I didn't know a word called stress. Nobody was talking about stress in 1968 – you just got on with it.

I felt under pressure, but one thing that helped massively was the running. I got clarity and got answers out of running that I wouldn't otherwise have found. That really kept me going.

WE GOT A house down beside Twickenham stadium and I used to work at the stadium, in the bar collecting glasses. There was a big rush on match days, particularly at half-time and at the end. I used to be able to go in and sit on the line, about a yard away from the action.

I had the usual challenges a student faced.

I had to get accommodation.

I had to study.

I had to train.

Jesus, it was difficult.

One time I was working for the Post Office and we'd had nothing to eat for a day and a half.

Pay day arrived and I was so hungry that I ran to the shop and bought a big box of shortbread biscuits. In I went to Rosaleen and we gobbled the whole lot in one go.

There was a certain pride in me. I wasn't going to beg or borrow. I'd struggle for as far as I could and as long as I could. That's how everyone in Ireland was reared, so I struggled on.

I was wandering around from place to place and didn't know where I was going. I didn't even know where I was going to live. I probably paid too much for the caravan, but I needed a base and I had no experience. I was living on the edge all the time. I certainly wasn't going to spend money on trains. Soon, I had things down to a fine art.

I'd be in the canteen and have the dinner eaten before I got to the checkout. So, by the time I'd get there, I'd have nothing to pay for. The trick was to wait for the rush and then eat like mad.

When you got to the head of the queue, face-to-face with the girl on the till, it was a case of turning around, pretending to recognise someone.

'Ah, how are ya, John?'

And away to the back of the queue again.

Christmas was a time to come home. I always came out on the midnight flight because it was cheaper. I'd get back in at one o'clock and sleep at the airport.

I was a temporary postman at Christmas time in London.

One Christmas, a thought struck me as I was on my rounds. It was the last day and I was ready to head home.

If I deliver all these letters, I'll miss the plane.

I just posted the letters again. These letters, including a lot of Christmas cards, wouldn't be delivered until after Christmas. I had a few streets done, but knew I'd never get them all done in time.

The shit hit the fan after Christmas, but I was long gone by that stage.

THE FIRST TIME we came home with Brendan, we went to Rosaleen's parents in Ard McCarron, Ballybofey.

Rosaleen's father, Mickey came up and collected us at the airport in his Morris Minor. We were home for a couple of days and there was no word. One day, out of the blue, I decided that it was time we went to my parents.

In the dark of night, we headed down. I was trembling and I'll never forget those few moments. It was awkward for a few seconds, but the whole mindset and attitude changed in an instant.

There was a certain innocence to it all.

But it was great that we were removed. We didn't have the priest at home in our ear telling us not to get married or to go away. That was the way it was in Ireland in those times.

Before we got married, I had to get a letter of clearance from the priest at home. Canon Gallagher was an elderly man at the time. He gave me the clearance letter, but the letter included some sharp opinions and he certainly wasn't welcoming us with open arms. He was just underlining what Irish society was like at the time. He was an old school priest and that was just the way he was.

I got a house in England and we shared with a load of Irish students.

We got enough to keep the house going and we all looked out for each other. And it was great to have that support for Rosaleen, with the baby, while I was at college.

I had the advantage in the summer months of being able to go to Finner Army Camp.

I was determined not to stay in England. I could have walked into any job in the morning. Being educated at St Mary's College was such a big deal in Catholic schools.

I had to get home.

I sent Rosaleen and Brendan home about two weeks out from when I finished my exams. I knew if I stayed a week or two, I'd end up staying there. That wasn't going to happen.

I did my final exam and finished it at five o'clock and I was on the midnight flight out of there. Just the same as my last day at St Columb's... I was gone.

I didn't even return for graduation.

THE COMPREHENSIVE SCHOOL in Glenties was a new institution and I managed to get a job. I sort of just walked into the job. Remember, at that time, PE teachers weren't ten-a-penny.

The people in Glenties were brilliant. I got very involved in the community there. I was passionate, I was young and I was seriously energetic. Before the 'Comp', as it became known, Glenties had the McDevitt Institute. The McDevitt family had a big hosiery business and they were benefactors of the Institute.

I loved my time in Glenties.

Myself and Bill Walsh started off the Homecoming Festival in 1969. We had everything you'd expect at a summer festival. We got athletics going and I helped form Glenties Athletics Club. Before then, I had them affiliated with Cranford AC, who I was running with in those days. I was very proactive in fundraising.

Fr Dan McDyre, who would later become Monsignor McDyre, was the Principal in the Comp. He was a local, from Kilrane in Glenties. I had his support and that was vital.

There I was, the first PE teacher in Donegal. While there was PE in the schools in Northern Ireland, there was nothing in the Republic of Ireland. There was no training college until Thomond College opened in Limerick.

The sporting hero in Glenties in those days was Columba McDyre – Fr Dan's brother – who was a member of the Cavan team that won an All-Ireland football final at the Polo Grounds in New York in 1947. He was the only Donegal man ever to win an All-Ireland medal until Donegal's breakthrough under Brian McEniff in 1992.

I WASN'T ABLE to drive when I started off in Glenties.

Mickey Houston sourced me a blue Morris Minor down in Strabane and that car – bought for £28 – was the conduit for everything, from gathering boys up, to leaving boys home. The thing was, though, I couldn't drive it.

I jumped and bounced about the car park, not a clue what I was at. Until, that was, I arranged a women's football match in Glenfin, in 1970.

A women's football match between Glenties and Glenfin in 1970... I had no barriers at all.

The car was still sitting in the school. It had never been on the road.

How am I going to get this team to Glenfin?

'Right girls... give us a push.

'Shape her up towards the old station.'

Away we went and there I was driving for Glenfin. We played the game on a wee small pitch beside the graveyard in Glenfin. In the middle of the match, however, I was thinking...

How do I get this car home?

Easy.

I got the girls to push it around... face it for Glenties.

When I got to Glenties, I didn't go back up to the school, so I was a driver from that day. You wouldn't believe the amount of people you'd get into a Morris Minor – I got 13 into it one time in the early days of Finn Valley. They were squeezed into the boot, wherever there was room!

Josie Duffy counted them outside the shop on Navenny Street.

There were no barriers in my head.

I used to keep the athletes after school and leave boys off around Ardara, Maghery... wherever they had to go. Running wasn't altogether acceptable. Some within the GAA community didn't want me to introduce athletics into their town. I was even threatened about it one night outside the Highlands Hotel.

It got so bad at one stage I thought I was going to get hit.

'You're fucking up the young ones.

'We need them for GAA training'.

I wasn't trying to be confrontational.

They were running for Cranford and winning Ulster titles.

At that time, the Department didn't allow boxing on the curriculum but, of course, I was caught out.

I was bumming away about the boxing to Mick McDonagh, now the Department Inspector. He was aware of my father. He was in charge of the physical training college at The Curragh and prior to this had been an army man.

I'd put boys in a square and get them to fight.

That was one PE class. We did gymnastics and football a lot, and we did running – which was basically, open the gate and away you go for a mile or two. There were no inhibitions. I was just this young fella with a lot of energy who was going to change the world.

I met up with a science teacher, Bernie O'Callaghan, who hailed from Killybegs and got him back into athletics. We began to work, think and plan a structure.

THAT YEAR IN Glenties, I trained the lads at Naomh Conaill, the local GAA club.

They were playing Ardara in the Championship. For anyone who doesn't know, you could say it was one of the most ferocious rivalries in world sport and on the right day it wouldn't feel like you were exaggerating.

God, it was hostile. It was just raw, local pride.

They expected me to run them around the field. I used wee hurdles, innovative things that the lads wouldn't have seen before and it was totally alien to them. Some fella came back from America, arrived at half-time and Ardara beat us. They were expected to beat us.

The pitch was a bog. We used it for running and I held some big athletics meetings on it in the summer. The Cardinal Dalton Games, for example.

I was completely and absolutely zeroed in to starting Donegal athletics, and we used to run the primary schools athletics on a Sunday in MacCumhaill Park. Certain teachers keyed in and others didn't, but I was flat out.

I formed a club in Glenties.

Killybegs got a club going.

There was one in Lifford, and one in Donegal town. Cranford, of course, were there. Ballyshannon and Holy Cross College, Falcarragh, also formed club units.

I WAS RUNNING away myself. It was so strange for anyone to be out running at that time. I often used to run along the old railway line into Fintown.

One beautiful summer's day, I couldn't hack the heat, so I took off my top. I tied the vest around me and was running away, along the banks of Lough Finn, as happy as Larry, until I got to the railway gate at the edge of Glenties.

The guards were there, laughing away like mad.

They saw who it was coming running towards them.

'It's the PE teacher from the school!'

Some woman had phoned them reporting, 'A man with no clothes on running down the railway line'.

THE DONOGH O'MALLEY Regional Technical College, the 'RTC' opened in Letterkenny in 1972.

I spotted an advertisement for the job of PE teacher in the new third-level institute in Letterkenny and, after being interviewed by Neil T Blaney – who was absolutely instrumental in its development – and the CEO, Eddie Gibson, I was heading for pastures new.

Initially, I was just a bog-standard PE teacher, but my role, over 40 years from 1972 until 2012 at the RTC, later to become Letterkenny Institute of Technology, developed as the institute developed. Back in '72, we actually had a Leaving Certificate class and everyone in the place knew everyone else.

The place evolved quickly and I only taught classes for a few years. Soon, I was in a full-time role developing sport and opening new sporting opportunities for the students.

Seamus O Cnáimhsí, who taught me for a period in St Columb's, was my direct boss. I was lucky with the people who were my superiors.

I didn't get involved in any development at the IT.

I felt I had a lot of ideas and thoughts and maybe should have been consulted on some things. Maybe they didn't know the calibre I was, simply because of the way I acted. Not the fault of the IT, mind you. I imagine that I contributed to the perspective that people had of me because of my attitude.

That said, I was called to a meeting with the Estates Department one day. I saw the opportunity for a pitch with a running track around it and put it to the committee.

I felt they should have developed a track at the IT and Letterkenny AC could have had a new base. I got no enthusiasm from the Letterkenny club.

I pushed for a track, but the department wasn't too keen.

Letterkenny AC have a great base now at the Aura Leisure Centre, a Council-owned facility in the town, but I felt they should have come to the IT at that time. All they had was a dust track at the Community Centre, but the idea was never entertained. That being said, their current status suits them perfectly.

WE HAD A small sports hall, with a net in the middle and there was volleyball from what seemed like morning to night.

Charlie Mulgrew, later an All-Ireland medal winner in 1992 with Donegal, was part of a team that won an All-Ireland volleyball title. We also played basketball and badminton, and I was very involved with the soccer team. Regularly, I even drove the mini bus, which I borrowed from Jim Lafferty in Ballybofey.

The only tape I had was one of the *Wolfe Tones* so we had it blaring the whole way down to Galway, Athlone, Dundalk... wherever. The boys were psyched to the hilt and, on one memorable occasion, we beat Athlone 3-0, pumped on rebel songs.

Getting them home again was a big challenge when we were involved in multi-sports days out. You'd have two coach loads of students away and it could get messy, with drink involved.

I left six behind me that time in Galway and there was no word about it. Sure, you couldn't leave boys in a better place!

John Jarman, who had been at Wolverhampton Wanderers and was the FAI's Director of Coaching, spent a lot of time at the RTC. John had a great relationship with Dick Duffy from Letterkenny, one of the driving forces in getting organised soccer off the ground in Donegal.

John was going around various coaching centres as part of his brief and he used the RTC as something of a base.

Dick wanted me to put a team into the junior league, which had just been launched, but I didn't have the time to be engaged full-time in soccer. In the 1970s, I had developed lunchtime runs with staff and students.

We had great buy-in to that. We had all sorts of variants of races, and I was involved in getting the inter-firms race underway – something that has become a real highlight event in Letterkenny. We had a Donegal athletics training session on Tuesday nights based out of the RTC.

Different groups would go running from the RTC and one of the attractions for those sessions were the showers. I remember Jim Hynes, who was from Ballindrait, standing so long in the shower that there was water streaming down the hall, about to flood a couple of rooms.

Jim wasn't too bothered as he emerged.

'Boys, oh boys...this is the best ever.'

I wouldn't have been able to do what I did if I'd stayed in secondary school. Third level allowed me to develop support and an element of pliability.

Basically, the RTC was a base.

That was where I ran my athletics. I had all the mod-cons... a phone, a fax machine, a computer. I could go into my office and batter on with no interruptions. I always ticked the boxes. I was good at my job and knew what I had to do.

I wasn't an alien to the odd row either, of course. I remember when they developed the new sports hall, An Danlann, someone came up with the grand idea of 'decorations' – I use the term loosely – on the outside walls. The two hearts that are supposed to read 'I love Letterkenny loves me' are bad enough, but I've never been able to get my head around the dozens of garden rakes that hang from the wall adjacent to the front door.

As the Head of Sport, I got moved into An Danlann when it was built and they had an office earmarked for me near the front door.

I couldn't have that.

If I had been inside the front door, I was going to be too accessible. I wanted to be in the furthest, darkest corner of the place, and ended up in a grand wee office out the back looking over the football pitch, that a visitor could have spent a day trying to find.

That was perfection.

With two of my best friends, Pierce O'Callaghan and Stephen Maguire, at the 2017
World Championships in London. 'The Athletic Ireland rejects' as we Christened
ourselves!

THERE WERE CHANGES – big changes – afoot in Athletics Ireland as
we came out of the Olympic Games in Beijing. For years after the Games in
Sydney, I had stayed on the case about making the set-up more professional.

I didn't just want proper people in the proper jobs – they needed to be paid
for their services.

Back in 2003, a High Performance role was advertised by Athletics Ireland
and I applied for it. I didn't really want the job, but I applied for it anyway. I
was just sussing things out at that stage. I do that often; just check out where
people stand on different things.

I knew I was never going to get the job and Elaine Fitzgerald, who was very
capable, was appointed. At the time, I was the Director of High Performance
of Athletics Ireland, a voluntary position, but I was thinking outside the box
all the time. Pre-Beijing, I brought in expertise from all arts and parts, in a bid
to add to the professionalism of the whole set-up.

I had Brian Kerr, the Republic of Ireland soccer manager, on a committee.

I knew Brian from his involvement in university soccer and we had a good relationship. The committee also included Brian Mullins, Frank Campbell, Niall Moyna, Anne Keenan-Buckley, Maeve Kyle and Jim Kilty. I felt that forming that group was one of the best moves I made. Others, though, didn't share the same enthusiasm for the idea.

It became very clear, I suspect, because of my personality, my desire to change, or the fact that I couldn't be 'controlled', certain people within the sport felt they had seen and heard enough from me. I was a very dominant, strong person within the structure of the national federation. I had been there since 1991 and was key in every element, as a manager, selector and influencer.

WE NEEDED A performance base. We had to link up with the Third Level institutes. I was trying to work on a lot of things, but it was becoming apparent that my task was getting increasingly difficult.

My relationship with the association, with the people at the top of Athletics Ireland, had broken down. But I still had work to do,.

At the 2009 European Indoors in Turin I got to work on what I had to do for the good of Irish athletes, and some! Zoe Brown, a pole-vaulter representing Ireland, ran into trouble. Aer Lingus wouldn't take her poles to Italy, so I arranged for David McCarthy's parents, who were flying with Ryanair, to bring them to Milan on their journey as they were supporting their son who was a middle distance runner. We rented a car and the poles arrived at the team hotel at 2.0 am on the morning of the competition.

With all that was going on, my immediate loyalty and concern remained with the athletes. I was starting to get concerned, though, and sure enough, I was asked to leave the Board of Athletics Ireland.

I wouldn't budge. I was an elected member and wasn't for moving. Pierce O'Callaghan and Stephen Maguire were two people who kept me right and were voices of reason and sanity during the whole difficult period.

Pierce, a consultant with the IAAF and EOC, has had lead roles at a host of major Championships. Stephen, from Strabane, was a coach with me on some Irish teams, and is now working as the Director of Performance and Coaching at Scottish Athletics.

It was the beginning of an episode in my life that was seriously stressful and certainly one I could have done without.

Athletics Ireland put out a statement in early November, 2008 to say I was suspended. I was under pressure now. Big pressure.

A lot of people wanted me gone, I felt, even some of my 'friends' in Donegal. Somehow, though, it never affected my management of teams. I was able to park it and keep going.

I don't really know how. I just got on with things. I didn't blink.

At one Congress in Athlone, I knew people would be mumbling about me in the crowd. I didn't hear any whispers, but the whole saga was dominating the athletics world so, in a congress with 300 Irish athletics people, it was obvious that it was going to come up.

I was one of the officers and had a seat at the top table.

To make a point, visually, I pulled my seat to the side of the stage and basically sat on my own, while the rest of the Board sat at a table. It was my way of saying I was standing firm in my position and was distancing myself from the Board.

I never missed training at Finn Valley all during this spell.

What I had done every single day of my life, I felt, was on the line. I couldn't let that happen.

But it was clear that athletics in this country might soon be hurting. In February, 2009 the Sports Council announced that they were withholding funding to Athletics Ireland. The whole business was stressful for everyone, not just me, but in the middle of it all there were moments of relief – that I can now look back at with a smile on my face.

After one unsatisfactory meeting of the Board in Dublin, I hightailed it to the airport and was in need of making some urgent phone calls, I thought. But my mobile phone was drained. At the departure gates, there were no plugs.

But I knew where there was one. Airline attendants have one at the desk where they make their announcements, so hurriedly I got down on my hunkers behind the desk, plugged out the audio system and plugged my phone in.

Before the phone could even switch itself on, this woman hurried over, needing to make an announcement to passengers.

'You can't announce anything yet,' I told her.

'You have no idea about the importance of the call I have to make.'

All I needed was a minute or two, and I got them. Of all people, Nick Leeson, who was sentenced to prison for bringing down Barings Bank, the UK's oldest Merchant bank in the early 90s, happened to be waiting for a flight to Galway at the same time and was watching all of this unfold.

'Jesus that was some act you played there,' he told me.

I took it as a compliment.

THE WHOLE BUSINESS was getting worse by the minute.

It was also a costly business, as I had a legal team at work on my behalf that included John Rodgers, the former Attorney General. Eventually I had to sit down with my family and tell them what was at stake. I felt that our house in Ballyliffin was on the line. The view around the family table was that I had put too much into the sport of athletics to let it get the better of me.

While I was in Doha at the World Indoor Championships, there was a court hearing being held. It had a big effect on me personally. Every day, there was something different going on... talking to a solicitor, preparing documents, and remembering that I was still the Irish team manager.

The phrase now probably would be that I was 'depressed', but that word was never in my vocabulary. People formed opinions and took sides. Some of those people didn't have the full facts, but that didn't stop them from forming firm thoughts on what was happening.

I drank a lot over this period.

In the mornings I was conscious that I had a hangover, but I didn't let on to anyone, even though my head was far from clear. I got into a bad habit of buying a bottle of wine after training and taking it home. It was a long and stressful battle that impacted on my health and my life.

The 'business' even reached an Oireachtas committee in June of 2009.

It was odd, therefore, that after such a long battle that the actual settlement of the case drew little coverage across the media. The whole, sorry saga ended with barely a whimper from the national media.

For me personally, it ended with an apology and a settlement figure. I handed the settlement cheque over to Athletics Ireland.

I embraced the working relationship and the discipline of the army.
The camaraderie and the people concentrated me.

THE NOISE OF mortar bombs blasting out of a Toyota Hiace van is a terrifying experience when it's close by. I was in a room upstairs in Lifford Army Barracks one Sunday evening in the 1970s and I was sure we were under siege. About 150 yards away, on the bridge between Lifford and Strabane, the mortars were pinging away.

Momentarily, I thought the barracks was under fire.

The bastards are taking us on tonight.

Before too long I was in position behind the sandbags, along a wall at the front of the barracks.

I was ready for action. The only problem was it wasn't a gun that I had pointed over the top, but the remote control for the television.

The man next to me saw what was in my hand and just said, 'Sir' and nodded, either in sympathy or disgust.

Another night as the mortars started to blast I was lying in watching *The French Lieutenant's Woman*, a film starring Meryl Streep. Another officer, who had just arrived, was staring out of the window, looking very concerned. I didn't move. I knew at that stage it had nothing to do with us, so I settled down to watch the film.

Your man at the window was ready for war.

'Naw, sir,' I told him, 'Settle yourself.'

I was 13-and-a-half, in my second year at St Columb's College, when I had joined An Fórsa Cosanta Áitiúl (Irish for the Local Defence Force), or the FCA as it was known.

You were supposed to be 17 before being recruited, but there I was, a dying-looking young fella, still four years away from being eligible, when I got accepted. I'll never forget putting on the uniform, all eight stone of me standing there, looking like a clothes hanger, as proud as punch.

The thing was actually hanging off me.

Seamus Hoare, a former Donegal goalkeeper and an officer in the FCA, came down the stairs to the foyer of Rockhill House – a 19th century country house outside Letterkenny and one of the army bases in Donegal – and looked me up and down.

'Jesus, young McGonagle, you'd think that uniform was made for ye'.

I felt six foot six. I didn't realise the whole place was likely sniggering and laughing at me. I wasn't unique because a lot of boys in the FCA were under-age, but it was certainly an exception for someone not even 14 years old to be in.

The first morning, a Sunday morning, we were all jammed into a big hall in Finner Camp for Mass. This was my first day as a soldier and my head was growing lighter by the moment.

I could feel it happening.

I hung on.

Hung on…

Hung…

BANG!

I fainted in the middle of Mass. A few boys had to carry me out of the place. I knew my father had to be embarrassed; his young fella getting carried out of Mass on his first day in the place. He had to be wondering if I was tough enough for it.

MY FATHER, A Captain, was stationed in Rockhill at the time. He was a Training Officer for all of the 24th Battalion of the FCA. There were hundreds of people in the FCA. Donegal was divided into A Company, B Company, C Company and D Company.

Around Ballybofey and the Finn Valley was A Company. But in every single Company there was only one rule above all others.

'Your rifle is your best friend. Don't lose your fucking rifle.'

At the end of the camp, there was a range where you fired the .303 rifle and, at first, I was scared of the thing as there was a powerful kickback from the gun. I put a beret under my tunic to cushion the force.

Here I was, not yet 14, in a dugout firing off live ammo. I was still at St Columb's College, so it was only really a summertime thing at that stage. We were expected to be there during the year for parades and all that, but if any of us were missing then someone else just signed us in.

We also took our rifles home with us.

I'm sure I was a sight, walking down Donegal Street in Ballybofey and a .303 rifle with me. A few boys sneaked some bullets out now and again, and they'd take off shooting rabbits.

When I got my first pay from Finner, I went away over to the shop to buy something. I left the rifle lying up against the hut. I got so excited, I forgot about my rifle. And, that one golden rule.

'Your rifle is your best friend. Don't lose your fucking rifle.'

Away I went, the son of the Officer, in for a pastry and forgot the rifle.

'Where's me fucking rifle?' I shouted when I came back.

One of the regular boys had lifted it to scare me. My father gave me an awful touch that day, but that was the only day I ever fell foul of the golden rule and I remained in the Army until I got to 57 and retirement age. I ended up Commandant of A Company.

WHEN THE TROUBLES broke out in 1969, my father was stationed in Athlone. He was immediately moved to the border because of his knowledge of the set-up around Donegal and Derry. Two army officers, my father and Captain James Kelly, who was posted to the Monaghan and Louth areas. worked the border lines.

My father was Commanding Officer in Rockhill to the 24th Battalion and became the conduit for recruiting Derry men to the FCA. In total he recruited around 15 from Derry, some of whom had been at St Columb's with me. They were all trained in arms.

My father trained them in Dunree, and the idea was that they would 'control' Derry. They were trained in all sorts of weapons in Dunree, and being in the FCA was really just a cover-up. My father gave them an address... 1 Fahan Halt, Fahan, which is basically the end of the pier in Fahan, a blink-and-you'll-miss-it village on the way to Buncrana.

Years later, back money arrived for those men that was due from their FCA days and the postman, naturally enough, couldn't find the address. The cheques kept going back to the finance department in Dublin. I'm not sure if the cheques were ever cashed.

My father reported back to Colonel Michael Hefferon, the Director of Intelligence, who was based in National HQ in Dublin. One particular day, I remember travelling in a car from Ardara to Glenties, where I was working in the school. The news came on the radio that the Minister for Defence, Jim Gibbons had denied in the Dáil that there were any Derrymen being trained up in Dunree.

My father had been in Cyprus where he served with the UN. The British Army were very big in Cyprus, and one of the Brits gave my father a little recording device which my father had used to record a conversation of him being given orders to train the Derrymen, who were non-Republicans.

The intention was for them to control things in Derry rather than let the IRA take control. When the shit hit the fan and it was being debated in the Dáil, Minister Gibbons rang my father and said that he'd have to resign from the army. He told my father he shouldn't have recruited the Derry men in the first place.

My father listened. His appointment to Donegal was Officer Commanding with an added intelligence brief. He knew what was coming around the corner. He knew Gibbons would deny all knowledge. He knew they would come after him.

My father took some advice from Neil Blaney, a TD based in Donegal, and got back onto Gibbons. He told him that he'd resign, but he also told the

Minister to listen in on the 1.30 news on *RTÉ*.

My father was prepared to put the tape out on *RTÉ*, of him receiving his orders to take the Derrymen on board.

That was the last my father heard about the matter.

OUR DAILY TIMETABLE was like clockwork.

We had two parades, at nine o'clock in the morning and two o'clock in the afternoon, every day. One particular day - July 31, 1972 - at two o'clock I checked and half of them weren't there. I knew right away what it was.

Operation Motorman.

We knew this was coming.

My father had recruited a good few Derrymen into the Irish Army and the tension was as high as it could get in Derry. The British moved in thousands of extra troops to regain control of 'Free Derry' and our boys went home to look after their families. 'Free Derry' was a 'no-go' area for British troops, a barricaded area in Derry manned around the clock.

My father was off on holiday and another officer took over from him. There were no Derrymen in the two o'clock parade and the replacement officer who was from down the country somewhere and didn't know the craic, wanted to mark them AWOL. I reasoned that if we could ring my father that we'd get it sorted.

Paddy McGroarty, an FCA officer from Moville, had worked with my father in the recruiting of the Derry boys for the FCA. Paddy was based in Moville and, in the early hours of the morning, saw navy boats coming up the Foyle. His message was stark. 'The boats are low in the water.'

The Brits were coming to get Derry back and looking to put a stop to the IRA activity in areas such as 'Free Derry'.

The word went out through the Republican community that they weren't to be in their homes. They made themselves scarce. The Brits came gung-ho, but the majority of the IRA men headed for sanctuary in Inishowen,

I rang my father, who in turn was onto Paddy 'Bogside' Doherty, a leading activist in Derry. I was stationed in Rockhill and Paddy 'Bogside' rang me. I could hear the panic and the degree of urgency in his voice.

'We're pinned down,' he told me.

'There's a gunfight going on here.'

He held the phone away and I could hear the ping of the bullets, but he then told me that he would sort things out.

'I'll hire a bus and I'll have these boys on parade in the morning,' he assured me. About half eight the next morning, this bus pulled up and, sure enough, the Derry crew, to a man, were all there.

My father's advantage in intelligence were the priests, who were a great source of local knowledge.

Generally speaking, the priests in the Derry Diocese were Inishowen men. Being a well respected Derry City footballer in his day also helped my father. It gave him a standing around the place. He could wander about and chat away.

'Any word of the B Specials?'

'What British Army Unit is active here?'

Amongst other things my father had organised Bernadette Devlin, the civil rights leader, to get out of Derry. He brought her to Rockhill. From there she was taken direct to Shannon and whisked off to America.

AT ALL TIMES, however, my father was cute enough not to get sucked in by the IRA boys, who would go to him looking to source weapons, as there was an expectation from them that the Government in Dublin would supply them.

It was a regular occurrence for me to come home and Martin McGuinness, a young IRA activist, would be sitting above the chemist shop in Ballybofey with my mother feeding him biscuits.

ALTHOUGH THERE WERE some obvious exceptions, life could get very boring in the army, given that one of the main remits in a place like Lifford was to support the Gardaí on patrols. At a point, I devised inter-platoon competitions to make things a little more interesting.

I sent them out to Murlog chapel, just outside Lifford, carrying their full packs, holding their rifles, and timed how long it took them to get back to the barracks. Another time, I put them all on a lorry and took them out to the middle of Barnesmore Gap. Again, they were in full regalia, carrying weapons, all sorts of ammunition, the works.

They got out of the lorry and had to get back to Lifford. Not, though, on the main road. Away they went, in over the 'Derg Line', as it's called, over the hills and trails for 26 miles. It was a full day away. When they got back to the handball alley at Crossroads village, they got a break.

We had competitions, too, that involved putting them into teams and running them around the beach at Dunree. Again, the time was on the last man and, of course, I was there driving the Jesus out of them. They may not have liked the challenge on the day, but they did enjoy it afterwards.

Then, there was the day I brought them to the top of Barnes.

It was getting late in the day and I figured I was going to be running it tight for time to get back to training at Finn Valley.

'If we get off this hill quick enough now,' I told them, '... we'll go into Biddy's O'Barnes and spend an hour there'.

I had it figured out, we could spend an hour in the famous *Biddy's* – a public house in the middle of 'The Gap' – and I could still be back for training. The tactic worked a dream. Once Biddy's was mentioned, men were practically coming down on the arse of their trousers, they were in such a hurry.

THE IRA USED the cover of Finn Harps games to bring boys in for meetings. At that time in Ballybofey, up to 10,000 people might watch Harps. The big games were against the likes of Waterford and Cork Hibs.

A cousin of Rosaleen's was stopped in Stranorlar and was lifted in London a year later. He was in a cell and being interrogated, tortured, the lot.

'You were in Ballybofey that day.

'Why were you in Ballybofey?'

He would never have been at a football match. He wouldn't have known what colour Harps played in.

'I was up to see the Harps,' he told his interrogators.

'Who were they playing?'

He had a priceless answer up his sleeve.

'I'll tell you now,' he began, '... when I go to see the Harps, I'm only looking at the wan team.'

9

With the first-ever Ulster team from Finn Valley, competing in Omagh in 1972: Manus O'Donnell, Georgina McNulty, Bridgeen Houston, Doreen Gallagher, Antoinette Duffy, Mary Anne McGowan and Susan Houston.

IN TURIN FOR the 2009 European Indoor Championships I was half-waiting for Athletics Ireland's guillotine to fall on me.

The backdrop was that seriously volatile row, but I was able to manage two parallel worlds. I had a serious amount of pressure on my shoulders, but I was able to 'manage' that and still manage the team. The Championships were in the Oval Lingotto, which had been built to stage the speed skating at the 2006 Winter Olympics.

We came into Turin in good form after Beijing and actually those Championships were, results-wise, the best under my watch. In the rankings table in Turin, Ireland finished joint eighth.

We impacted well.

Derval O'Rourke was in top form and won a bronze in the 60 metres hurdles. She ran a season's best 7.97 seconds, her fastest time since 2006 when she was the World Indoor champion in Moscow. You just expected Derval to deliver on certain stages and Turin was one. The curtain went up.

The gun sounded. Derval performed.

But, as invigorating for me, was how Mary Cullen did.

A CALF INJURY had kept Mary Cullen out of Beijing, but she came back with a real bite in Turin. She won a bronze in the 3000 metres in Turin having lowered Sonia O'Sullivan's record earlier in 2009 at the Boston Valentine Invitational.

Mary went to Providence College and, under the guidance of Ray Treacy, John's brother who was the coach in the college, became a lead athlete in the States. She came to Turin aiming for a medal – she got a bronze.

That outlined the talent that she had. She was cut from tough stuff but, ultimately, injuries beat her. Her international career was brought to a close in a bedroom in Amsterdam, on the night before she was due to run at the European Championships in 2016.

There were doubts before the Championships, but she was on board and desperately trying to make the qualifying time for the Rio Olympics. I went up to her room to discuss running or not running. The answer was inevitable.

She just sat there with a resigned look on her face. There were tears.

A lot of tears.

'You'll come back from this,' I told her. 'You know, Mary… you could jog around the marathon and get the time.'.

None of it ever materialised and Mary Cullen never got to her cherished Olympic Games. Athletics was her life. She was capable. She was prepared. But, Jesus, she was unfortunate. Going in the marathon didn't excite her, but if she had gone to the Olympics I feel she'd have been fulfilled.

None of us knew it that night in Amsterdam, but Mary Cullen's international career was ending.

We had to get her a flight home, and that was her gone.

Injury messed her up for Beijing and she just didn't make the time for London. In December 2015, Mary, from Drumcliffe in north county Sligo, came to the St Stephen's Day 5k at Finn Valley and smashed the women's course record. She finished in 15 minutes and 45 seconds – taking 29 seconds off Vivien Cheruiyot's time from 2007.

That night in Amsterdam was the end of a long road for Mary. Time had been running out and a coach in Sligo, Dermot McDermott organised a meet at IT Sligo, with the sole aim to get Mary over the line and qualified for Rio. This was in late June, with the Rio deadline looming fast. Dermot took in pacemakers from all arts and parts, but it just didn't work for them.

That night in Amsterdam, her mind was probably – like mine – going back to those moments before Beijing when hope briefly flickered for her. I was sitting in Northwood in the Crowne Plaza in Santry in 2008 when, out of the blue, my phone rang.

It was a voice from the Olympic Council of Ireland.

I was told I had a decision to make.

I was then given three names.

The OCI had decided that they'd take three B standard athletes to Beijing and gave me three names… Pauline Curley, Michelle Carey and Thomas Chamney. They said something to the effect that, if I didn't call it, there'd be none of them going.

I put the names of other B athletes to them, including Mary Cullen's, but it was quite clear the OCI had their trio already selected. I don't even know why they rang me. They probably needed some semblance of a buy-in from somebody.

Ireland had never taken B standard athletes to an Olympic Games before Beijing and haven't done since. Mark English was a young up and coming athlete in 2012 who would have benefited so much from going to London.

It was a short hop across to London, but the OCI wouldn't entertain the idea, even though, at the previous Games, they'd taken three athletes half-way round the world to Beijing.

ROISIN McGETTIGAN WAS fourth in the 1,500 metres in Turin but, five years later, was upgraded to a bronze after the race winner, Anna Alminova – yes, a Russian – was found to have been doping.

Roisin was at Providence, at the same time as Mary, and was also coached by Ray Treacy. Roisin was from Wicklow, but has strong family connections to Kilmacrennan in Donegal. The 3,000m steeplechase was new in Beijing and, as the Russians and Kenyans were arriving, I could sense that the event was going to go through the roof. Roisin came into it at the right time, took advantage of it and did extremely well. She exceeded herself, in fact. She reached the final in the Olympic Games at Beijing. The problem was, she knackered herself in qualifying.

Her final was very hard to watch. She had a very good ranking from the heats, but the final became a nightmare. That's the thing about Championships; coaches need to remind themselves preparing that you can have two races in three days, or three races in five days. It's not all about going out and getting that one big bang.

I HAD A women's 4x400 metres relay team in Turin that people told me I was mad to take in the first place. Marian Andrews (later to become Marian Heffernan), Brona Furlong, Gemma Hynes and Claire Bergin didn't win a medal, but they came from nowhere – and I mean absolutely nowhere – to finish fourth.

I was trying to develop a 4x400 metres squad for the future and I had a real battle getting that team. I adopted the old GAA approach. It was all mental motivation. I was trackside, roaring like an absolute maniac at them. That didn't happen in athletics, but I could always make an exception and it worked with those four.

Just 18 months earlier, Brona was winning an All-Ireland camogie medal with Wexford. Then there was Claire, who had also competed at the winter Olympics in bobsleigh. I got serious engagement from that team in Turin and they set the second fastest time ever (3:36.82) for Ireland in the event. They were easy to get through to and they transcended the excitement into performance.

At the 2006 European Championships in Gothenburg we hit high notes with the relays. The women's 4x100 metres team set a national record with Derval joined by Joanne Cuddihy, Ailis McSweeney and Anna Boyle.

There were no expectations for our men's 4x400 metres team, but they made the final, with Brian Doyle on board. Brian was from Scotland, but had family connections in Donegal and ran for Finn Valley. He was very loyal and came regularly to us. Gillick, Paul McKee and David McCarthy were on board and it was a solid team.

McKee and McCarthy were on a 4x400 metres team with Robert Daly and Antoine Burke, who broke the national record in 2002 at the European

Championships in Munich. Pre-Beijing, I spent a lot of time trying to piece together a relay team to make the Olympics. I had them set up all over the place, from Belgium to Zaragoza.

The door for a lot of athletes was in relays.

Individually, certain athletes mightn't be great, but they could impact in a team. I remember some lads who tried to make individual qualifications, which was never going to happen, but they could have made relay teams. They lost out because they wouldn't listen.

A lot of people criticised me for entering that 4x400 team in Turin, but they were close to the podium and two of them reached individual semi-finals.

As I wrote in a blog that night… 'To blazes with the begrudgers.'

Myself, my brothers (John, Charlie and Eamon) and sisters (Mary and Susan) with our parents.

POLITICS WAS ALWAYS a hot subject in the McGonagle household.

My mother was a staunch Fianna Fail supporter. She was a very strong-willed woman and a real matriarch who called things how they were, which wasn't always the popular line.

She was also very active in the party and became the Chairperson of the Comhairle Ceanntair. That was very unusual for a woman in those days, but she carried the role with no discomfort. Being the local chemist, she had a big influence within the community anyway.

Neil Blaney, our TD from Donegal, used to have a clinic in my mother's store and he asked her to run in the 1979 Local Authority election.

Neil had been elected to the Dáil in 1948 as a Fianna Fáil TD. He was a Fanad man, who held numerous senior ministerial positions in Fianna Fáil governments but, with the beginning of the Troubles in 1969, he was concerned by the plight particularly of the people in Derry.

My mother was too busy to take up Neil's offer, but she volunteered me. I was too consumed by my athletics, so I suggested that my sister Susan could be a candidate. A woman had never been elected to serve in Donegal County Council, but we tore into it and we got Susan onto the Council.

IN 1972, BLANEY split from Fianna Fáil and formed Independent Fianna Fáil, a breakaway party. My mother had to make a choice. Immediately, she also broke from Fianna Fáil and sent her notice to the party by telegram, indicating to Neil that she was with him.

That was perhaps a surprise to people because Ballybofey was big Fianna Fáil country. We fought elections for Blaney, put up posters, canvassed and rallied support though in the beginning people were reluctant to show their hand because of the strength of Fianna Fáil in Ballybofey and Stranorlar.

One night around 11 o'clock we were putting up posters and a car load of Fianna Fáil people came along. There would have been a fight only I stepped out of the car outside Andy Bonner's shop in Stranorlar. The Fianna Fáil members sped away.

Up in Knock, a few miles outside Ballybofey, which was solid for Fianna Fáil and the home ground for Senator Patrick McGowan, we put up a rake of posters. They were always torn down, but we tore down posters too. That was all part of the carry-on. I had our boys, Brendan, Conor and Niall all out putting up - and pulling down – posters all the time, too.

We chased votes and we stood in booths. I used to stand at the Butt Hall, which was the biggest polling station in the area, eyeballing everyone on the way in.

I was driving out with the loud speaker blaring.

'VOTE BLANEY'.

'VOTE BLANEY'.

'VOTE BLANEY'.

ALICE STEPS OUT, PATSY STEPS IN.

The headline in the *Donegal People's Press* screamed something I never thought I'd see. I maintained an interest in politics, but without ever thinking about any involvement until Alice Bonner, a Fianna Fáil Councillor, decided that she was stepping down. I was very friendly with Alice and, after Mass one Sunday, she mentioned to me about running in her place.

Harry Blaney was on at the same time, asking me to run for Independent Fianna Fail. I was at Finn Valley when Harry rang and he had sent people over to talk to me.

I had an allegiance and maybe even an obligation to the Blaney camp. But I decided that I was going to run for Fianna Fáil. It was all in place, but, when it went public, a panic whipped up behind the scenes. I was at a Cross-Country athletics meeting in Mullingar and got a call from Alice at 11 o'clock one Sunday morning. She wanted me to call to her that evening.

In the middle of the shop in Stranorlar, she said she was reconsidering and thinking of putting herself forward. I had to make my position known, and I did.

'The way it is, Alice,' I told her, ' Harry Blaney was onto me too. I'm psyched to go and I'll work my head off to make it work. I'm torn now because I don't want to run against you.'

I wished her good luck.

There were around 300 people at a convention in the Finn Valley Centre. I did a speech but got out of there at the first chance. It was just a waste of time. I could see that the convention was stacked against me.

I also felt I wouldn't have been happy as a Councillor.

Sadly, the Finn Valley area still doesn't have a representative in the Dáil. That was and is a failure and a disappointment.

THE POLITICAL GROUNDING stood to me in later life, in athletics.

I felt that Donegal needed someone on the Irish Sports Council and, naturally, believed that I was the man for the job. I already had the feelers out for a while, about getting onto the Council.

I was driving past Clontibret on my way to Dublin when Jimmy McDaid rang to tell me I had been elected onto the Council. I found that a good experience. It was influential in one way, but the Council was driven by civil servants and the department.

I enjoyed the connections I made in the Sports Council and it was valuable to a point. The position was all part of the profile too, and it helped network me into things that I wouldn't have got at otherwise.

Building the story with an early Finn Valley group at Sean MacCumhaill Park.

BEFORE I WENT to London, I wanted to form an athletics club in Donegal so, in August of 1971, I called a meeting in Jackson's Hotel in Ballybofey.

I had settled on a name and the colours before the meeting even took place. The Finn Valley Athletic Club would wear blue and white. To this day I am so grateful that I had the initiative and sense to christen the club Finn Valley.

I wanted to avoid the parochialism that can come by labelling a club with the name of a town. Finn Harps were flying at the time and their colours were blue and white, so that seemed like a natural thing to tag onto.

Manus O'Donnell and Eugene Quinn, two local teachers, were at the meeting. Fr Kerr from St Columba's College, Sister Catriona, a nun from Ballybofey, and Mickey Houston and Hughie Gallen were the other key attendees. I was based in London at the time, so they were on their own most of the time.

None of them had any athletics background, but they got on with it. I came over and back as often as I could in the early months to keep the clock ticking. As soon as I came back, I'd take training out in Drumboe Woods. We were living off nothing… begging, borrowing and surviving just to get the club, pardon the expression, up and running.

All the while, I was trying to get through college, doing a thesis on the kinesiology of the golf swing of all things. Thousands upon thousands of words on a golf swing.

Imagine!

ONE THING I realised early on was that I needed an outlet in the media. It was no good me preaching to the converted – I needed to get the story out there to the general public.

I went to Sean Curran, who was the editor, and the everything, of the *Derry People*. Sean put the whole newspaper together from his sitting room at Lower Main Street in Letterkenny. He also ran the Donegal Printing Company and was a former inter-county footballer, having played for Donegal.

Getting a column in the *Derry People* was a big break for athletics. I wrote every week under the moniker *'The Olympian'*.

It was so helpful, and I was disappointed when I lost this soap box and the column was discontinued. I felt Donegal athletics had lost its way of reaching the public, until I found my way onto DCR – *Donegal Community Radio* – a pirate radio station. Charlie Collins was putting huge effort into a Saturday programme about sport and gave me an outlet to preach athletics. And when Charlie moved to *Highland Radio* in the early 1990s, I maintained the link and it became an important vehicle for me and the sport of athletics.

AFTER FORMING FINN Valley AC, we were very grateful for access to the practice pitch at MacCumhaill Park. Joe Doherty was the groundsman and was so supportive of us and we also used a piece of land across from MacCumhaill Park, where the shopping centre is now, for Cross-Country races. It was owned by the Butt Hall Committee, but Finn Harps used to train in there and had put up lights.

We also used the perimeter of Ballybofey & Stranorlar Golf Course, but we had to be careful and only use it when there was nobody else about.

Drumboe Woods was, and still is, a regular spot for Finn Valley athletes.

The club started off with youngsters and John Gallagher, a local teacher, was one of the first adult athletes. Manus O'Donnell was the first secretary and he was very positive and proactive which was important as there was some antipathy against athletics in the area at the start. We were building a new sport in Donegal and some feathers were ruffled in the process. It was no harm.

We built a strong club and soon took in people from east Donegal, who historically had always competed for Strabane, notably Francie Irwin. John Carlin from Castlefin was an Ulster high jump champion and was one of the people who understood what I was attempting. The Reid family were also hugely supportive.

Along the banking at MacCumhaill Park, we developed long jump and high jump 'facilities'. Well, we had a dust run up and a sand pit, which was about as much as you could hope for in Ballybofey in 1972. We had Anthony Dunne, Sean Carlin and PJ Sweeney – three of the top four long jumpers in Ireland – training from that sand pit in a corner of the training pitch. We really made the most of what we had.

The Twin Towns Youth Club had a sports day that we built on and I had county primary schools competitions, initially on a Sunday. Finn Valley AC did well immediately and started to win medals. We were on a roll.

I would have gone anywhere to get athletes into competition and to win. Cranford had dominated in Ulster and we soon had Neil Martin, who ran with me in Glenties, with us. Michael Crampsie, Patsy Doherty, Paddy Bonner, John Gallagher and Anthony Rushe came in quickly. Later, Pat Hegarty came in, too... Rushe had something. He won an Ulster Senior Cross-Country and, on natural ability alone, there were few who could touch him. He was good, but he just never 'got it'.

I remember him coming off the bend with Steve Ovett, the Olympic 800 metres gold medallist, one night at a meet in Belfast. With about 100 metres to go, there was nothing between them.

SOURCING MONEY FOR the club was a mission.

We used to gather up all the children to lift glass bottles from houses around the area. We could sell them again, so we'd go around every couple of weeks and collect the whole lot.

District Justice Liam McMenamin, on behalf of the Butt Hall Committee, gave us money at one stage and Frank Reid, from Donegal Creameries, supported us. Frank wasn't a man for a long conversation. I went to him one day looking for some help.

'Stay you there, young McGonagle.'

He came back down with 80 pounds and handed it to me for the Community Games. I would jam the athletes into buses. As many as we could get on, and more if it was possible. We were heading to Carrickfin one Sunday. Hugo Mulligan was a great character in Ballybofey, who drove buses and I asked him if there was enough on.

The kids were wedged as tight as they could.

'Naw, naw,' he replied nonchalantly. 'Keep putting them in 'til she sinks in the tar.'

At another stage, we got seats put up the middle of an old County Donegal Railway (CDR) bus. We were coming out of Strabane when I counted 124 people on the bus. One hundred and twenty-four. The capacity was around 50.

Coming into Lifford, I looked at the driver, Willie Duncan.

'What would the inspector say if he saw this?'

'I tell you what, Patrick, he wouldn't give me time to put on my coat.'

People like that took a chance on me.

Also, from day one, I involved parents.

As a result of that, men like Patsy McGinley and Peadar McGranaghan came on board and were instrumental. Peadar started up another training centre in Porter's field, just beside his house in Castlefin, which became an important venue for us. Liam Merritt had competed in track cycling in Strabane, and saw what I was at and got behind me. Carrigart and Downings youngsters came to us. Hughie McClafferty, who taught in Castlefin, started a training group in that area.

ALL THE WHILE, I needed a base.

In 1981, I struck gold with a disused factory at the Millbrae in Stranorlar.

When I first walked up to it, it was so badly dilapidated there weren't even doors on the place. Northern Construction owned it, but the business shut down and the building was left derelict. It was just a shell of a building with no windows and there was a limited amount of land to the back. It had gone to rack and ruin by the time an English company bought the place off the bank.

We bought it for £32,000.

We got money from half-a-dozen people around the town, and we got a loan for the balance. Rosaleen's father, my parents, Mick Gallen, Danny McIntyre, different people signed off on the necessary requirements for the bank to free up the necessary funds.

We also bought two acres from Kee's Hotel, but the town dump was next door and it was infested with rats. The dump was closing down and the Council agreed to give us the site. We had a LOT of work to do before it became usable as everything was buried there. Glass was the biggest problem and it just kept coming to the top. Francie Irwin and Patsy McGinley used to go down every single day, walk a yard and just clean it. That went on for months.

THE TWIN TOWNS Boxing Club had been using the place and we had to move them on. They had built a ring with cement blocks, put a floor in it and roped it off. It was rough enough, but it did the job for them.

The boxers were very negative towards me in the community when they left. I offered them an alternative, but they still weren't happy. Some years later, Conor Quigley came to me and was looking for somewhere to set up another boxing club. The conversation was pretty short. It was a case of them coming in and following my way of working.

Which they did, and they developed an extremely successful club. Conor had a lot of enthusiasm and it was brilliant to be associated with Finn Valley Amateur Boxing Club. They held a few tournaments at Finn Valley and they were hosts for Ulster Championships at the centre, too. It worked extremely well.

A young boy came out of that to be a World Championship silver medallist. I was on site to witness the joy of that and had been there for the disappointment when, as a younger boy, he had lost an Irish final. He would do nothing else only boxing. He was so focussed. He fought on and by God he made a success of himself. I developed a relationship with Conor and Jason Quigley from the earliest days.

They left to go to a place across the road, but I maintained my contact with Jason.

When he needed help and advice, I was always there for him and I watched his development very closely. I've been very proud to watch Jason develop further into a professional boxer as he signed up with Golden Boy Promotions in America, before basing himself in Sheffield within the brilliant Ingle 'boxing family'.

He's a fine example and role model to any aspiring young sportsperson and is currently the North American middleweight champion and listed inside the top 10 in the World rankings.

THE OFFICIAL OPENING of the Finn Valley Centre was held in September, 1982. Rev John O'Donnell, a Kilmacrennan native based in Manorhamilton who was the BLÉ President, performed the opening ceremony.

We had, even then, a gym, changing rooms, showers, a shop, a trophy room, a meeting room and a games room, with table tennis and pool tables. We had a crèche running from Monday to Friday and, rough and all as the place might have been, it was starting to become a community facility.

We filmed everything, thanks to Anthony Murray, who was doing wedding videos at the time. We were always pushing the boat out and doing new things. Neil Blaney gave us a grant of £20,000 to employ people, but there was a problem. I needed the money for materials, doors, windows, ceilings and what have you.

If I had given the money to boys for this scheme, I'd have had no money left for the essentials. As always, I had a plan. I used the names of a load of men who were in Boston at the time to get the grant. Basically, I needed to use the names of local men on the live register, who weren't working, showing that there were men available to do the work. I knew enough fellas who had left to work in the States.

We got the money, and we got the derelict building structured into a usable community facility. We made a reasonable job of it. No one asked a question.

I never questioned what I was doing. To me, it was for the benefit of the community, so it was grand. That was just the way I rolled.

The first long jump pit that we dug out in the corner of Finn Valley had a conveyor belt for a run-up. The run-up that we had wasn't long enough, so we simply started the run up from the middle of the children's play room and came bursting out the door, giving us the required length. This 'exciting' facility was officially opened by seven-time national long jump champion and club member, Hugo Duggan.

We managed to develop a nine-a-side football pitch with temporary lights, but we wanted more, and we needed more. I put a big push in for a grant, so I had a conversation with Mick Gallen, a big Fianna Fáil man in Ballybofey. We had to get Senator McGowan on side, too.

We opposed him in the last election and that was a worry for me.

Me and Peadar McGranaghan went to Lifford one Sunday night to try and get him on side. It worked. We got Senator McGowan on board and, with him, Pat 'The Cope', who was Minister of State at the Department of the Marine. I followed 'The Cope' around the country. I used to joke with boys that when Pat woke up in the morning I was at the bottom of his bed. They delivered for me.

That phase of the development, officially opened in 1989, was key for us.

Mary Coughlan, from Mountcharles, was a young politician who later became Tánaiste, but she probably summed up what we'd done in one simple sentence that Sunday afternoon.

'The club has put athletics on the map here.'

FOR AROUND 40 years, there'd been talk in the Twin Towns about a swimming pool. The project never went any further than talk.

It was something I never got involved in but, over time, it became obvious to me that it made sense to progress a swimming pool idea at Finn Valley. I began to make contact with officials in the Council. There had been money spent to do bore holes at the Finn Valley Centre so someone had been thinking about a swimming pool at some point. I took that as being an encouraging sign.

One Saturday morning I found myself in Noel McGinley's office with a load of Fianna Fáil people and it was suggested to me that there could be a way.

Jimmy McDaid, who was the Minister for Sport, pursued it and followed through. There was a couple of million euro of a shortfall, so we formed a company that was made up of Donegal County Council representatives and Finn Valley AC people. It was 50 per cent community and 50 per cent Council. The first Board was myself, Conor McGonagle, Neil Martin, Bridgeeen Doherty, Anne Marie McGeehin, Paul Doherty and Sean Carlin from Finn Valley; and from the Council we had Cora Harvey, Bartley McGlynn, Paul Kilcoyne, Frank McBrearty, Matin Harley and Patrick McGowan.

We put the plans forward and the Council suggested they'd obtain a loan from their lending agency.

The swimming pool was built for around €7 million and I was in it every single day. I had announced the launch of the development at Finn Valley AC's 40th anniversary celebrations in Jackson's Hotel.

Some clubs can lose focus when they're building facilities. To begin with, we couldn't lose sight of the fact that we were an athletic club. The club never took a step back through all the development.

It was very important that the two sides – the wet side and the dry side, I called them – were hand in glove. When the swimming pool was finished and ready to open, I said to Conor and the grandchildren that we'd go down one Saturday and be the first in there to swim.

There they were, in the pool, as some people outside were peering in the window wondering if the place was opened or not. Our family took great craic out of the fact that they were the first ones in.

CLARITY AND TRANSPARENCY about a club's financial dealings, especially in a club like Finn Valley where so much money has been on the move, is always vitally important. There are always a few people who will be inclined to have a pop.

'Patsy McGonagle is making a fortune over there.' That kind of throwaway remark can easily run amok.

So we had to be so careful.

It's all about accountability. Neither me nor any one person in my family ever held a financial position in the club. An approach we deliberately took in the early days was to appoint a bank official as the treasurer. It was taken out of the hand of even the athletics people.

We developed a business ethos and that thinking has seen us progress successfully. Between part-time and full-time, there are 45 staff at the Finn Valley Centre.

Local enterprise doesn't really engage local organisations like us, but we could always have done with more support. I wanted to develop a hostel here so that athletes could stay here to train. We had 10 en-suite rooms, a kitchen and a general dining area put in.

We ran it as a hostel for a while. We'd take a bus load of Shamrock Rovers fans in if they were down for a game against Finn Harps but, ultimately, the venture was going to be more torture than it was worth. The hostel idea just never took off so, eventually, that part of the building became offices.

Three or four small businesses use the facility, and other people run classes, and give us a little bit of rent. Taking all those people in, there could be up to 70 people with a return from the centre.

We have tried to develop opportunity and community.

The pool allowed us to do a lot more. We needed a car park, so the Council bought a chicken farm next door and we developed the car park on that site. We used the fill from the swimming pool and managed to level out the pitches that are now used by Finn Harps FC, Finn Valley Rugby Club, Ballybofey United, Finn Valley Ladies FC and various school groups.

We organised a land-swap to enable the development. Throughout this period, the relationship with Donegal County Council was excellent, thus we developed a legacy for the community beyond my time.

I would still like to see a cycling club, swimming club and a triathlon club developed at some point.

Eventually, in the late 1990s, I felt that I had taken the development of the centre to a point, and it was time for stronger, younger people. My son Conor came in with renewed energy. With my support, Conor drove things on further still.

I had a spell as Donegal team trainer in the mid-90s and again in the early noughties. I took part in a lot of stuff myself, like this run along the beach in Fintra.

'Pressure?

'You want to be in the changing rooms in Clones at half-time… and you're three points down to Down with Manus Boyle firing water bottles at you.

'That's fucking pressure'.

Interview with Irish Independent, Sydney Olympics, 2000

Clones, a market town in county Monaghan, is the epicentre of summers for Gaelic football supporters. In athletics terms, Clones is Ulster's Santry.

St Tiernach's Park, a claustrophobic arena at the top of the hill in the town, is their stage. It is a monument to a previous generation but, in the heat of the sporting battle, it's one of the most demanding places in the world. Even on that epic evening in Sydney, my mind wandered back a few years to a day spent in the Clones cauldron.

It was one of those afternoons when it felt as though the world was going to end. I was in the GAA trenches after being roped in to assist PJ McGowan, a Ballybofey man who was appointed as manager of the Donegal football team in 1993.

Those trenches were ferocious places. When Tom O'Riordan of the *Irish Independent* started questioning me about 'pressure', while in Sydney at the 2000 Olympics, my mind spun back five years, to 1995, when I was with PJ as we faced Down in the Ulster Championship.

Down were defending All-Ireland champs.

We had beaten them in the League earlier that year, but Down were still cock-a-hoop after winning the Sam Maguire Cup in 1994. Down always had a bit of a swagger but, boy, did we catch them that day? We beat them by 1-12 to 0-9 and Manus Boyle scored 1-5.

John Joe Doherty, an All-Ireland winner with Donegal in '92, got injured in the second-half, but he wouldn't come off. He was hardly able to walk.

John Joe could hardly move but he remained so psyched up.

'FUCK OFF... PATSY!

'I'm going... NOWHERE!'

I turned to the crowd and told them to encourage him to go off. Men like John Joe would have died for the county jersey, and it was a 'live or die' job in the Championship then. There was no qualifier series in those days. No back door, no second chances.

It was tense at half-time, as I was trying to drive on a message about not letting the game drift away. There was just overwhelming frustration in the room. The space was tight and we had 30 or so brutes of men, all fit to be tied. We were in front by a point, but it was as tight as you could imagine. The half ended with a bit of a skirmish so the mercury was high anyway.

A whole shouting match quickly broke out.

Manus fired a couple of bottles across the room and hit the far wall.

Manus, John Joe... those boys were absolute winners, and I loved that edge in them.

DONEGAL FOOTBALL WAS a bit fractious at the time. PJ had taken over from Brian McEniff, who was manager in 1992 when Donegal won that first epic All-Ireland. There had been a clamour for Martin McHugh, one of the '92 stars, to take the job, but he ended up managing Cavan and, as luck would have it, we ended up playing Cavan in the Championship in 1997.

Martin was a brilliant figure within the game, but there was a feeling that he had done the wrong thing by going to Cavan. They beat us fair and square in '97 and, after the game I went to shake his hand, but the same rush wasn't there from others.

There was a lot of resentment towards Martin from certain quarters, but I admired him. He put his head on the block and made what I'm sure was a difficult decision to go and manage Cavan. Martin knows the game inside out and he was the best individual footballer I ever watched. He controlled and contributed all the time.

He was an absolute leader and was always planning the strategy for the team. I have no doubt he would have been such a driving force in the dressing room if he had taken over Donegal. He lived for Donegal and his heart would have beat a little quicker if he'd been the Donegal manager.

I had a good relationship with PJ and I got involved with a view to just helping him, but sure I was neck deep in it before I knew it. I couldn't help it, and soon the training was 'mine'. It was my call what happened on the training pitch and I got a great reaction from the players.

Tom Comack, later to become a journalist with the *Donegal Democrat*, Michael Lafferty, Sean Ferriter and Seamus Gallagher were all involved with us. But it was probably the worst time to get involved in the county team, simply because of '92.

There was still a lot of back-slapping to be seen and heard. The men who lifted that first Sam Maguire Cup were a great bunch, no doubt about that. I understood and admired those fellas. They trained hard and never looked for short-cuts.

WE GOT TO two National League finals during my time with the county, in the spring of 1994 and again in '95, but we lost them both. I was disappointed the first year we lost to Derry, but I was devastated the second year, when once again Derry did the job on us even though it was a great Derry squad that included Anthony Tohill, Brian McGilligan, Tony Scullion and Joe Brolly. The game was all over after about ten minutes. Tohill and McGilligan destroyed us at midfield.

But, apart from Derry, we had another big problem. Our own County Board. The Board had the players skimping and scraping for simple things like bits of gear. If I thought it was going to be such a problem, I'd have bought the gear myself. Honestly, it would have made life easier.

Manus Boyle was always pushing them on it. If the Board gave them a polo shirt, they thought they had given them the world. The Killybegs boys, of which Manus was one, were strong personalities on the Donegal squad of the 1990s and drove the thing.

But the shit hit the fan in 1995.

We were coming up to a game against Monaghan in Ballybofey, a game that was widely and foolishly considered a walk in the park. I could see what everyone was thinking.

We'll beat Monaghan.

Of course we will... no problem!

I couldn't get them ready mentally and I was struggling. They were just there in body and they weren't 'into it'. I knew we were in bother. It was all about... 'gear, gear... fucking gear'. It would be wrong to say they wanted *more* gear. They simply wanted gear.

They had nothing at the time. At the last training session before the Monaghan game, a fight broke out. Manus and John Gildea got stuck into one another. I wasn't unhappy looking at them.

Thank Christ for this... bit of aggression at last.

Manus was a contrary boy and pushed Gildea 'til he reacted. John wasn't on the '92 squad and was one of the new guys. But he had that bit between his teeth, too.

It was too late and the incident didn't snap everyone to attention.

We lost to Monaghan. We were annihilated. 1-14 to 0-8. Hammered in our own back yard by nine points. Towards the end of the game, I went as far down towards the River End as I could go. I was just totally ashamed.

MY FIRST EXPERIENCE with Gaelic football was a crowd of us playing down on the practice pitch in Ballybofey. God knows how many of us played in those groups. With only one ball between us. If you weren't able to catch the thing, you were running around like a wasp all evening.

The Sean MacCumhaills club won senior championships in the 60s and 70s, but they were a Finn Valley team in those days and had players drawn from Glenfin to Castlefin. I had no knowledge of them at all. Football wasn't prevalent in Inishowen at the time, bar in Burt, Carndonagh and Urris.

As the years passed, I began to delve a little deeper into the game, and it was hard not to become involved. I went up to Glenfin, who had a good team at the time, to be their trainer.

It was all physical-related training, getting them fit and getting them focussed was what mattered. Glenfin didn't win too many Championship games at the time, but they had a serious team. They had the likes of Seamus Marley, who also did a bit of sprinting, the Ward brothers (Frank, Liam, Seamus and Dermot), Francie Martin, and Joey McDermott. Terry O'Reilly, who would later become the Garda Sergeant in Ballybofey, was at midfield.

I started winter training with them after Christmas – that was another first for a GAA team in Donegal. We had no floodlights or anything like that in Glenfin. One night I landed out and you couldn't see the place for snow, but in my head there was no question of training being called off. The boys were all standing at the door, just staring at me.

'Don't tell me the snow's going to fucking beat you all.'

I went apeshit. I can still see them now, doing press-ups in the snow and me barking away at them.

In athletics there was very little, or absolutely no, drinking in the background, but the GAA boys always went for a drink. Normally, I just went home, but I did join them on the odd occasion.

The problem I had with Glenfin was that Kilcar were in their pomp. Martin and James McHugh were flying, and that meant Kilcar were a giant-sized stumbling block. We did eventually win a Donegal Senior Gaeltacht Championship when we beat Naomh Columba in Glencolmcille. That was a massive achievement. We went to the All-Ireland Gaeltacht Championship in Carroroe and lost to Kilcar. Them again.

I felt that me being with Glenfin was never going to last, and I was right. We were playing MacCumhaills one evening in the League. Two of my sons, Niall and Conor were playing for MacCumhaills, who hadn't been going well and they got the bit between the teeth to bloody beat us.

The thing was just too confrontational with the two lads being with MacCumhaills. Soon enough I was managing MacCumhaills.

WE WERE PLAYING Ardara in MacCumhaill Park and Martin Gavigan was sent off. In those days, if you were sent off you weren't eligible to win an AllStar. Although he was playing against us, we tried to protect Martin. Myself and Charlie Faulkner, a MacCumhaills man who was the Donegal GAA chairman at the time, pleaded with the referee to let Martin stay on the field.

I knew it was going to be a big national story. Martin was one of the star men. Donegal were going well at the time and he was known all across the country. His nickname, 'Rambo' helped in that regard and, of course, his playing prowess made him a prominent national figure.

After the game, my message was very clear in our dressing-room.

'There will be people looking for this story about Martin Gavigan,' I warned. 'But, as far as we're all concerned he wasn't sent off.'

All the national newspapers were ringing around the whole place, but they never got the story. We were so solid on that. If that was nowadays, the ball wouldn't be at the lower goals when the news would be out... there'd be a #Rambo on Twitter.

I USUALLY FOUND that GAA people generally had no interest or understanding of any other sporting activity outside of their own bubble. They were in a world of their own. They didn't gravitate towards other sports. It was very insular.

Stephen Roche was going into the final day of the Tour de France, one of those famous summers for cycling in the late 1980s. Same day, Glenfin were playing Kilcar in a Championship game in Ballyshannon, and I got the driver to put the race on the TV on the bus, thinking it would act as a bit of motivation for the boys.

I looked around me a few minutes later and not one other man cared what was going on. They'd make the effort the odd time and ask about some athletics meet but, by and large, they didn't give a hoot. They were mainly just being polite.

IN THE WINTER of 2002, PJ McGowan came to my door again.

Donegal couldn't find a manager so Brian McEniff, as he often did, was stepping in. He needed help and PJ had suggested my name. Like the old eejit I was, I jumped at the chance.

The big wake-up call was how the preparation of teams had changed since my previous encounter with a county dressing-room.

Joe McBrearty from Killybegs was county trainer. Fortunately for me, Joe knew all the new routines. He had all the stuff backwards. I learned a lot from Joe and soon I was up to speed. Strength and Conditioning had come in and the Ulster Council were pushing out a big coaching message.

It wasn't all about training for me. I had to make the work on the field interesting. I needed ball work, small-sided games, and Joe was a Godsend. However, this period with the Donegal team was probably the most demoralising time of my whole sporting career. It was an absolute nightmare.

They were a talented bunch, but their lifestyle screwed them. They were very immature. Some of them went on to achieve everything under Jim McGuinness, but it took them a long time to cop on. The rest retired and never reached anywhere near their fullest potential. It was their own fault because they had talent. They just didn't wise up early enough as a group.

All the time, I had people ringing me and telling me stories about players out drinking. They were up to all sorts of stupid antics. It made me mad as hell.

Eventually, I told Brian to drop nine of them.

That came after we lost to Fermanagh in the opening round of the Ulster Championship.

On the Monday evening following the game we had a recovery session planned, but it looked like it might be abandoned. In the end, some of the boys turned up, some of them still the worse for wear. One or two of them were still drunk.

I read the riot act.

'We need to get the act together here.'

There was two weeks to go to our All-Ireland qualifier match against Longford, but the next evening the boys were off on the mess again. I was still getting phone call, after phone call.

When the Wednesday came Brian and I were walking up the side of the pitch in Ballybofey, when I dropped the bombshell.

'I have nine names here for you,' I told him. 'Drop them.' I knew the team was wrecked without those nine men, but it couldn't go on.

'We'll get players from somewhere,' I assured Brian.

He took the decision to drop two of them, and I compromised. Seven of them survived.

I knew that Brian wouldn't be through Donegal town before he'd relent and have the two of them back. So, I rang Tom Comack.

Tom was with me on the backroom team in my previous time with Donegal and was now working as a journalist with the *Donegal Democrat*.

'Get the story out there,' I asked him.

Brian heard the news on the radio going through Barnesmore Gap. Five days later we were in MacCumhaill Park on the Sunday for a training session. Joe McBrearty and I got an inkling that something wasn't right. We were out setting up for training, and were by ourselves. Not another sinner was out.

Something's going on here.

I went into the dressing-room, and World War Three was in full flow. Some of the lads were being disrespectful and abusive towards Brian, who was standing up on the bench in a corner of the room. The boys, seemingly, had a meeting before training and decided that they'd put on a bit of a strike.

'Bring the boys back or we're not training.'

I interrupted the whole thing.

I did not tread gingerly. 'You boys must be the most stupid bastards in Ireland.' I spoke to them as if they were two-year-olds. Nobody stopped me. One did try, but he copped on very quickly.

'If you aren't on that field in two minutes, you know what's going to happen then? You'll read about this in every national paper going.'

I grabbed the door and swung it, hitting PJ on the way out.

'You better be out after me,' I told them.

Half of them came out. The boys who had a meeting in Letterkenny stayed in. I started the session and, eventually, the rest of them came out. One of them wandered past me.

'You're lucky you didn't get hit in there,' he told me.

I replied loud enough for them all to hear.

'There's something you don't understand... I DON'T GIVE A FUCK!.'

I spoke to him, but was addressing the group. 'Just get on with fucking training!'

The two boys came back in a few weeks later.

I formed the impression that the boys from north Donegal were the problem. The boys drinking were the 'north of the Gap' boys. There was no indication of the same going on in the south. The 'north Donegal' boys used to socialise a lot in the Letterkenny area.

We went to London one time for a League game. We were driving from the Crown in Cricklewood to a match in Ruislip and they weren't switched on. With the greatest of respect to London, if we'd lost to them, we may as well have just left the country. I got wired up, I stood up on the middle of the bus.

'Think about how stupid you fuckers will look if we're beaten by London.'

We made hard work of it, but we won. I sat up the night before that game watching in case any of them would sneak out on me.

Brian put serious effort into it. He approached the job very professionally, but the boys just didn't match his hard work or ambition. And yet, we should have reached an All-Ireland final.

We were in a parallel world to the one Armagh were living in. Armagh had developed a real, hard-hitting mentality. We always came off second best to them.

We tried to set up a gym programme, but the problem was the players went in, looked in the mirror for an hour and went home. We'd have needed someone driving it on and reporting back.

Somehow, we got to the semi-finals in 2003.

After the Fermanagh defeat, there had been another little problem. Two anti-doping officials came to our dressing-room and in a room full of remorse and anger they did not get a great reception. I knew it was a requirement from my athletics background, and that the GAA had finally bought into the same procedures as the International sporting world. However, we had a wild problem convincing boys to comply. Luckily, I knew the anti-doping officials and I delayed them, and apologised for the abuse.

The officials left with what they had come for, but they must have been left wondering about the mad, unruly room they had visited.

13

Olive Loughnane entered the pantheon of great Irish athletes with a silver at the 2009 World Championships. The silver later turned to gold.

LOCATION, SOMETIMES, IS everything.

For Olive Loughnane, the 2009 World Championships in Berlin provided the most iconic, historic and picturesque backdrop to a silver medal. With the Brandenburg Gate gleaming just beyond the finish line, Olive walked the race of her life to win silver in the 20 kilometres event. Six years later, Olive's medal was upgraded to gold after the Russian, Olga Kaniskina was retrospectively banned, though I must admit I had no expectations of a medal for Olive going to Berlin.

Olive always believed in herself and I have no doubt that she was feeling a medal was possible. That was the way she rolled; with utter belief in herself.

Olive was more relaxed than ever in Berlin as she had a really positive race plan, and it worked for her. Kaniskina was so good on the day. Liu Hong from China and Anisya Kirdyapkina from Russia were also in the mix, but Olive dragged herself through the field into a medal position. From around the 16 kilometres mark, I was getting excited.

I knew then that the possibilities were opening up.

MY FIRST ENCOUNTER with Olive was at the 2000 Olympics in Sydney, where she finished 35th in the 20 kilometres walk.

Her sister, Anne was a great athlete and medalled at World youth level, winning a silver in the 5,000 metres walk in 2003. I was more aware of Anne, who sadly went out of the sport at a young age. Soon, though, it was evident that Olive had a fire within.

She was so driven.

If she was six inches short of a line and you blew the whistle, it wouldn't have done. Olive always demanded the best of herself and she certainly always believed in herself. In Athens at the 2004 Olympics, she was so nervous and anxious that she got up in the middle of the night, just hours before her race. She couldn't sleep, which is not unusual for an athlete.

She was knackered before the race ever started and she didn't finish in the 20 kilometres. Although she was a seriously hard trainer, Olive was a difficult management challenge for me. In Beijing, she was seventh and that was an indicator that she was at least capable of competing with the very best.

In her mind, she was always looking for improvement and she was always going to go the extra mile to get that improvement. She ended up being based in the mountains in Colorado. That didn't work out and she reverted back to Ireland. She still wanted to be the best she could be, and was willing to go out on a limb, to sacrifice, in order to achieve.

At the midway mark in Berlin, Olive was in fifth and she was really impacting on the race. We had been up since five o'clock that morning but the focus in her eyes was very clear. The canteen was eerily quiet at that hour. I liked that. The calmness allowed us to keep things controlled.

I had a lot of things to check for walkers. Their drinks, for example, Everything had to be absolutely spot on, but, anyway, Olive already had it all worked out. She had it figured to the very last millimetre. That was one of the reasons she was successful.

However, I hadn't seen the form to suggest that she could medal. Then, she came like an express train. Her training and her preparation, everything had been on point. I had her as top eight material, but she had an unreal second phase. Her last five kilometres were unbelievable in Berlin.

I ran like a madman across the Pariser Platz to get to the finish line. I broke the barrier, and the IAAF officials were trying to get me out of an area I shouldn't have been in.

'Patsy, you'll have to go back.'

'Sir, there's an Irishwoman going to medal here,' I shouted back.

'Jesus... sir'.

I went back one step and forward two. Olive's father, Matt, a Fianna Fáil County Councillor from Loughrea, and her brother, Brendan jumped the barrier to embrace her. That was a special moment. Olive was 33, standing at 5'3" and weighed about seven-and-a-half stone. The Russians, Kaniskina and Kirdyapkina, were full-time athletes. So, too, was the Chinese woman, Hong.

For Olive to go and do what she did in 30 degrees heat and with 40 per cent humidity was amazing. Only Eamonn Coghlan, Sonia O'Sullivan and Gillian O'Sullivan had ever medalled for Ireland at the World Championships before that. Now, Olive Loughnane was entering that pantheon of great Irish athletes.

IN ALL, 2009 was a very good year for Irish athletics with Olive the obvious highlight, but Derval O'Rourke had a seriously positive display in Berlin, too, finishing fourth in the 100 metres hurdles. In the final, at the Olympic Stadium, Derval set a new national record of 12.67 seconds. As the only European in the final that in itself was a major achievement. David Gillick was sixth in the men's 400 metres final.

The stadium in Berlin and the whole environs had an Olympic aura. Indeed, construction of the Olympiastadion had been ordered by Adolf Hitler for the 1936 Olympic Games and I remember walking around the place at different times trying to visualise what it had been like 73 years previously.

Throughout, we always had our suspicions when it came to the Russian walkers. Olive had mentioned in one interview how Kaniskina had been 'looking at me a bit dazed' on the podium.

In that moment, though, it was just important for us to make a big deal of the silver medal and celebrate it for what it was – one of the great Irish athletics moments.

IN 2011, OLIVE went to Olhão in Portugal for the European Race Walking Cup. She walked an unbelievable race and was heading for a medal with one kilometre to go.

Again, I ran like a madman to the finish, and at the same time I was texting boys at home… 'This woman's medalling here'.

Olive had caught Maria Vasco and had overtaken Kirdyapkina. She was all set for at least a silver and maybe even gold. I got to the finish and she wasn't there. She had been disqualified. I was waiting for her and wanting to say to her, 'You've deserved that Olive'.

And then, there was nothing.

I was distraught for her.

Something similar happened in 2002 with Gillian O'Sullivan in Munich. Gillian was in a medal position with about 600 to go in the women's 20 kilometres walk. Again, I ran like hell to the finish.

Gillian went in under the tunnel to come into the stadium, but by the time she came onto the track she had been caught by the Italian, Erika Alfridi and finished fourth. She managed a national record of 1:28:46, but that feeling, watching three other athletes and with Gillian just behind them, was gut wrenching.

Olive's performances in Berlin and Olhão rose expectations.

With that, Olive became more ambitious. We had set up a very good training camp in Daegu for the 2011 World Championships, but Olive wanted a different approach. Instead, she flew to Seoul first and there was a whole plan that had to be developed for her there. I wasn't in favour of it, but Olive had a world silver medal to bargain with. She was pretty much on her own in solitary confinement in Seoul, and that was a mistake in my view.

She finished 16th in Daegu and I felt she had overcooked it with the trip to Seoul.

IN SARANSK FOR the 2012 World Race Walking Cup, Olive finished seventh.

Saransk was where the Russian race walkers were based. Even getting there was an ordeal. We flew into Moscow and the IAAF had a plane chartered to take us to Saransk.

That plane journey was the worst of my life. The smell of what seemed like diesel didn't help any nervous fliers amongst us. I remember looking out the window and the barren nowhere beneath us.

I'm going to go out of the world here.

People were smoking on the plane. It was just a completely different world altogether and Saransk was, to put it mildly, remote. I turned at one point to the fella beside me.

'Is this plane even moving?'

I was sure we were goners.

In the early days, athletes used to go to Saransk by train. The train might take close to a day, but people took a view that it was safer to go on a train that took a day than a plane that never got there. The trains had stopped running, so we had no choice.

The train stopped for Olive when she retired from athletics in early 2013, a few months after finishing 11th at the London Olympics. She had a long career and a successful one. The upgrade of the medal from silver to gold from Berlin was a fitting reward, even if she had to wait too long for that moment.

14

*With Sean Carlin from Killygordon, who was my first big
success story at Finn Valley AC. Injury prevented him from
qualifying for the 1984 Olympic Games in Los Angeles.*

SEAN CARLIN FROM Killygordon was the first athlete who had me
dreaming the dream and uttering the words… 'The Olympic Games'.

Sean remains the best ever all-round Donegal athlete.

Even when he was at Dromore National School, Sean was mad keen into
athletics. He was ambitious and he was prepared to make sacrifices. He won
a national Junior discus title and he eventually became a decathlete.

Funded by his family and by Finn Valley AC he went off to California, to
Santa Barbara, to train alongside a group of West German and US athletes.
He followed a trail and he was so driven to succeed. He lived for athletics.
We were full-on.

I brought Sean into the army with me, and our lives were totally
interlinked. He won the General Mulcahy Trophy three times, an award for
the best athlete in the Irish Army.

Due to the volume of disciplines, our training schedule for Sean was tough
and had to be organised two or three weeks at a time. We trained twice a day

and there were never excuses. Not once did Sean ever pull out of a session.

At the National Championships in Tullamore in 1981, Sean won the Senior decathlon and broke the record. He went to the top of the Irish rankings with 7226 points: 11.5 seconds, 7.02 metres, 11.17 seconds, 1.97 metres, 50.43 seconds, 16.21 seconds, 39.58 metres, 4.20 metres, 50.84 metres, 4.21 metres.

Sean still holds the Donegal decathlon (7226 points) and discus (42.62 metres) records. He was a special talent and his dream could have been reality.

THEN CAME 1984, the year of the Olympic Games in Los Angeles.

Sean came back from America to compete in the National Championships in Tullamore. As he was leaping over the bar in the pole vault, his hamstring pulled. It was more than your normal, run-of-the-mill injury, simply because of what was at stake. Years of work were gone.

The Olympic dream was over.

There was this great, imposing man just standing there with a knowing look on his face. He wasn't going to the Olympic Games. Not that year or any year.

I am still connected to Sean, who is on the Board of the swimming pool at Finn Valley, but that moment in '84 will haunt me forever because, deep down, I knew how good he could have been.

I saw how good he could have been. It's a shame that BLE, the Irish athletics federation, didn't. There was, of course, no financial support or any performance advice available in those days.

IN DECEMBER, 1969, a group of people met in Logue's, a little public house in Cranford, to form the Donegal Athletics Board.

The first Championships held under the auspices of the Donegal County Board was in 1969-1970 and I won a Donegal Novice Cross Country race. That was interesting because it was a novelty in a place like Glenties. It was held in the middle of the town in a field across from the school. The place was a bog; so bad you could lose a man in it.

It was really extreme.

We formed a good committee at that meeting in Logue's. I was the secretary. PJ O'Carlin was the chairman, with Eamon Giles, Ben O'Donnell and Bernie O'Callaghan also on the committee. Up to that point, athletics was only about the parish sports.

Parochial sports were just a community event that related to a parish. There were confined events and open events – the confined events solely for people who lived within the parish. There was tug o'war, weight throwing over the bar, stuff like that. It was great entertainment and an opportunity for families to meet.

Those type of days disappeared with the social fabric of the country.

Back in 1961, Cranford, because of the shared vision of Eamon Giles and Bill Hunter, formed a club. There was absolutely no history of organised athletics in Donegal until then, not in terms of national affiliation. There had been a club in Donegal town, which went under the John Bosco banner, with Mickey Cooney the driving force.

Until then, people drifted to places like Derry, where there were all sorts of variations of clubs, and Strabane. Those clubs were on the look-out in Donegal, for people who seemed to have potential.

Cranford opened the door, and they certainly led the way.

After 1961, Danny McDaid, then in his early 20s, was eyed up by Cranford while he competed at the local sports in Glenswilly. He ran in two Olympic Games in the marathon.

In 1968, Lifford formed a club, and I formed a club in Glenties in 1969. Bernie O'Callaghan was a science teacher in Glenties, who had previously boarded at Gormanston, and he formed a club in Killybegs. In those days, you could have put every single athlete in the county of Donegal, from Bundoran to Malin, in a 14-seater bus and nobody would have missed that bus.

I was recruited to Cranford by Captain Sean Hurley, who was stationed in Milford and was very involved in army athletics. I was proud to be a member.

AT THE BEGINNING of organised athletics in Donegal, one of the things I was tight about was timing. Something would be advertised for three o'clock and, by four we'd be lucky if we were up and running, but that was just society back then.

I maintained that if the advertisement said a three o'clock start, the whistle would be blown at three.

'You better be there because it'll start on time.'

How many times did I utter those words?

One day arrived, in Killybegs, and of course I had warned everyone in advance. I blew the whistle and the Cranford boys missed the race. At an Ulster meeting in Omagh the following week, I was handed a letter telling me I was suspended for six months.

That finished me in Cranford.

I was shocked that they didn't understand what I was doing. I tried to explain, but nobody was listening.

I felt that I had been so loyal to Cranford, taking the Glenties kids to the club and buying Cranford vests out of the Glenties' school funds.

WE HAD THE first Donegal Championships at Fintra in 1970. We had no shot, so we improvised. Someone went down to the beach and brought up a big stone. Someone had to be the best at it, so we rolled with it.

A Mr Emens, a British soldier, who came to Killybegs from the British Army barracks in Derry, entered and won with a couple of throws. He was a brave man to make that trip, but he did, and he left with a couple of medals.

There was a level of intrigue to athletics in the early years.

People talked about the sport as though I was developing this alien concept around the Twin Towns. Francie Patton, the local butcher, met me out on Stranorlar street.

'You're doing well with them runners, young McGonagle. There's a whole load of weans running.' Like with most people of the time, there was a sting to what had initially come as a compliment.

'Do ye know this, young McGonagle,' he continued. *'There was many the thing that started around here… but they could never keep it going.'*

Francie's son, Brendan is now a coach at Finn Valley. Francie was preparing me for the eventuality that it would fail. It was as if the athletics was just the latest craze.

But it was all new, and exciting.

Getting running spikes wasn't easy in the late 60s. Billy Doherty had a sports shop at the top of the Port Road in Letterkenny, and he sold spikes. Buying spikes was a big deal. Football was established and sourcing football boots was never a problem, but parents weren't convinced about this fella in his 20s who wanted them to buy spikes for their kids.

Mick Duffy was at a wake one night in Ballybofey and the conversation started about athletics.

'It's going well now, Patsy?'

'Aye, Jesus it's going great, Mick'.

'If you ever give this up, there'll be the greatest sale of second-hand spikes there ever was!'

I remind his family about that.

WHILE THERE WAS that intrigue and, at the same time, part-wonder at athletics, when you cut it all down nobody actually gave a toss.

In 1976, Sheila McMenamin went to Dublin and won the Irish Under-14 long jump title. I was made. At that particular moment, it felt like this was one of the greatest days of my life. I came home, heart still beating, assuming everyone would be talking about it. I quickly realised that nobody cared.

Sheila was brilliant. She was jumping close to six metres; a real, natural, stand-out athlete. She won silver and bronze in the long jump and triple jump in 1977, and came home with two silvers in the Under-17s in 1978. She had a jump of 5.97 metres. Sinead McLaughlin went to 5.98 metres and Shauna Carlin went around the six-metre mark.

Even now, nobody is jumping to that level, and the nearest would possibly be Janine Boyle and Sommer Lecky, two up and coming athletes at Finn Valley.

HUGO DUGGAN, WHO was from Milford and who previously competed for Cranford AC and Lifford AC, won his seventh and final Irish long jump title with Finn Valley in 1984.

My family slept in a tent in the field behind Morton Stadium in Santry the night before Hugo competed. It wasn't quite a money-saving exercise.

We didn't have any money.

We woke up to the sound of cows on the Sunday morning before Hugo went and excelled. Hugo used to drive a bakery van around Donegal. He'd do a few hours early in the day, we'd train during lunchtime and Hugo would get back in the van again. I remember him jumping into horrible water on one particular afternoon.

The pit had sand in it at the time and I had to pull him out at times.

'If you can jump there, sir, you can jump anywhere'

In 1987, Hugo went to Melbourne and won gold at the World Masters Championships, leaping to 6.69 metres. That was massive for athletics in Donegal. There were thousands of people out to greet Hugo when he came back. They were lined, cheering from the Port Bridge in Letterkenny to his home in Milford.

For many years in the 1970s and 80s, I entered Finn Valley in the British League.

The British thought we were from Northern Ireland and, obviously, I wasn't going to put them wise, so we rolled away to Gateshead, Carlisle, Glasgow, Edinburgh, anywhere to have a chance of winning.

We got away with it for years. Until, that was, the phone in the house rang at five o'clock in the morning before we left one year. The caller was questioning our eligibility. I just lied through my teeth, and we got in... again! That was the only time our entry was ever questioned.

In 1988, the women's team reached the British League final. We had left Edinburgh dispirited, thinking we were out. A couple of days later, a letter arrived to Christine Lynch's house, telling us that we had qualified for the final.

The final line-up was completed after the points had been tallied... Hull, Haringey, Hallamshire, Woking, Lisburn, Chelmsford, Leicester... and Finn Valley.

We finished fourth in the final and had some excellent displays. Sinead McLaughlin won the long jump and was third in the high jump, Noelle Harron and Belinda McArdle were second in their races, and there were thirds for Margo Davis and Kay Byrne.

Getting there was a problem in more ways than one.

Cost would have been a factor, but we made sure that money never became a wrench. We overloaded buses and we sneaked people onto the boat; anything to make it cheaper.

Getting people on and off boats was a challenge, of course. We had the kids piled into the toilet of the bus, just to avoid detection. I'd have put them in the roof rack if I could've.

That all changed in 1979 when the MS Herald of Free Enterprise capsized just after leaving the harbour at Zeebrugge in Belgium to head for Dover. A door was left opened and the water gushed in – 193 people died in that tragedy and security seriously tightened up in terms of doing head-counts of passengers.

The challenge to get people on board was tougher.

You had to get off the buses and walk on. We still managed, but not to the same level. One night coming from Liverpool to Dublin, they put us into a shed to count us. Some got back in and lay on the bus floor, others got out the back door.

It was a great experience for our athletes. It was a great outlet. Nobody in Ireland was getting that chance in the early 80s. But travelling was always an issue, even in Ireland.

During the Troubles, we had difficulties with people who couldn't go across the border into Northern Ireland. Sometimes, for us to get to Dublin we couldn't go the direct route. We had to go via Leitrim.

There were different times where a panic got up if a driver happened to take a wrong turn and we thought we might have ventured across into the North.

That was just life for a border club.

I WAS SUSPENDED from Irish athletics for a year in the 1980s. In an Under-12 race, I ran a wee girl from Buncrana, Anne Marie McDaid, who was a member of the Buncrana club and I got screwed for it.

I swore blind that she was a member of Finn Valley AC, but they caught me on the fact that she was Under-11, not Under-12. The Donegal Board were out to get me and they got me.

I was too pushy and too driven for a lot of them. They just weren't able for the enthusiasm I brought, not to mention that I was obviously in the wrong.

For a lot of them, it was a case of anyone but Finn Valley, and particularly anyone but Patsy McGonagle. I was taken up to a meeting in Gormanston

College. I had a car load of boys and we all gave evidence.

I had to give the medals we'd won back, but I went out and bought more medals for the Finn Valley athletes.

'There's a far nicer medal now,' I announced.

THE CLUB WAS barred from entering teams.

The Nationals were being held in Thurles one year, and Belinda McArdle was the best Juvenile in the country at the time in her age category. I went down with a Finn Valley crowd and jumped a ditch to get into the racecourse. Belinda 'won' the Nationals, and we got into the car and up the road again.

I brought the whole shebang to the Ulster Championships.

I told them on the bus that we'd do a tally ourselves and if we were supposed to get medals, we'd get medals. Finn Valley proved dominant. I was there afterwards with a pocketful of medals and handed them out. In their minds, they qualified for the Irish Championships.

The individuals could enter, but they wouldn't entertain teams. I announced there and then on the bus...

'Fuck the nationals... we're going to Gateshead.

'We'll be on the BBC!'

And there we were, 78 runners heading to Gateshead on Charlie McNamee's buses.

15

David Gillick and I after he won gold at the European Indoor Championships in 2007 in Birmingham.

THE 2010 EUROPEAN Championships in Barcelona presented me with one of the most devastating moments in my career.

I had David Gillick as a gold medallist in my mind, and he cruised his way to the 400 metres final. This was his moment. It was 'eyeballs out' stuff with David before the final. We hugged, and I banged him on the chest with my fist.

I saw that he was focussed and saw that he was ready to go.

Or, so I thought.

It soon became obvious that he wasn't in the zone at all. My preparation with David had been intense. It reminded me almost of my time with the GAA teams, when I used to hit big Martin Griffin in the build-up to Championship games.

Griffin would just stare back.

'HIT ME AGAIN!'

On one occasion, I did the same with Brendan Dunleavy, who was also a county player, and he went down in a heap as I had struck him unawares. I was wired and, in the process, was attempting to wire up the team.

'JESUS... Patsy!'

That's what I could be like in 'the moment'. Just pure raw passion and aggression could power through me. There were times where I was nearly singing *Kevin Barry* to athletes. I developed a more controlled approach over time. That was a good thing – for the athletes and for me.

THE ESTADI OLIMPIC Lluís Companys in Montjuïc overlooks the harbour in Barcelona. A stunning setting and, yet, for me it brings only haunting memories of 2010. It just didn't happen for David. He didn't handle Barcelona.

I can still see him floundering coming up the home straight in the final. I was standing on the steps absolutely gutted. He just didn't execute the race. He didn't bring the aggression or the mentality that he needed. David finished fifth. He worked so hard to get himself among the world's best and this was a race he could have won, and should have won.

David was devastated.

I was dumbfounded.

He broke down and I hugged him. There was nothing that I could say. Words were pointless and meaningless. Worse was to come, though.

There was a relay the next day and I needed David.

But he was in the doldrums.

We were out on the warm-up track and it was almost pitch black. Martyn Rooney, a British man with Mullingar parents, who was a training partner for Gillick in Loughborough, came in and things were a bit abrasive.

I had allowed David McCarthy to go home because of a family issue, which was the wrong decision. It was a humane call and it looked like a no brainer because I had my men. But with Gillick out, I had to ring Steven Colvert, who was out on the town with his girlfriend. Steven was in no frame of mind to run a relay. I got him and, thank God, he came in. They were flying for three legs in the race until poor Steven got the baton. It wasn't Steven's fault at all, but the relay team's Olympic dream was over. Steven was very responsive and I will be forever grateful to him for filling the card that day.

Gordon Kennedy was crying on my shoulder. He had great form going into Sydney, but he didn't get to run because he messed up in a trial. He knew his dream was gone.

David stated that he never planned to do the relay, but he was the best 400 metres runner in Ireland. He was one of the best there was anywhere. Earlier that year, he proved it in Doha. He breezed through the heats at the World Indoor Championships and was all set up for a medal. The final was another 'what if', though. I went to the far side of the track to watch it and, with 200 metres to go, my heart sank.

I knew before he was at the line that he'd be disqualified.

It's all over.

David infringed on the American, Bershawn Jackson and there was a bit of a shoving match. The Americans actually went apeshit. We tried to counterappeal the disqualification, but it was never going to work. The dream, once more, had died on us.

The IAAF actually warned David officially. The technical people said he had to tidy himself up a bit.

I WASN'T IN Madrid when David won gold in the 2005 European Indoors, but I was there in Birmingham in 2007. He was all singing and all dancing. He was absolutely brilliant in Birmingham. I also had to fight for him so hard in Birmingham.

British athlete Steve Ovett once compared indoor racing to running around a bathtub without the faucets. Some runners can be sucked down the drainpipe indoors. In the semi-final, Britain lodged an objection because they felt David impinged on Robert Tobin.

The race was so tight; David edged Tobin out by just 0.03 seconds, but the British were incensed. I had to fight it into the early hours of the night. David had gone to bed and knew nothing about the whole thing.

But he was an intelligent lad and he knew there was something amiss.

At the end of the race he had come to me.

'There was a bit of bumping there. Am I alright?'

'Aye, you're grand, sir.'

We won the case and David aced the final.

He was relaxed all through the Saturday. I made sure everything was nice and calm. Believe it or not, that was something I was good at. I had an ability to treat even the day of a European final as just another Saturday.

We knew David would have to be on top of his game for the final. 'The German looked good,' I had informed David after the semi-final. Bastian Swillims had looked phenomenal, in fact.

Before the final I changed my approach. I built the momentum from a calm base to get him into the zone with a winning instinct. As he was ready to go I just looked at him and barked, 'Get the fuck out there and win the race!'

It was only afterwards that he realised why I was so fired up. David was unaware that I'd been up half the night trying to make sure that the ceiling didn't cave in on him - Swillims was in the lane outside David, and we said beforehand that if David could get to the bell in the top two, he'd do it.

Bang! The gun went and David was away just how we wanted.

Just get close.

GET CLOSE!

At the bell, David was second.

I knew he had it in him.

This time, he delivered. Over the last 20 metres, David kicked for gold and he had his moment again. I was overjoyed for him on a personal level.

People often ask me what I say to an athlete in that moment.

With David in Birmingham, I had two words.

'Deadly, sir!'

I was genuinely over the moon for David. We walked back to the hotel, my arm around his shoulder, just living in the moment and enjoying it for what it was: An Irish athlete delivering the goods on a big stage.

Two years later, he ran an unbelievable race in Berlin at the World Championships and made the final. He was sixth in that final and the second European athlete to finish.

People talk sometimes of me being able to douse a sensitive moment with a sprinkling of humour. You can cut the tension at a major Championships with a butter knife, but I managed to scythe right through it in Berlin. The heavens opened with the athletes in the warm-up area before the final.

The athletes were all in a tent in the warm-up area with the races having been postponed due to the thunderstorm. In an attempt to protect myself from the elements, I dressed myself in a black bin liner and crashed into the tent resembling a drowned rat. The whole place just burst out laughing.

At least I lifted the mood.

David went out in that final like an express train, but just didn't have the gas to get onto the podium. Fifth in the world final was amazing and set him up perfectly for Barcelona.

Or so we thought.

David had the potential always to do it. At a time, he was one of the best 400 metres runners in the world.

The problem in Barcelona was the excitement. The medal was put around David's neck too early, and people had David winning the race way before the final was even run.

The noise around him was a massive issue.

I TOOK STEPHEN Maguire with me to Barcelona.

Stephen coached the sprinters and the relay teams, but he was effectively the head coach. Barcelona was the first time I had him on board with the senior team and it was obvious he'd be a good addition.

Stephen competed as a long jumper and triple jumper for Strabane AC, and he had won a few National underage and All-Ireland Schools titles in his youth.

Gerry McDonnell, who was the team leader, built a club in Strabane and he always had good athletes in a very difficult environment. At a point in time, before organised athletics really hit the scene in Donegal, Gerry gave opportunities to young athletes in Donegal, like John Gallagher from Cruit Island and Cyril O'Boyle from Glenswilly.

A Strabane AC team won the Lisburn Cup and five of the six scoring athletes were from Donegal. When Stephen wanted to start afresh we registered him to Finn Valley AC and I maintained contact to a point where I took him to Barcelona.

Stephen used to compete for Ulster at the O'Duffy Cup in Claremorris when he was a teenager and I had him on the bus with me. It's funny now that we would strike up such a connection in later years. Back then, I was just this madman roaring at the top of a rickety old bus that was making its way west.

Stephen got injured young and he drifted out of the scene for a while, but eventually he rang me up and told me that he was eager to pursue jumps coaching. I sent him the way of Maeve Kyle and made the introduction between the two.

After that, he used Finn Valley to do bits and pieces of training he was doing with individual athletes, and I put him forward for his first International in Germany in 2000. Stephen was like a sponge when it came to taking in information. At the 2002 European Championships in Munch he sat and studied the whole warm-up areas of the various teams. He also went off to work in Tampere at a European Juniors with Sean Naughton. I had him with me at the 50 kilometres walk in Berlin in 2009; again, it was part of the education and the experience he needed.

ATHLETICS IRELAND HAD a process where they would give everyone a chance. It was a back-clapping exercise. They imposed coaches on me, but Stephen and I on occasion ignored them. I felt bad about that, but at elite level you have to have a ruthless streak.

There was always silliness in the background with Athletics Ireland and it is primarily for that reason that Stephen is now working with Scottish Athletics as their Director of Performance and Coaching.

He is a passionate Irishman, who would love to have come on board and would have had the courage to change things, but he is now working with another federation. Stephen went to Scotland, turned around their whole set-up and was head-hunted by British Athletics.

He worked with Jason Smyth. He spent months with the best American sprinters in Clermont, Florida, working with Lance Baumann, one of the top sprint coaches in the States. He was assistant to Baumann and was on a difficult learning curve.

He wanted Jason Smyth to win the Paralympics – which he did – but also to qualify for the Olympics and he came so, so close. Jason is still the second fastest Irishman ever. Jason had four B standards for the Olympics, but he tailed off in 2012. He ran 10.21 and the A standard was 10.18: he was a fingernail away from qualifying.

At the 2017 World Championships in London, Great Britain's four relay teams won medals. That was largely down to Stephen. The point was recognised when he was named Coach of the Year at the BBC Sports Personality of the Year Awards.

As I heard his name being called out, I started thinking about all the frustration, all the hoops we had to jump through to keep him in the game.

As I watched the BBC awards, the more and more I got annoyed about the nonsense. Athletics Ireland had made a High Performance coaching position available in April of 2017. Stephen tossed the role about in his mind; he wanted to come home to do the job, but he couldn't apply because of his commitments in Britain.

We had an experienced Irishman, who had a track record of changing cultures and mentalities, and who did a phenomenal management job on top of his coaching with Britain to bring egotistical personalities together to win the relay.

This man wanted a role in Irish Athletics, but a space couldn't be found and we have had to watch his work and his talent succeed with other countries.

16

Finn Valley AC competing in Europe was a real highlight for me in the 1990s. We came sixth in Portugal in 1995, during a period where we won eight Irish Senior Cross-Country titles in a row.

DEEP DOWN, I always knew that Finn Valley could win a National Senior Cross-Country title.

It wasn't an impossible dream in my mind.

The feat had never been achieved by a club from Ulster before, in either the men's or the women's race, but I *knew* we could do it and I *knew we would* make it happen.

In 1992, I thought we had it won in Santry.

We had it in our grasp with 200 metres to go and we celebrated like we'd won it at the end. We were certain. Finally, we had broken the mould, and I felt on top of the world. Ten minutes later we found out that there had been a miscalculation and we lost – by ONE point.

I was disappointed and depressed all at once.

I was at the back of Santry Demesne and walked from the finish line across the field to get a team photograph. The image is still ingrained in my mind, the picture of Catriona McGranaghan looking absolutely devastated.

She wouldn't smile and she couldn't smile. She was just dejected.

It was the fact that we thought we had it and we were brought crashing down again that made it sting so deep. The others made an effort to look happy, but Catriona couldn't bring herself to do it. Catriona was just a winner. Her family had a lifetime of association with Finn Valley and they were so successful.

That she journeyed from being a little eight year-old who went to a Cross-Country in Mallusk, to being a key woman on the most successful group ever in Donegal sport, is one of the real highlights of my career.

PORTER'S FIELD WAS just behind the McGranaghan family home in Castlefin. A group of athletes used to meet up there once a week as Porter's Field was illuminated by a street light fixed to the gable wall of the McGranaghan's house.

There was even history behind the streetlight, which had previously hung at Anfield, the home of Liverpool FC, but had, via Finn Harps FC, made its way to the outskirts of Castlefin.

Catriona was part of a great group through the age groups, with the likes of Maeve Lafferty, Stephanie Crossan, Teresa Callaghan, Margaret Gallagher and Angela McGinley.

Catriona was a winner, but she was a confidence runner, who also used to have doubts and would constantly question if she was good enough.

Catriona was more than good enough.

She was an exceptional runner – and, best of all, she *got it*. At team meetings I used to remind Catriona of her best moments – her big wins, her fast times - and she'd leave the room feeling 10 feet tall. And if Catriona was going through a spell of bad form, I used to make her take off her stopwatch during training.

Instead, I'd 'time' the session. At the end, I'd tell Catriona a time that was far faster than it actually was. That trick worked every single time.

TWELVE MONTHS LATER, in the Phoenix Park in 1993, Catriona McGranaghan wasn't going to leave disappointed.

After Santry, I had changed the tune a bit. We did the National Road

Relays in Gowran Park in April and won. A blistering leg by Belinda McArdle led the way. That was our marker thrown down. I wasn't coming home with nothing again in '93.

I knew we had the group and I was in touch with those athletes non-stop. Every one of them, every single day. They were my priority.

Catriona was working for the Derry Housing Association and all of the calls to her office had to be vetted. I rang Caitriona so often that my calls didn't have to be put through the system in the end; the girls at reception just put me straight through.

Just before Christmas in 1992, we went to the Inter-County Championships in Ballyfin. I entered the Finn Valley team as the Donegal representatives. Not only did we win it, three of the girls were in the top four – Belinda McArdle, Dawn Hargan and Kay Byrne.

The difference in '93 was Dawn Hargan. Dawn was from Derry and was the real deal; an international athlete. Of course, people didn't want me to sign her and were telling us we couldn't sign her because she was from outside the county. I dismissed that view as complete nonsense. It has been said to me that I excel when people are trying to slow me down. That was the case with Dawn.

The talent on our team was obvious to anyone who knew anything about athletics, and it shouldn't have come as a surprise when we came out on top. We got there ahead of Dublin and Cork, which was always the target.

Belinda McArdle had been at the World Juniors in 1988 in Sudbury in Canada, competing in the 3,000 metres. She qualified when she did a 9:36 and I can still remember the sensation of that moment. Realising that we had an athlete going to the world stage was something else. That was a massive breakthrough and showed the way for others coming behind.

'Yes, it is possible from Finn Valley.'

Dublin City Harriers won the European Championships – twice – and people thought I was insane even thinking about challenging them for that crown. They had a Derry woman, the 1992 Olympian Roisin Smith, in their number and they were clearly the real deal. They had, after all, won the damned thing for 16 consecutive years.

We, too, had to get real.

BELINDA WAS A class act all through her career. She was the same age as Sonia O'Sullivan, and they went to the World Juniors in Canada together in 1988.

Temperament was the only thing that separated Belinda and Sonia. When they were in action, there was very little between them. In terms of moving on, Sonia was just able to go out into the big, bad world and embrace it. But Belinda was invaluable to me, without ever really *getting it*. She never had a deep desire, but I just forced it with her. I had her tortured and never let her off the hook.

I was in the family house in Ard McCool most days with her and I remember saying to her mother, Linda at one point, 'You do realise, there'll be no discos and she'll have no friends around here. She will be in a different world completely'.

Belinda was a lead runner.

One Saturday, 24 hours prior to an Ulster Championships, Belinda was in hospital to have her appendix removed.

I was anxious. I needed Belinda for the race.

'Have you not had the operation yet?'

'Naw, not yet.'

'Have you any pain today?'

'Naw, I'm not so bad.'

'Fuck sake, Belinda. Get your clothes on you and meet me downstairs. You've been lying here three or four days... and they've done sweet fuck all.'

I saw the team going down the tubes without her. Away we went and we got the win. To this day, I don't know if she's ever had that appendix operation, but she has the Ulster medal.

ONE FRIDAY EVENING, I had to be in Dublin for a meeting and Gerry Byrne drove me up and down. On the way back home, Gerry took ill. He was out of the car, and throwing up and looking as weak as water.

Gerry worked for the Donegal County Council and, while he was down a sewer in Buncrana, he contracted Weil's Disease. He was in a bad way. I mean, a seriously bad way. He was at death's door, it seemed.

We had the National Cross-Country Championships the next week in

Ballinlough and his wife, Kay was running. Again, I ploughed on.

'This woman's going to have to run, sir,' I told Gerry.

I also spoke with Kay. 'I need you to run.'

Suffice to say, Gerry was totally with me on this.

I always had a strong relationship with Kay, who started running with me at eight years of age when she was at school in Glencovitt, where the teacher, Manus O'Donnell was an athletics enthusiast. Manus later became the County Secretary.

Kay won an Ulster Under-9s on the same day Donal Reid, who would win an All-Ireland with Donegal in '92, won the boys' race. Kay had been with me all her life. Her family were big into football and didn't really get behind her athletics career. It was possible that they just didn't understand this new craze in the community.

Kay was still at St Columba's College in early 1977 when her talent shone first. She was running in a school's competition and finished at the front, which qualified her to run for Ireland in Wales.

In Wales, Kay – 'that marvellous little Ballybofey girl', as the *Donegal News* called her the following week – proudly wearing the Irish vest, finished 15th. She was only 14 years of age but competed in an Under-17 race.

She gave up athletics in her late teens, went to Dublin for a year-and-a-half and stopped running completely. There was one exception. The girls in Dublin didn't believe that Kay was a runner so, to prove herself, she went out and competed in a 10-miler. That was Kay Byrne in a nutshell.

One dark night I was doing a hill session on the Millbrae and this girl came walking up the road.

'Yes Kay?'

'Hi Patsy. God, are you still at that?'

'Jesus, Kay… it's about time you came back to the running. Tuesday night at half-seven! See you then Kay.'

'Aye, you will, Patsy.'

The following week, Kay Byrne came back to us – and that would prove one of the key moments in the Finn Valley story. By 1993, Kay Byrne was a cornerstone and in 1994 she was an inspiration.

All through Gerry's illness, Kay ran. And ran. And ran some more.

Her mind was obviously just in a spin and the race wasn't even on her radar. She asked me to take her out of the equation in 1993, but then she changed her mind late. She went out in a mud bath the next day and put in the performance of her life, finishing fourth, one second from bronze. If only she had taken on Kerry athlete, Maureen Harrington just a fraction sooner, she would have been on the podium.

We still had to be delighted with her performance. Fourth at any stage was a great finish in that event but, considering what she was going through at home, it was mind-blowing that she could even have the capacity to park it and run. Not only did she run, she made the Irish team for the 1994 World Cross Country Championships in Budapest out of it. Kay was in America with Northern Ireland at the 1984 World Cross and it was brilliant to see her go to Budapest 10 years later as part of the Irish team.

In the middle of that bog of a field in Ballinlough, I rang Gerry Byrne and told him the good news.

'God, she'll be annoyed that she didn't get the bronze,' was his first reply.

He knew Kay alright.

Ten years later, in 2004, Kay's mental fortitude showed up again. Her brother, Patsy died tragically the week before the Nationals. She was on the floor, devastated.

She was actually inconsolable.

Neil Martin was looking after the team that year and I went with him to see her. Neil offered his sympathy and said what any reasonable human being would have said in those circumstances.

'Do whatever you want at the weekend, Kay.'

I was different and I also spoke up before the poor woman could respond.

'Naw, you'll be running, Kay.'

Kay ran and the team came second. I waited at the finish line for her. I didn't need to say a thing. It was just a presence she needed.

Kay could have walked away from athletics during her husband's illness, but she stayed with it and Gerry supported it. Gerry continued to struggle with his health and he 'died' on me after one St Stephen's Day 5 kilometres run. He got sick just after the race and was rushed to Letterkenny Hospital. The staff did their best, but it was no good.

Of course, I was in the room when they were trying to bring him around. It's a wonder I was never barred from that hospital. They were just about to give in when one of the nurses ventured that they should, in the festive spirit maybe, try to revive Gerry one last time.

Against all the odds, Gerry responded and came around.

He opened his eyes and about two seconds later there I was lying on top of him. I'd had a few drinks after the race, and I ended up falling over on Gerry in the bed and the poor man at death's door. Naturally, I was calmly ejected from the situation.

IN BALLINLOUGH, WE had Rosaleen Campbell, a teacher from Castlebar, Rosemary Boyle, a youngster from Castlefin who was with us from a young age, and Margaret Synott, who hailed from Malin in north Inishowen and who worked in the swimming pool in Letterkenny.

We had good strength in the team, and it was a good job because the conditions in Ballinlough were the worst ever. The place was pure bog.

Dublin City Harriers regrouped after 1993, but they were never mentally able for us. We warmed up on the grass in the field, but the Dublin City Harries girls stayed on the road.

That just fed the team talk.

'Those Dublin fuckers are soft,' I announced. 'They're used to their parks in the city. They're not able for us.'

My team was wired to the moon. I used that anti-city line so many times. I'm not sure if it was reasonable or not but you have to throw out whatever is going to resonate with your group.

The Nationals were our litmus test. I was motivated to be involved in Nationals from my time in England, as traditionally over there everything related to the Nationals. That was massive.

I brought that psychology home and didn't want to know about anything else bar the Nationals.

We went to Ballinasloe one year to a race won by the great Leevale athlete, Donie Walsh and finished 12th. We went, just to be in the Nationals, which are the true judge of where you stand as a club.

Winning the Nationals also meant qualifying for the European

Championships. We went to Italy the first year, to a place called Monte Cassino, and we just took it as a trip away, no big deal. We learned from our – *by our*, of course I mean *my* – mistakes and realised that it was more than an outing. It was an opportunity to rank Finn Valley and, by association, Ireland. Hence, there was a different attitude the next time we travelled.

We had to get our act together. And we did, and we went to Europe with a vengeance. After the race in Italy, Catriona collapsed. It was nothing too serious, but she was low on iron and dehydrated. It was serious enough at the same time for the medical people to put her into an ambulance, but I couldn't have that. I pulled her out.

I'd never have got her home on time otherwise. She probably did need medical attention, but thankfully she was alright and we got her home. Caitriona is a strong woman. Years before, at an Ulster Juvenile race in Enniskillen, she got spiked.

At the end of the course I was wrapping her foot and it was a case of, 'Ach... sure you'll be grand there now, Catriona'. But I couldn't see her foot with the blood. It was a day of howling winds and rain, to add to the drama. She ended up needing 10 stitches and the doctor at Enniskillen Hospital sought us out afterwards and was not best pleased with our care and attention.

WE FINISHED 14th in Italy. Albertina Dias from Portugal won the race and Francesca Ribeiro, also from Portugal, who the fastest 10,000 metres woman in the world, was there too.

We came sixth in Portugal in 1995, competing in Maia.

I could be hard and harsh on them at times, but the girls responded. We just moved on every time. We dominated the National Cross-Country scene, but we never really thought too much about it. We just moved on. I never believed in dwelling on defeat and, on the other side of the coin, I never let anyone get carried away when we won.

It was always, 'Right... what about these road relays now?' or whatever the next mission might have been.

We were unique in the Donegal sporting world, where there was a tendency at times to over-celebrate. That certainly didn't happen with us. But in Portugal, I had to acknowledge what had been done. They were in roaring-hot heat. The race had been held up and the girls were there at the start line, throwing water on each other as the sun beat down on them.

Catriona was sixth, Dawn 31st, Kay 39th and Ita 47th. This was Finn Valley AC, from Stranorlar in Donegal, remember, finishing SIXTH in Europe. I had to sit them down and say what I was thinking.

'You need to take this all in,' I began.

'You need to take in where you are... and what you're doing. Here you are, six athletes from a small town in Donegal... and some of these you are running against are professional athletes.'

FOR NAAS IN 1995, when we made it three-in-a-row, Kay, Dawn, Belinda and Catriona were the foursome again. They all wanted to be on the team - and we had always more than four.

By the time '98 in Bree arrived, we could only start four athletes and we were on the edge, but Helena Crossan, Rosaleen Campbell, Ita Boyle and Kay saw us home.

We had wins in Santry, Cork and Bree to take us to six-in-a-row, and then came the moment we had all dreamt of. The National Cross-Country Championships were held in Stranorlar in 1999.

One of the reasons I brought the Nationals to Stranorlar was motivation.

You need something to keep a team motivated.

'We're on home territory. We have to win!'

A week out from the Nationals, I had to go to Dublin because of serious pains in my chest. I was there for an angiogram, but the doctor looked at me and didn't seem too content.

'Mr McGonagle, you'll have to come back another day so I can put a stent in.'

I was having none of this nonsense.

'Wait 'til I tell you, Mr McCann... I'll not be back. The way it'll be, whatever's going to be is going to be done today'. I had a blocked artery but, sure, I didn't have time to go back for surgery.

'You have no idea how busy a man I am, Mr McCann.'

The man probably wanted to refer me somewhere else. I was arrogant, passionate and driven to a point where nothing else mattered only the Cross-

Country race. I got the stents put in. I had no clothes or anything with me, but all I could think of was the Nationals.

Charlie Collins rang me from *Highland Radio* to do an interview about us hosting the nationals. I wasn't supposed to have the phone, but I had it hidden underneath the pillow. I had Nationals to organise. There I was, walking about in one of those hospital gowns, my backside bare, figuring things out. I had a pillow in front of my face as I spoke to Charlie, who clearly knew that something wasn't right.

'What the hell are you whispering about, Patsy?'

'I'm in intensive care here in the Mater Hospital. I'm after getting stents in.'

I can still hear the laughs of him yet.

I got the interview done out in the corridor, but I needed out of there.

PJ Sweeney, a national senior long jump champion from Drumkeen, worked in the Posts and Telegraphs in Dublin. It clicked with me that PJ would be going back to Donegal at the end of the week, so I rang him. That Friday, I was sitting on the steps at the Mater waiting on PJ. I didn't mention to anyone that I was going home.

There was no way that they'd have let me.

I've had stents inserted again in more recent years and the procedure is much smoother now. But I got into the car with PJ and was sleeping before we got to the first set of traffic lights. I slept from there to Ballybofey.

The weather on the day of the race was the worst possible, but we had a massive day. We won the Junior men title, Gary Murray won the individual race, we won the Senior women's team and we got two boys – Simon Ward and Murray – on the team for the World Juniors in Belfast. On top of all of that, we got Helena Crossan and Kay Byrne on the Irish team for the World Cross Country Championships.

There was no stopping me that day. Everyone was telling me to calm down, but I neither listened to nor heard them. I settled myself when it was all over, but I was back at work the next day. I had to write the reports and get the photos done up.

The only concession I made was that I didn't take a drink that night.

I FELT INVINCIBLE with that group.

I knew we had created something special. It was down to energy, passion, drive and a group of unbelievable girls. They trained hard, on the golf course, and in the forest, in Drumboe and Welchtown. We adapted training as often as we could to try and make it interesting. There was a lot of hard work and the titles were earned.

They would meet together, too. Kay and Catriona teamed up a lot and there was a great team spirit there. My message was always the same.

'We have to make the most of this because this is not normal life. Let's make it last as long as we can.'

I continually repeated it to them.

'This is not normal life.'

But they made it the norm.

17

Rob Heffernan and myself in London in 2012.

AN AIR CONDITIONING unit on The Mall in the heart of London became the snapshot of my Olympic Games in 2012.

It is now an iconic image: Rob Heffernan – glasses on his head, his face in his hands and a towel across his thighs – is the picture of utter devastation. He has just walked a race for the ages, shattering his previous personal best for the 50 kilometres by seven minutes, but has finished fourth. The worst possible place for an athlete. Fourth place in the moments after a race may as well be 'Nowheresville'.

This time, however, it's different and I know it.

Rob is just sitting there on the air conditioning unit, crying his heart out and I have my arm around him. I'm speechless and helpless, too.

At that stage, a couple of Olympic volunteers tried to block a photographer from capturing the moment. I barked at one of them to get out of the road. She got the message very quickly.

My message to Rob was equally as clear.

'This isn't going to be the end of this,' I told him. 'We could have a medal out of this yet.' I knew it was important to keep talking to him.

'You're fourth… but you're not really fourth.'

'You walked some fucking race there.'

Rob was just sitting there, nodding away, but in a world of his own. He was listening to me but wasn't hearing me. It was Rob's time to win a medal.

It was Rob's medal and we all knew it.

All through the race, Rob had been phenomenal. I'd been up and down The Mall like a madman roaring him on.

'Drive on to fuck.'

'Don't let that fucker get away.'

'Hold it now, Rob.'

'Control it.'

'You're okay, Rob, keep it going.'

WITH AROUND EIGHT kilometres to go, Rob was in sixth. He caught up with one of the Russians, Igor Yerokhin with just over a kilometre to go, but he couldn't overhaul the three in front of him. Russian Sergey Kirdyapkin was the gold medallist in a new Olympic record time (3:35:59), Jared Tallent from Australia was second and Tianfeng Si from China won bronze.

We knew in our hearts that Kirdyapkin was doping. His coach, Viktor Chegen was renowned for it. He was infamous for doping with his athletes. Eventually, in 2016, Chegen was banned for life having coached over 25 Russian walkers who had failed dope tests.

It was all part of the culture.

I understood that ever since our visit to Saransk years before for that race walking competition, when we were on a plane for over three hours, travelling about 630 kilometres east of Moscow. Saransk was the very definition of the Middle of Nowhere. For anti-doping officials to even get to them would have been a fair ordeal. The doctors and their medical people were in on the whole thing too.

The location just added weight to what they were doing.

This was known through the sport, but that didn't make it easier for Rob Heffernan as he took his rest after his mammoth effort in London.

Rob was a model athlete. He could have the craic, but when he needed to be, he was seriously focussed. London was a case in point. He said at one stage, just before the race, how he was going to try and win a medal for Ireland on The Mall and have the Queen waving out from the window of Buckingham Palace.

Other managers would have taken the view that Rob was losing focus and would have put him in a box. I, on the other hand, knew that Rob needed to be a character. He needed to be himself. His game plan was to hold back a little. He had blown up in one 50 kilometres before London when he was on world record pace. London was about controlling that excited emotion which would only be raised because of the noise from the crowds. Rob came through that and he came through the race.

That made it so hard to take.

But the emotion was about so much more than knowing we'd been cheated out of a medal.

IT WAS ONLY 11 months earlier, in a hotel in Daegu just before the World Championships, that I had to tell Rob that his mother, Maureen had died. I got a phone call from Liam Reilly to tell me the news.

Rob was one of our lead athletes and a medal target. Marian, his wife, was also key in the 4x400 relay team and we needed to perform. My reactions in that moment after I got the news remained sharp. I began to dictate what was going to happen.

At first, I went looking for Rob, but couldn't find him. I ran up the stairs of the apartment block and broke the news to the rest of the team, emphasising to them to keep a lid on it until I dealt with it. Rob came in eventually and I just had to go for it.

'I've bad news for you, Rob.'

'What is it?'

'Your mother is after dying…'

Rob immediately went into denial.

'No. You're wrong Patsy. Do you mean my grandmother? You're mistaken.'

'No, Rob… your mother.'

Maureen was found at the bottom of the stairs at their home in Cork after suffering a heart attack at the age of just 63.

I had to get Rob back home as quickly as possible. Aoife Hoey, in Athletics Ireland back in Dublin, was brilliant and had a flight arranged within a couple of hours. We got them both out of Daegu, through Seoul and via Istanbul. They had to sit it out there, but we got them home and I'd given them a few quid to make sure they were as comfortable as one could expect on such a painful journey back to Cork.

I pulled the team together the same day and talked about focus, about the fact that Rob's tragic news couldn't override why we were there. We had a job to do.

An advantage I had was the 4x400 relay wasn't until the end of the Championships. I needed Marian, so I started to float the idea about bringing her back. People thought it wouldn't work and expressed concern about her mentality, but I was continually in conversation with Liam Reilly in Cork and knew what Marian was capable of. There was a brief notion that Rob might also re-join us, but that was never going to happen.

I went into the rest of the women's team in the apartment block and began to lay the land for Marian's return. I also found Marian a room of her own, just to give her the space to deal with everything. I made it clear to the athletes that I didn't want a whole drama about her return. I was keyed in on settling Marian back in with the least amount of distraction.

Marian, after travelling half-way across the world twice, handled it so well. She was tough. She was as hard as nails. Marian, Joanne Cuddihy, Claire Bergin and Michelle Carey ran that 4x400 metres in 3:27.48, a National record and a performance that qualified the team for the 2012 Olympics in London.

THERE WAS ANOTHER image of heartache from London that was beamed across the globe. It was a tale of bravery, courage and determination.

Caitriona Jennings wasn't just another athlete to me. She was a Donegal woman so, of course, I had an extra bit of warmth towards her. Despite struggling with an injury, Caitriona finished the women's marathon. She finished in last position and came across the line 59 minutes behind the race winner. From a long way out, it was clear that Caitriona was in distress.

Again, I was at the finish line on The Mall, down towards Admiral's Arch – where I consoled Rob – wondering away if Caitriona was going to drop out. There was no way Caitriona Jennings was going to let plantar fasciitis, an inflammation across the bottom of her foot, beat her. I also knew a long time before the finish that I needed to be on the line when Caitriona came in.

The problem was that I wasn't allowed to be at the finish line.

I needed to work some magic, but I was in a secure zone, behind an extra layer of security. I began to edge up through the crowd towards the line and I got chatting to this fella, who seemed to be in charge of the volunteers. As I was trying to make friends with him, it emerged that his mother was from Killybegs and that he had gone to St Mary's College.

I'm in here.

In the middle of the conversation, he told me that his uncle, Michael Gallagher, ran for Killybegs. He told me how his uncle gave him a vest one time.

'Was it green?'

'It was.'

'That was a Killybegs vest.'

By then, I was on the line. Caitriona came in and I hugged her. It was seriously emotional. She was devastated and I was in absolute bits. The vultures were lurking, however, and I had to keep Caitriona away from the baying mob of journalists, who all wanted to speak to the woman who had finished last after a quite heroic run.

Caitriona had refused to give in and the crowd all the way along the route were just amazing. The vast majority stayed on and their support helped carry her around. In many ways, she won the Olympic Games that Sunday morning. But the emotion was raw at the end. She was crying in the team tent when her mother, Teresa and her sister Sinead - also a phenomenal athlete who just missed out on competing in the rowing in London – burst into the tent. They broke the security barrier and came in with two soldiers hanging from them. The way security was, Teresa and Sinead could have been shot, so I had to do a bit of pleading to calm the soldiers down.

'Settle down, lads. That's her mother and sister ye have there.'

It wasn't working.

I needed another approach. I always carried Irish Olympic pins with me. 'Did you get pins, lads?'

Then they engaged, and they left with their two Irish pins.

I took a photograph of the Jennings women, but decided not to put it out anywhere. It just wouldn't have been appropriate. It was only for them.

There should have been a conversation about whether or not Caitriona should have started, but she never indicated an injury prior to the race. These conversations came up regularly. In Beijing, we had Derval O'Rourke, Joanne Cuddihy and Eileen O'Keefe all injured beforehand.

Journalists would often ask, 'Should you have allowed them to compete?'

These girls began their athletics careers at eight or nine years of age. They weren't going to perform to their full potential, but I wasn't going to take the Olympic experience away from them. They had worked their whole lives for that moment.

Another time, in Gothenburg, I received medical advice to pull Ailis McSweeney out of the 4x100 metres relay team.

I offered to sign a declaration taking full responsibility, and I informed Ailis of the medical advice. Ailis insisted that she was going to run the race. Amy Foster, Niamh Whelan and Claire Brady were also on the team and they ended up missing out on the final by one hundredth of a second. I was biting my fingernails when she was coming around the bend, but Ailis ran and helped the team break the Irish record.

THE EUROPEAN ATHLETICS Council changed the European Championships to being held every two years, so weeks before the Olympic Games in London we were in Helsinki for the European Championships and it was rather farcical.

The timing totally diminished the event. It was overshadowed by London. On deck, the team didn't perform in Helsinki, although some athletes didn't travel to compete. Fionnuala Britton finished fourth in the 10,000 metres, Jessie Barr had a personal best in the 400 metres hurdles and reached a final, and Brian Gregan was sixth in the 400 metres final.

Overall, it was a mixed bag, but it wasn't a worry for London.

I had Tori Pena with me in London - and again in Rio in 2016.

Her story began with an email to me in late 2009, before the European Championships in Barcelona. Tori had family connections in Burnfoot; her grandmother hailed from Derry and she actually had been in Ireland for an Irish Dancing Championships. Tori asked me to help her with a passport.

Soon, she had established herself as a serious Irish athlete. Tori regularly made qualifications – something that indicates and proves a serious, elite athlete. She travelled everywhere and was extremely loyal, to me and to Irish athletics.

The first time I met her face-to-face, myself and Kieran Carlin had headed off to collect her at Dublin Airport. The car wasn't big enough, so we came from Dublin to Finn Valley with her poles stuck out of the boot, hanging out the back of the car.

Welcome to Ireland, Tori!

She was living in Huntington Beach, California, a world away from the Finn Valley Centre in Stranorlar. Tori was American born and American based. Because of that, she never got the credit in Ireland or in Donegal, unfortunately.

Elements of the local media would list athletes and would regularly leave Tori out. That was so unfair - and it really bothered me. Tori was American, but she competed with Finn Valley. I used to always say that if an American footballer came to play for Finn Harps, they'd be interviewed and featured regularly in the media – and rightly so – but the Irish and Donegal media at large never took to Tori.

She was an Irish passport holder, competing and winning medals for Finn Valley and representing Ireland regularly on the big stage.

Some years earlier, I had the same issue with Katie McCandless, who was a world class athlete representing Ireland and from a family that had emigrated many years previously from Culdaff in north Donegal.

Tori could easily have opted out of Championships, but she never did – and people don't realise the hardship and sacrifice she endured. In 2011, we were in Izmir for a European Cup and Tori came to Turkey from Los Angeles. She ended up in Izmir alright, but her poles didn't get out of Istanbul. The customs wouldn't release them. Tori, cool as you like, walked into the stadium in Izmir to compete and had no poles. Her relationship with the other pole vaulters was so good that she was able to borrow some from another competitor. It was remarkable to see her focus and general state of mind. Imagine a footballer walking into a game with no boots, or a snooker player going into The Crucible without his cue, or a boxer ending up having to borrow gloves from a rival. It really was something else to see Tori go about her business.

For Barcelona, I was Tori's manager, coach and mentor. That happened a lot, but I just rolled with it. We were at a training camp in Murcia and I videoed the sessions; Tori talking me through everything and basically telling me what to look out for. We struck up a great relationship and that remained through her time competing. It was never easy for Tori, but she accepted it and I always admired the way she handled herself.

I WAS WALKING around the Olympic Village one day in London and came upon a group of Jamaican athletes, including the sprint sensation Usain Bolt, the world's fastest man.

Suddenly, a familiar face appeared from the crowd.

'Guys, this is my uncle, Patsy.' Ricky Simms is a young man I am extremely proud of. Ricky, from Milford in Donegal, competed as a middle-distance runner at Finn Valley and wore a couple of Irish vests at Under-23 level. He is now one of the leading figures in athletics, as the head of PACE Sports Management, who count Bolt as one of their clients.

Ricky has showed a lot of resilience to get as far as he has, but he always stood out, even going back to his days at the Royal & Prior School in Raphoe. He went to work for Kim McDonald – Sonia O'Sullivan's former coach – in 2000, but Kim sadly died shortly after that. Ricky, his partner, Marion Steininger and Duncan Gaskell took over the running of PACE Sports Management.

I've been in touch with Ricky regularly since he did a year of his college placement at Finn Valley. He was in the mixed zone, a no-go area, with Kieran Carlin at the Sydney Olympics the night Sonia O'Sullivan won her silver medal.

Ricky has never really got proper credit for his coaching, as the general public see him as an administrator. His talent and his achievements have been completely lost. Ricky wasn't just an agent and a manager, he was an exceptional coach.

He coached Vivien Cheruiyot, a world champion, but that has never actually been recognised in Ireland. Ricky brought Vivien and Mo Farah to the St Stephen's Day 5 kilometres at Finn Valley in the mid-noughties.

Mo and Vivien stayed with Kieran Carlin, who was always a great host. Kieran was so good like that and he has made a massive contribution; I was so glad Finn Valley honoured him with a Hall of Fame award in early 2019.

Mo broke the British record when he ran our 5 kilometres in 13 minutes and 29 seconds. From the bar at Finn Valley, Ricky was circulating the news to media outlets across the globe. It was big business – and the coverage reflected that fact.

I remain proud to be close to Ricky and it was probably a reflection of our closeness that he referred, even jokingly to his 'uncle' Patsy.

We had hoped to get Bolt to Donegal, and for a while it looked like it might just happen. In one of those random *Highland Radio* interviews in 2012, Myles Gallagher ended up speaking to Bolt and asked him about coming to Donegal.

'We will see, next season maybe,' Bolt told him. 'Yeah... I'm looking forward to it.'

The media, local and national, jumped on it.

BOLT SET FOR DONEGAL VISIT.

It never quite worked out, but it was great publicity. It's a pity we couldn't get him to visit, but logistics just never made it happen. If we'd got him, it would have been like Lionel Messi visiting Finn Park to play a football match. However, our relationship with Ricky allowed us to get a recorded video message from Bolt at Finn Valley's 40th anniversary banquet in 2011. The fastest man in the world even wore a tuxedo to record the message.

'I would love to be there, but you guys haven't invited me!

'If you had invited me... I would have come.

'Happy anniversary and enjoy your night.'

THE TEARS FROM Rob Heffernan were of a different kind in November, 2016.

My words from London – 'This isn't the end of this' – proved prophetic and

51 months after he headed away from The Mall to drown his sorrows in Bag O'Nails, a little pub in the shadows of Buckingham Palace, Rob was presented with his Olympic bronze medal at a function in the Concert Hall in Cork.

I travelled down to Cork for the night and it was emotional as Rob got his just rewards, albeit belatedly. When Rob got to the top of the room, there was a special embrace for a man who had been by his side through the bad times and the good.

Liam Reilly was Rob's right-hand man and played a huge part in the story. He was central to it all, and that night in Cork I had a quiet word in Liam's ear.

'That man would have had nothing without you.'

It had indeed been a long, long road for Rob Heffernan.

I HAD ROB at the 2002 European Championships in Munich, where he competed in the 20 kilometres walk. He was in the hunt for a medal before finishing eighth.

Rob came back into the call room, and I caught him by the cheeks.

'You're there now, sir... YOU'RE THERE!'

Rob worked hard to get to a position where he could challenge the world's leading athletes. He went off at a stage to train alongside Poland's Robert Korzeniowski, a four-time Olympic gold medal winner. Rob wanted to see a professional at work in order to be professional himself, but his problem at times was that he trained too hard.

In Sydney, Rob finished eight minutes behind Korzeniowski in the 20 kilometres. Rob, even then, was one of the fastest in the world. His times were phenomenal, but he just went out too hard too soon. He was determined to get it right, and he did.

At the 2007 World Championships in Osaka, he finished sixth in the 20 kilometres. That was a seismic day for him, and I took the opportunity to let him know.

'You did it!'

I shook Rob as I spoke every word.

'You've showed you can stay with the best in the world now. Next year... we'll bring home an Olympic medal.'

DOPING HAS BEEN a scourge on our great sport over the years and we haven't been immune from it in Ireland, though thankfully instances of Irish athletes being found guilty have been pretty rare over the years.

One of my early memories of seeing an athlete I was convinced was doping was at the 2002 European Championships in Munich. We had Adrienne McIvor entered in the 800 metres. We kept a close eye on the event which was won by a Slovenian, Jolanda Cepla, who was a beautiful looking girl, with long, flowing blond hair.

She looked picture perfect from trackside. After that 800 metres final in Munich, I went down to the mixed zone and was a couple of feet away from her.

Holy fuck.

The hair on her face was so obvious and I realised that her body wasn't normal. British athlete Kelly Holmes, who went away with the bronze after that final, called out Cepla, however it wasn't until 2007 that she tested positive on erythropoietin and was banned for two years.

I had my own dealings with Irish athletes and drugs stories, too, of course.

The day before I was flying to Cyprus in 2004 for a pre-Olympic training camp, my grandson, Michael, was being Christened in Ballyliffin. At six o'clock in the morning, Sinead Kissane from TV3 rang me, asking about an Irish athlete failing a drugs test. That phone call was the first I'd heard of the story.

It would dominate my day.

My phone started hopping. I was making calls, too, trying to figure it out, and I copped on that the athlete in question was Cathal Lombard.

I was the anti-doping officer with Athletics Ireland for a while and knew how it all worked. I knew what to say and how to say it. One of the conditions of all of this is that you don't name the athlete at all. You're very clear on that. There is a process. I had to hold a line, but coming up to dinner time, everyone in the media knew it was Lombard.

The word was going to get out eventually.

Lombard's performances had been exceptional. We were of the opinion in Ireland that we didn't do drugs, and whenever a story such as this emerged, it was always a big shock to Irish athletics. It got to mid-afternoon and Greg

Allen from RTÉ rang me.

'You need to go on the air about this, Patsy.'

I was avoiding it all and trying to be very cute.

As Michael was being Christened, I was sitting in the car in Ballyliffin and didn't even get eating the meal. I had no time to eat. The pressure that day was just incessant. Everyone wanted the name, but I was confirming nothing.

I had an official line that I spun out to everyone about the process. Greg mentioned Cathal Lombard's name to me.

'Patsy, it's Cathal Lombard.' I went on air with Greg, but confirmed nothing. The Lombard story went on for a week. The BBC wanted me at six or seven one morning, and I ended up doing talk shows with other people about the drugs issue.

It was a bigger story because we were coming into a Championship. I had Lombard on teams since he was a student. From the moment that story broke, we had no contact. It was all over. Hour by hour, that story developed. He flew back to Cork from France and there was a stampede. It was such a big story, reporters tracked him.

Cathal made a comeback after serving a two-year suspension. He trained so hard and won the National Cross-Country title, beating Alastair Cragg, who was as good as there was in the world at the time.

I had to pick a team for Brussels, for the Europeans, and Cathal had served his time and he was clean by that time. He was a qualified solicitor who had been two years in limbo. He was a fella who messed up and it had a massive impact on his life.

He chose not to be considered.

There was also Martin Fagan, a lovely fella from Mullingar who put his whole life into athletics. He chased his dream and was a former scholarship student at Providence College. In 2011, while trying to get up to speed for the London Olympics, he tested positive for EPO and he served a two-year ban.

He put his hands up straight away.

Martin competed in Beijing, but he didn't finish the marathon. He qualified at the Dubai Marathon, running through a fracture. He had worked hard to get money to pay for an American visa and he went to work with Greg McMillan. He prepared for Dubai, but he dropped out around 35 kilometres into the marathon in Beijing.

He did a lot of training in America, where it was only him and the dog in Boulder, Colorado. It was a tight life. I remember one time seeing him off at Faro airport when he was heading to compete in the Great Edinburgh Run.

'Keep in touch, Martin. Good luck sir'.

I never heard from him. I looked at the results and there was no sign of Martin. He was injured and didn't say. Martin qualified for Rio, but he retired from athletics in 2015.

He seemed a bit lost, though a few shorts words from a statement he released explained where he had landed in his life.

'I woke up and didn't want to run.'

No matter where in the world I was, my heart and mind were always at Finn Valley Athletic Club. From a disused tool factory, this world-class facility was born.

ATHLETES AND ALCOHOL during a Championships is never a good pairing.

Late on a Sunday night, after the final day of competition at the 2003 European Cup in Aarhus, in Denmark, a row started because an Icelandic athlete was acting the maggot.

We were flying back to Ireland the next day.

One of my men put him outside, but the Icelandic fella came back. It felt like World War Three was threatening to break out, and it did when one of the Irish lads punched the Icelandic fella.

The police came, and I took my man up to the room to try to calm things down. I had to get him out of Denmark. I ended up that night, trying to keep a lid on things, speaking mostly in Irish.

I didn't want the police to know what was going on.

'An dtuigeann tú?'

I took my man to the police station the next morning. We were going home at lunchtime that day. We were apologetic and played ball with the police. It worked. The boys couldn't believe I bullshitted my way around the police.

I wrote a report, as I always had to do, and just mentioned that I was 'relating to an alleged incident'. I never named our athlete in the report.

But the next year's European Cup was in Iceland, and I figured that might be a problem. When it came to appointing the Irish manager for the European Cup, I made sure not to be considered..

'I have no mad interest in Iceland, boys.'

WE HOSTED THE National Intermediate and Masters Cross Country Championships in 2002. We had a good Masters men's team, but no Ulster team had ever won the Masters before then.

Clonliffe Harriers had won the National Masters for six years prior to that and were coming to win it again. In 2001, we finished third in Tymon Park, but I knew we were capable of winning it in Stranorlar.

We went out and won the Masters with Seamus Kerr, Dominic Bonner, Pat Hegarty and Mark Connolly scoring. That win was the catalyst for another great sequence of wins. We won seven Masters titles in-a-row and Dominic Bonner scored in all seven. Dominic also won a bronze in the 10 kilometres at the European Masters at that time.

We came back from Phoenix Park, Dungarvan, Tinryland, Cork, Santry and Piercetown with golds. The team changed from year-to-year, but Dominic was always there.

Winning back-to-back titles was always a massive achievement. But we had done that in 1989 and '90 when we won the National Intermediates. John McGlinchey, Pat Higgins, Joe Brennan and Mark Connolly led the way in 1989 and, again, it was made special by being on home soil. A year later, we came back with a different team.

I didn't do a pre-race team talk in Westport in 1990. Instead, I did the team talk on the bus, as we travelled through the wilds of Barnesmore Gap on a bitch of a morning.

'Let no-one here walk away from this today!

'Don't think about the weather.

'Other people will have looked out the door... they'll be wiped away mentally before they even get to the start line.'

Kieran Carlin, Neil Martin, Dominic Bonner and Anthony Murray scored and we had another unique win. Of the eight who scored on those Intermediate teams five – McGlinchey, Brennan, Connolly, Carlin and Bonner – were scoring members of the seven-in-a-row Masters wins.

ANTHONY MURRAY'S SON, Gary was a key athlete at a time and in the European Cross Country in 2007 he finished 12th in Tilburg. Unfortunately, my relationship at that point wasn't great with Gary – who was probably the last great Donegal athlete, before Mark English came along.

Gary had left Finn Valley and joined St Malachy's in Belfast. He was teaching in St Malachy's College for work placement and joined the local club. Gary grew up 100 yards from Finn Valley on the Millbrae and his father was a very capable coach who had a very good group in the club.

I didn't really take much to Gary's decision.

Injury was a big issue for him, but he had great longevity and it hit me hard when he left. We just drifted apart. Gary won the National Cross Country Championships in 2005 and 2007 – Cyril O'Boyle in 1951 was the only other Donegal man to have ever won it. That was how good Gary was.

Gary was still training away at Finn Valley, but he wasn't connecting with anyone at the club. There was even a discussion about whether or not we should have banned him from training. There was such antipathy against him locally. It was sad because he could have been used brilliantly for the new generation coming up.

A week after Gary's first victory, Mark Connolly came around the corner and put it to me that some in the club felt that we should have a celebration for Gary winning the Cross Country title. I sat down on the window sill in front of the Finn Valley Centre, and I thought about it for about half a second.

The boys want a function for a fella who has left us?

'There'll be no fucking 'do'.

'Ahh, the boys were just saying we should do something,' Mark suggested.

'I don't know where you'll have it,' I responded.

'It won't be here.

'If I'm over-ruled, I'll burn this place to the ground before there'll be a celebration here for Gary Murray.'

Mark didn't speak. He was completely taken aback. Mark is from Aghyaran, just on the Tyrone side of the border. Aghyaran is deep GAA country.

'You're from Aghyaran, sir,' I reminded him.

'You get the GAA. Do you think if Oisin McConville left Crossmaglen... joined Mullabawn and won a title that there'd be a celebration... in Crossmaglen?'

Gary's achievement in Tilburg wasn't the 12th-placed finish. It was the effort, the focus. Gary could do that all the time. He could dig deeper than anyone on his day. He was as tough an athlete as ever came into my space.

I was so in awe of him in Tilburg. It was a massive performance and when he came into the tent I congratulated him, and he walked on. He was an introvert and conversation would have been light anyway.

It was a massive gunk to us that he left. Gary perhaps didn't understand that at the time. We have a very reasonable relationship since. There was a time where there was a rumour that he was coming back at the start of the season. Every night it was the same.

'Gary Murray is coming back.'

'Gary Murray is joining us again.'

One night, I walked into the Murray house. His mother and father gave me a cup of tea. Gary was in the shower so I waited.

I got straight to the point.

'The word's out that you're coming back, Gary...'

'Nah, I think I'll stay where I am,' he told me. 'We're putting a team together to win the Nationals at St Malachy's.'

'That's dead on, sir.'

I wished him well but, as I was walking out the door, I had a pop. 'If St Malachy's are putting a team together to win the National Senior, it'll be the first time. But good luck anyway.'

I went back down the road to Finn Valley again.

'Right, boys... if I hear Gary Murray's name again, I'll knock one of ye into next week. He's not coming back... end of story.

'I'm fed up listening to this shite.'

As it happened, Malachy's didn't win the Nationals. They had some serious individuals, but they could never get it together as a team at the National Senior Cross-Country Championships in those days.

Gary is teaching now in Deele College in Raphoe. I'd love to think we'd see him back at Finn Valley as a coach some day. How incredible that would be, to have Gary doubling down on the enormous positive contribution that his Dad, Anthony has had as an athlete and a coach all his adult life.

19

In Moscow with Rob Heffernan after he won his
World Championship gold medal.

WHEN ROB HEFFERNAN arrived in Russia for the 2013 World Championships, it was clear that he was either going to win gold or die in the attempt. If you could bottle what Rob had in Moscow, you'd be a millionaire.

His mentality was right. His health was perfect. His mind was sharp. Rob created such a good environment for himself and I just knew, that morning by the Moskva River, that he was going to be on song.

He was up at 5 am, three-and-a-half hours before the men's 50 kilometres race. We met in the cafeteria and shared breakfast with some Jamaican athletes. The sound of cereal crunching was all that filled the room.

Rob nibbled at some toast and was as relaxed as ever. The banter was flying across the table between myself and Rob, his wife Marian, the physio Emma Gallivan, and Ray Flynn, a Sligo man who was a mentor for Rob.

Bar the walkers and their various support people, there was nobody else stirring at that hour of the morning. We tied up some loose ends, went to the Olympic Stadium and warmed up. The whole thing had become so routine for Rob, but he got a bit edgy as the race loomed

At one point, he bent over and vomited on the warm-up track.

Some people would have panicked, but I felt it was natural. It was important for me to remain calm and not lose the head.

'Are you alright?'

'I'm fine!'

IF I BELIEVED, then Rob was just convinced.

In the Luzhniki Stadium before the race, Rob appeared on the big screen. Where the word 'Ireland' was written across his vest, Rob just ran his hand across the lettering.

He explained himself some time later.

'I wanted the rest of the world to know that we could do it, too. We were as good as any other country and I always believed I could do it, that Irish people could do it.'

I loved that attitude.

Marian and Ray Flynn were looking after the water stations. Everything was in place, but in that moment all you can do is let the athlete take care of business.

I kept it brief with Rob before he set off.

'This is fucking it, sir.'

Rob was in control from then right through the race. London had energised Rob, but there is always a danger that an athlete can suffer from what we call the 'Olympic dip'. Rob had prepared for that and made sure it didn't happen. Instead, he kicked on from London.

His game plan was the same as it had been in London, but the race in Moscow didn't go off as aggressively. In Beijing, Rob found himself in the lead at a stage and got carried away. It threw his whole game plan off course. Pre-Moscow, he worked with a sports psychologist on coping with the various pressure situations a walker can find himself in. For each kilometre, Rob concentrated on something different… legs, hips, arms, fitness, a to z and back again. Basically, it was about keeping the focus on himself and on the here and now.

Moscow was just perfection and, as he came across the finish line, it was clear to see the emotion on Rob's face. He executed the race of his life.

It meant *everything*.

We were waiting for the bus back to the hotel and a group of supporters had gathered around. I was oblivious to them all because I had a message I needed to give Rob. It couldn't wait. The message needed to be delivered now.

I jabbed my finger into him just to emphasise the point.

'Now, Rob… before we get onto this bus, let me tell you… I've seen a lot of silly bastards in my time.

'You keep your feet on the ground.

'You settle down and be a humble boy.

'If you don't… I'll be the first man on your case!'

Rob just shrugged and in his best Cork accent jabbed back.

'I'm from a tough part of Cork… I'll handle it.'

That was Rob Heffernan having won the World gold.

TO PUT IT bluntly, the walkers had balls. They were in a very unsexy sport and they were very tough people.

Rob and I went back a bit and I always felt that his longevity was key to his success. I remember at the 1999 European Under-23 Championships in Gothenburg, Rob and Jamie Costin competing. Well, they took part.

The performance was poor and, as a result, I became quite negative.

'If you can't do better than that, you'd be better off sitting at home in the house,' I told them.

'That was pure shite. You weren't even in the hunt.

'You're just not training hard enough…there's something badly wrong. You have my heart broken.'

That was something that was often quoted back to me… 'Those fucking walkers have my heart broke'.

It became good banter between us over the years. I remember telling Jamie after the 2007 World Championships in Osaka, 'Your mother can't look at you doing another race, sir.'

But the Irish walkers had a seriously professional mentality, a mindset that developed initially through Jamie and Pierce O'Callaghan. They lived in a garage in New Zealand in 1998 and they travelled the world just to learn their trade.

I was at a bar in Ashbourne with Pierce and Jamie one night, before they left, and listened to them as they outlined their dreams. My message was simple.

'Get off your arses and do something that no-one else is doing'.

They had real initiative.

New Zealand was important. They learned a lot – especially about how unprofessional they were. They quickly came to realise the gap that was in their training. I was back at the bar in Ashbourne some months later and told Jamie he'd be at the Olympic Games.

'You're going to be on the plane with me next year, sir'

His eyes lit up.

Sure enough, Jamie qualified for the 2000 Olympic Games in Sydney. He was training all winter in Melbourne. When we were flying to Australia for the Olympics, Jamie was going to Melbourne again. We were off to our training camp in Newcastle.

The arrangement was set in stone. We were in the air on a flight from Bangkok to Sydney when we realised that Jamie's connecting flight to Melbourne hadn't been arranged.

Shit.

What could I do?

Off I went, up the aisle of the plane, and into the cockpit. The pilot took a nervous look around at me, but I spoke before he could even open his mouth. I explained the gravity of the situation, and urged him to radio someone in Sydney.

When we landed in Australia, we got on a bus and Jamie got his flight to Melbourne. Easy as that.

JUST TWO WEEKS before the 2004 Olympic Games, Jamie nearly got wiped out by a lorry in Porto Heli, a country town 300 miles from Athens.

Jamie was being coached by Robert Korzeniowski and he got a loan of Korzeniowski's car one afternoon in northern Greece. He collided with another car and it was touch and go if he would ever walk again. Jamie was transferred back to Ireland on a plane and he lay on the flat of his back for a full year.

It was no surprise to me that Jamie fought back to compete in Beijing.

I remember telling him during that difficult period. 'You're fucking thick enough to go back... You will be back'.

Jamie was a tough boy.

In Osaka, Pierce and I had to help him away after he collapsed around eight kilometres from the end of the 50 kilometres. He was on a stretcher, but we got him off and we walked him back.

He gave it his absolute all and he finished in Beijing. He was out of it at the end, after finishing 44th. But it was a remarkable journey, one that went way beyond the 50 kilometres he'd just walked.

Eight years previously, in Sydney, I saw a completely depleted Jamie Costing cross the line. The night was baking and the air as thin as could be. Jamie was staggering around the finishing area. Fifty kilometres just takes everything from an athlete.

Jamie hardly knew where he was. I was in the middle of a group of Irish journalists about 20 yards away when I spotted some medical people going at Jamie with a wheelchair, to take him for recovery. I caught sight of the wheelchair and I got into madman mode.

'Don't get into that fucking wheelchair!'

He was absolutely wrecked, but I got louder.

'DO NOT GET INTO THAT FUCKING WHEELCHAIR!'

I knew someone would take a picture of Jamie in the wheelchair. That picture would have been the story of the Irish team.

Jamie brushed the wheelchair away.

'Get to me,!' I shouted over, '... GET TO ME!'

I took him.

In Sydney, pre-competition, Jamie was offered an Olympic tattoo on his arm, but he famously said he declined as he wouldn't consider himself 'worthy' until he completed his race.

He was two hours on a drip when he was done in Sydney, but he went back to the well and competed again in Beijing. He doesn't have a tattoo, but he's an Olympian and a hero. I wanted Jamie to qualify for London 2012 so much. We wanted a fairytale, but sport doesn't work like that.

I COULD SEE the influence and impact Rob could have when he took Brendan Boyce under his wing.

Brendan, from Milford in Donegal, got involved at Cross Country and wasn't a stand out athlete. He was well into his teens when he took to walking but he embraced the sport big time. He went to university in England and he pursued the world of walking.

When he finished his studies, I was worried about what he'd do next, but he continued to take the sport so seriously. He met Andi Drake when he was in Coventry and when Drake moved to Leeds, Brendan went with him, training at the Race Walking Centre of Excellence.

His speed was never the thing that marked him out, but he had serious work ethic and he had the focus. He drove on massively and got himself into a position where he was top 20 in the world. Brendan lived on the breadline continually. He never had a job. Instead, he has followed the world of elite walking.

He is supported by the Sports Council to the tune of €12,000 a year. That's €1,000 a month or €250 a week to live off. He has to travel on that and support himself on that. It says a lot about how determined he is that he just went to get what he set out to get. He works so hard and he's seriously well established.

He has a lot to offer, but he has been reliant on the leadership of Rob. He has been in a very professional environment and has taken advantage of that. He's been Irish Senior indoor and outdoor champion, but it's the progression that tells the real story of him.

It was in his first ever 50 kilometres – imagine that, the first time he had ever done that length of race – in Dudince in 2010 that he reached the qualifying standard for London. He achieved a new personal best in London and he was in the top 20 in Rio.

Brendan's family were always so supportive, especially his brother, Brian. In Podebrady, in the 2017 European Race Walking Cup, Brendan walked an absolutely unbelievable 50 kilometres. He was at the head of it and in the medal positions for a long time.

The 20 kilometres team – Rob Heffernan, Alex Wright and Cian McManamon – won a bronze in Podebrady but, for me, Brendan was the story. He came fourth, missing a medal by inches, but it was all so positive. He engaged at the front of the race and did everything that he should have being doing. It was his best ever competitive race.

Brendan epitomises the drive of the walkers.

I loved the walking environment. It was so competitive, totally my kind of scene. Walking is so special and far from breaking my heart, it has kept that organ pumping brilliantly.

I love it.

'That fucking Russian is coming.'

'Get that fucking Spaniard by the next lap.'

'The Russian boy is dying.'

'Keep driving on.'

'Don't mind that Portuguese boy.'

'Get away from that Hungarian.'

20

With some of the family and Councillor Frank McBrearty after I was awarded the Freedom of Donegal. I'll never forget Frank for such an honour.

NORMALLY, I DON'T do nerves, but I had a lump in my throat in June of 2013 when I had to address a crowd at the County House in Lifford. I was at the top table in the Donegal County Council Chamber.

The first words I spoke weren't prepared. I rarely prepare notes or speeches. I don't like being scripted and feel better just talking off-the-cuff.

The words that day just sort of flowed.

'My mother and father would have been proud of me today …'

Until that moment, it was something I hadn't properly thought about. I was an athletics man and what I had done was all athletics related. People like me didn't get acknowledged. People like me were just part of the woodwork, the backdrop.

But there I was, a Freeman of Donegal.

GETTING THE FREEDOM of Donegal was beyond special.

The calligraphy on the award itself says it was given, *'in recognition of his contribution to athletics at a national and international level'.*

Something struck me that day in Lifford.

They would have been proud of me.

My mother died in her sleep.

She slipped away in October, 1993. It was around two o'clock in the morning and my father, from the house next door, rang me with the news. He said something to the effect of, 'We need to get the priest'. I knew what he meant.

Fr Kieran McAteer had only been in the parish for a week or two, but I met him at the old Balor Theatre in town and he came up to the house with me.

My mother's death was serious on me. She was such a strong personality. I didn't cry until they were closing the lid of the coffin, and then I roared for maybe five minutes before I quickly settled myself. Kay Byrne hit me with a reality a couple of weeks after the funeral.

'You haven't grieved at all.'

She was right. I was briefly emotional, but I hadn't handled my mother's death at all. I sort of just shrugged the whole thing off, and tried to get on with things as normal as possible.

It was two years later, in December of 1995, when my father passed away. In truth, he had died with my mother.

We lived on a hill on one side of the town and my mother was buried at Sessiaghoneill. He was devastated, but he didn't show it very openly. There was a tree outside the sitting room window that impeded the view of the grave, which was three miles away. He got the tree cut down so that he could sit at the window and see the grave.

Men of that generation didn't talk openly about things like that. All of a sudden, his whole dynamic had changed. He began to lie in bed until lunchtime and it quickly dawned on us that he was depressed. He even stopped taking his medication for a spell.

My father was dying for a period of time, but he was rushed into hospital just before Christmas. He was living next door to me, and Conor was staying with him.

It was tough at times but our neighbours, the Gallagher family, were brilliant. They'd have done anything and often went out of their way to help.

That was a real insight to Irish society, more prevalent in years gone by, of people actually being 'neighbourly'.

Conor came in one day and said that my father was looking a bit pale. We got the doctor out and we knew by her expression that things weren't good. It became very clear, very quickly that he wasn't going to last.

'What did the doctor say?'

'Jesus, Daddy, the doctor says you're not great.'

The fact that he was dying was never mentioned. But he knew what I meant. Even at that stage, however, mad as this sounds, I rolled away with the athletics. My father had days to live and I had a training session with a group of Finn Valley athletes in the field next to the house.

My father was buried on New Year's Day, 1996. The higher ranks of the Irish Army flew in for the funeral. The army took complete control of it all and appointed an officer, Tony Kiely to look after the arrangements. Even the army band came and played *The Last Post* at the graveside in Sessiaghoneill.

All the stops were pulled out.

He got a great send-off; a military police guard of honour, pallbearers from the 28th Infantry Battalion, and a gun salute before his burial.

There are always regrets looking back at family times. I didn't talk to my father enough and didn't ask enough questions about his life. I regret that, and I regret not visiting him enough.

My parents shaped me, and the influence, the discipline, and the values that they instilled in me and the rest of our family stand with all of us, even long after their passing.

COUNCILLOR FRANK McBREARTY was the Mayor of Donegal in 2013. He instigated the whole thing about the Freedom of Donegal and saw to it that it didn't fall through. He rang one evening and said they were, 'thinking of doing something'. I hadn't a clue what he meant.

I had no real connection, affiliation or association with Frank. I had been friendly with him in a sporting sense, but he went out of his way to give me that honour. I appreciated his effort so much and I was over the moon about it; seriously chuffed.

The fact I was nervous in Lifford the day it was being presented shows the esteem with which I hold that award.

In 2002, I had been presented with the Donegal Person of the Year award.

Generally, people who have won the Donegal Person of the Year award were key people. For me to get the call from Mary McGinley, the secretary of the Donegal Association in Dublin, was another massive honour. There were 560 people at the Burlington Hotel the night I got that award.

The citation – 'Athlete, Administrator, Motivator, Manager and Visionary' – was rather overwhelming and I felt a real sense of pride: In myself; in my county, my club and in my sport. I spoke well. There are times when you make a speech and you know that you've nailed it. That was one of those nights. Again, there were no notes. If I had to look at a piece of paper it would completely break my momentum.

'I'm over the moon about this,' I told the attendance. 'For 30 years, I have been following a dream. Tonight, I'm really proud to be a Donegal man. I got an opportunity as a teenager in sport and I have ran with that all my life. This award ranks up there with leading the Irish team at the Sydney Olympics. It's overwhelming to be honoured in such a way by your own people.'

I didn't always nail it when I was on my feet.

There was a time, after the Olympic Games in 2012, when the Council gave us a Civic Reception. We had an event at Finn Valley organised for afterwards, but the problem was that I stopped in Castlefin for a couple of drinks. A couple became more than a couple, and when I arrived at Finn Valley I made a speech and was walking around talking to people. In the middle of someone else's speech, I remembered something that I forgot to say. So, of course, I had to get saying it.

Quite rightly, my sister Susan told me to shut up. Some of the boys had to take me home. I handled that very badly and I was upset with myself for quite a while.

AWARD CEREMONIES CAN be awkward at times.

I got a Rehab Donegal Person of the Year award in the Abbey Hotel in 2011. I knew I was getting an award - as others were on the night - but I didn't realise that I was getting an overall award at the end of the whole show. I picked up my award and was throwing wine in me to beat the band.

I made a good job of going to collect the award, made a half-baked speech, which involved everyone in the room – including Jim McGuinness - but it was totally against the grain on the night.

There was a table of GAA-types down in one corner of the room. They'd come there to see Jim McGuinness being honoured. Of course, I didn't cop that at the time. Me being me, I landed down in the middle of them all and tried to make conversation. There was no response from them.

The reaction told me that Jim was the only man expected to get the award. GAA people have that mindset and that mentality about them - when it comes to awards, grants or most things in my experience.

It was time to go home and we only had one car between the whole plant. I ended up, me and Conor, in the boot of Aoife's car, with this award in my hand.

'If the guards stop us, fire this aul award out.'

DEATH IS SOMETHING I have found hard to deal with in my life.

Tensions were running deep in Donegal athletics in 1981, and there were recurring rows. The inter-club atmosphere was toxic.

I suppose I was partly at fault given that it was Finn Valley versus the rest of the world, in my head. That worked for me but no doubt it rubbed other people up the wrong way. Finn Valley were winning a lot as well, which didn't help.

The Ulster Senior Cross-Country Championships were on February 1, 1981 at Bonagee, on the outskirts of Letterkenny. But the drama began the night before for me.

Margaret Gallen, one of my key athletes, was working in Jackson's Hotel and couldn't get off for a team meeting at the GAA centre. Of course, that didn't wash with me. I wanted everyone at the meeting and just thought everyone could and should be there. Belfast Olympic were coming to beat us in the Ulster Senior and I had to rally the troops.

Hughie Gallen was a key man for me since day one. We had words about Margaret not being at the meeting, and ended up driving like madmen to Bonagee. Hughie pulled in just behind me and walked up to my car with this smile on his face.

'Did you forget anyone or anything?'

Who was with him in his car, but Rosaleen and my children. I was so hyped I drove out of the carpark in Ballybofey and left them all behind. That's how wired I was. All I thought about on days like that were the athletes.

The race had just started, when I looked to my side and Hugh was on the ground. My first reaction when he hit the ground was that he'd been hit. I called for help.

'Finn Valley... QUICK, QUICK, QUICK!'

There were Finn Valley boys running towards us from all directions.

'Somebody's hit Hughie Gallen.'

I didn't assess the situation at all. A doctor from Belfast came on the scene, but it was too late. Hughie had a massive heart attack and died. We got him to the hospital. I told the doctors not to declare him, but I knew he was dead.

He was just 47 years of age.

That had a huge impact on me. His family was immersed in the club and Hughie had been with me from day one. He was so close to me all year around, and we could always count on him arriving at the house with a bag of spuds on Christmas Eve. Many mornings, his children used to run to our house in Sessiaghoneil from theirs in the hills above Ballybofey. Rosaleen would make them breakfast and I'd take them to school.

Hughie's death remained in my head, all the time. His girls, Margaret and Christine were on the Finn Valley team that won the Ulsters that afternoon in Bonagee. They were seriously talented athletes: Christine ran 400 metres for Ireland and Margaret ran Cross-Country for Ireland.

Hugh was a big loss to the club. He was keyed into everything we did. He entered Lismulladuff National School for the school sports one year. The problem was that Lismulladuff school was closed. Hughie took all the children from the area – who all attended Dromore school – and entered them in as Lismulladuff. He was making a point about the closure of the school.

Lismulladuff won the thing.

That showed the edge Hughie Gallen had. We lost more than just a man when he dropped in Bonagee.

TED McGARRIGLE WAS absolutely central to the development of the club and he practically moved in when we started our own facility in the 1980s.

He was always present. Ted used to get up every morning and spend his day doing odds and ends at Finn Valley. Quite naturally, he took responsibility for the place.

I was abroad in Portugal with the Irish team when Ted died.

Francie Irwin was originally from Castlefin and lived in Mulreaney Terrace, right beside the centre, after coming home after living in Scotland for a period. He was another man who took ownership of the centre and had immense pride in the place.

Every day, Francie – who had been a very good athlete in his younger years - was on the case. Francie died when he was out running in Drumboe.

He had heart problems and years earlier had gone for a check-up in Letterkenny. Francie came back from the hospital and told me that he got 'bad news' about his heart.

'What am I going to do about the running?'

'There's nothing else you can do, but keep on running,' I told him.

'They told me to take it easy, Patsy.'

'Nah, sir. I'll tell you why… we're all going to die. You love your running and you'll be far happier just running on.'

That's how blunt I was with him.

Francie lived for years after that conversation, but we were in Portugal for the European Cross-Country Championships when the word came through that he had dropped in Drumboe. I kept the news from the team initially because we were a close-knit club and I knew it would take a grip on the group.

IN ALL MY time at Finn Valley, there are few memories as vivid as the events of Thursday morning, February 17, 2011.

The previous day, I sat in my office at LyIT talking with Shane Bonner, who had just got his exam results and was talking about going out that night to celebrate with his friends. Shane was in a very good Cross-Country group that was winning all the way up the ages. He was studying engineering in the IT. He was a bright lad and was a very talented runner.

That winter, Shane scored on the Donegal inter-county Cross-Country team in the snow in Derry. In the office the following Wednesday I was doing my usual, warning him to do this, do that and do the other. In the middle of the night, Shane was struck by a lorry on Lurgybrack, just outside Letterkenny.

We sat in the hospital for a couple of days.

We hoped and we prayed.

Subconsciously, we probably knew what was going to happen, but we kept hoping. We had a couple of hundred at training the next night and I brought Fr Kieran McAteer in to say prayers. We all gathered in the hall where everyone was upset. Shane impacted to such an extent, you couldn't but have felt the emotion in the hall that night. It was just so raw.

He started up a blog called "The Running Man'" which was ahead of its time. Shane showed great initiative to do that and the whole country was chatting about it. It was something that could have developed commercially.

Shane sadly slipped away and on a cutting February afternoon almost 2,000 people turned out in the usually sleepy village of Convoy to say their farewells. It was the biggest funeral I ever saw. Convoy just came to a complete standstill. One thing that stands out for me was the number of athletes who came from around the country.

That showed the young's man's standing. But Shane's death impacted massively on the whole club. Finn Valley members came out in their droves and formed a guard of honour.

I often thought how touching the sight of the club singlet on the coffin was that afternoon. He had worn it to win medals so often.

Beside the coffin at the altar were his running spikes. He should've been getting ready for another roaring match with Peadar, his revered coach.

Sometimes sport is put in perspective by such tragedy. But at those very same moments perspective can be the hardest thing in the world to find.

IN OSAKA, DURING the 2007 World Championships I didn't even look for perspective. My niece, Leona – my brother Eamon's daughter – who hadn't been keeping well, dropped dead in her bedroom while I was in Osaka. The news came through and Max Jones asked me a very pertinent question.

'Were you close?'

The athletes talked to me about it for a day or so, but that talk, sadly, just had to stop, because the athletes were there to do a job.

That's how cold my world had to be on occasions.

21

Mark English is and was the most talented athlete that we have ever produced in the north west of Ireland. Ever.

THE SAME THOUGHT crossed my mind after each Olympic cycle came to an end. The same doubts surfaced.

Is this it?

Is it all over?

But, after London I just kept going, no doubts whatsoever.

I was on a roll.

There is always something to motivate, but London really struck because of its proximity, its hype and the fact I had such a personal connection to the place. After London, there was a danger that it would have been hard for me to go again, but the European Cup was being held in Dublin in 2013 and I wanted to manage the Irish team in Ireland.

Ireland compete in League One of the European Cup. The top 12 compete in the Super League so we're somewhere in the mid-to-late teens.

I always dreamed of getting into the Super League.

The European Cup was something I really enjoyed. I worked hard at getting our best athletes out to compete. When I started out, not everyone would turn up. Some would come to me with silly excuses, and the American-based athletes simply couldn't be bothered.

However, I made connections with the athletes and built momentum for the European Cup. It wasn't easy, but I also took control of it. I was lining up our team from way out for Dublin. I told them what was going to happen. It was all with a view to putting the best possible team out, to develop the relationship with the individual athlete and to get them all on the one page for it.

We wanted a strong ranking given the fact that 2013 was at home.

I was able to facilitate a couple of bus-loads of young athletes from Finn Valley coming in and meeting the Irish athletes. They were all excited about that and it was something nice for me to do.

I nailed my team talk to the athletes in our base, at Roganstown Golf & Country Club. My talk was about looking out for one other. About the race never being over until it was over. About getting the extra point. About fighting for the team. About driving for everything we can get.

About pride.

About passion.

About remembering who you represent.

'Never underestimate this privilege. You have to deliver for Ireland here.'

We had a good team in Dublin, and it was a really good event for us. Brian Gregan won the 400 metres; the 4x400 metres relay of Gregan, Dara Kervick, Jason Harvey and Richard Morissey won; Tori Pena was second in the pole vault; Jason Smyth (100 metres), Ben Reynolds (110 metres hurdles) and Jesse Barr (400 metres hurdles) were all third; and our 4x100 metres and 4x400 metres women's relay teams also came third.

That took us neatly towards Gothenburg for the European Indoors in March of 2013. We stayed in a massive hotel and in the function room they were able to build an indoor track. I'd walk from my room and look through this big window down onto a track. It was an impressive piece of work and they were able to take it away again after the Championships. On the Monday morning, I looked through the same window and it was just back to a bare room.

They basically folded it up and took it away again.

WE CAME HOME from Gothenburg with three bronze medals, from Ciarán Ó Lionáird, Derval O'Rourke and Fionnuala Britton.

Ó Lionáird was an unbelievable talent.

He went to Florida State and he had some super results in America, where he was supported by Nike. He got to the World 1,500 metres final in Daegu in 2011, but over his career he was so unfortunate. In Gothenburg he delivered and I was delighted on a personal level for him.

At times as a manager, you align yourself with some people more than others. It could be to do with their back story, their personality, or something that's going on with their lives. It depends on the individual and the circumstance, really. Basically, I liked Ó Lionáird and I wanted him to do well.

He was expected to perform at every Championship. He was *that* good. He always portrayed confidence and I think people latched onto that.

At the 2014 Europeans in Zurich, a French guy, Mahiedine Mekhissi-Benabbad impeded Ciarán and messed the race up on the run for home. Ciarán had just taken the lead at 800 metres and was spiked and pushed over all at once. Ciarán was always going to be in a medal position if that hadn't happened.

Paul Robinson actually came fourth in that race. We lodged an objection for Ciarán, but it went nowhere. He was an inch of being the top 1,500 metres runner in Europe. That maddened me. I knew what he could have done and would have done.

I HAD COMPLEX characters to deal with over the years, and Mark English was a Rubik's Cube among my many puzzles.

English won a European 800 metres bronze in Zurich.

I left him out of the start team for the 4x400 metres relay heat to give him an extra bit of recovery time. After that race, I had a team meeting and announced that Mark was back in. The team was Brian Gregan, Mark English, Richard Morrissey and Thomas Barr.

Mark came in instead of Brian Murphy, who helped the team to a National record (3:03.57) in the heat. The boys came fifth in the final – and set another National record of 3:01.67. English had a phenomenal run – a 45.0-second split. And that was with a twinge in his hamstring. It was a courageous race that portrayed exactly what Mark English is.

It made sense for English to come in, but Brian wasn't delighted at being left out of the final. We were in a meeting with the team, and Kevin Ankrom was there. I had no patience for any discussion.

English was in.

End of story.

'Brian, you did an unbelievable job but, lads… here is the team.'

Mark English got his first opportunity through Evelyn Roche, the teacher in Woodlands National School – a school that was always on board with the schools athletics – but he first crossed my radar at a Juvenile Championships in Tullamore. It was one of those madcap weekends where I just decided to leave Tullamore early to get back to Ballybofey at something resembling a respectable hour.

When I left, Mark still had the 400 metres to run. I was nearly in Roscommon when someone rang me and relayed what was going on.

'Mark English has broken the Donegal Senior record!'

I knew immediately the significance of what was happening. That excited me. I called *Highland Radio* straight away and got the news and the significance of it across.

In Zurich, I knew Mark was ready.

He's an intelligent man and a great racer. I took a view that I was with him, but should remain very much in the background. I let him dictate his own routine.

Our conversations were usually light.

'How's the form sir?'

'Aye, grand.'

He was like a fighter going into battle when he was going to race. He was in a zone. Some fellas you'd embrace before a race, but there was no hugging or anything like that with Mark.

Knowing what to do came with experience.

Early in my career, it was almost a case of when a man was wrecked at 600 metres I'd have been out to do the last 200 metres for him. I mellowed in that respect later in life.

Mark's family were always there with him and I was close to the family.

I coached his aunt, Bernie English at Finn Valley. It's funny how little links like that come back in sport.

In Moscow for the World Championships later that year, Mark was capable of making a semi-final but he finished fourth in his heat. He stayed until about 120 metres to go and then revved it up.

We were in the coffee dock together afterwards, when I just tore at him.

'You need to realise these boys are all able to run the last 100 metres.

'You need to wind this up from further out.

'You can match them all… but if you leave it too late you won't get them.'

I didn't know if he was even listening, let alone taking on board what I was saying to him..

'This is the World stage… Mark…

'Not the Community Games in Milford!'

Moscow was a letdown and I was annoyed by it because he hadn't done himself justice. A few hours later, someone on the bus related back to me that Mark had commented that what I had said to him 'made sense'.

He did listen to me, but I wished he had listened a little bit more.

In Moscow, I talked to Ricky Simms about possibly representing Mark. Mark wouldn't have been on the radar, but Ricky would have been happy to go with him because of the Donegal connection. I suggested a link-up with St Mary's College in London, and the whole thing was worked out in my head.

But it has never seen the light of day.

Mark is now working with an American coach and their relationship is long distance. Of course, I have my views on that. With the proper approach, attitude and commitment, Mark English is a potential finalist anywhere. He can turn over the speed and he is that good.

I just hope that his time doesn't pass. He showed his worth again in early 2019 – after a period out with some complicated injuries – by winning a bronze at the European Indoors. His third European medal is certainly a fine calling card.

Mark English is the most talented athlete that we have ever produced in the north west of Ireland.

Ever. That isn't even in question. I am very, very clear on that. In 2014, he finished second in an 800 metres at the New York Diamond League. Only the

Olympic champion and world record holder, David Rudisha was ahead of him. Duane Solomon, who was fourth in the London Olympics, was third, but Mark English showed that night how special he can be.

In terms of world ranking and ability to make major finals in a seriously-hyped track event like the 800 metres, he is unrivalled. He medalled three times at major championships and his win-loss record stands the test.

He could be tough work for me, though.

He put word out in 2017 that he wasn't going to do the European Cup. He was going to do some Mickey Mouse race in Sligo instead. In fairness, it was his loyalty to the local lads that engaged him there.

I needed English. He was one of my main men.

We had this funny understanding; an unspoken thing. We didn't need to speak at times. But I rang him one day.

'I need you, sir. We'll fly you in on the Friday and sure... you'll do the relay. It's not on 'til Sunday evening.'

He agreed to do the relay. He was talking about doing a meeting in Malmo so, thinking on my feet as usual, I told him to fly to Malmo from Finland, instead of coming over and back. Any excuse he might have had was eradicated. Nothing was going to be a problem.

I tried him again.

'So, you don't want to do the 800 metres?'

'Naw, I don't.'

I left it another few days and told him that I wasn't ruling him out of the 800 metres. He still wasn't doing it, but as the event got closer he agreed. He ran a brilliant race in the 800 metres and a great relay leg. He was absolutely outstanding in Vaasa on that weekend.

AT THE START of those Championships in Zurich, I thought I was a goner.

Alongside the managers from the other federations, I went to a technical meeting. We were listening away to the information and next thing... Bannnnnggggggg!

I hit the floor.

In fairness, I couldn't have collapsed in a better place.

The Championships were about to start, but I was whisked off to a private clinic in Zurich. I was green-gowned at midday, but I had a team meeting at six o'clock in the evening. Pierce O'Callaghan came to the clinic and, in his head, was making all sorts of plans about taking my corpse home. There was panic at home, too, even when I came around. Rosaleen and Aoife, my daughter, had a heap of missed calls and poor Aine, my other daughter, who answered, thought I was on the way out as I slurred down the phone at her.

I was just dehydrated and didn't take long to come around.

I was so weak that I couldn't even send a text. Pierce filled in for a couple of hours, texting all and sundry, including the media – from my phone. He made sure to give the key messages: I was fine and I *would* be at the team meeting. There was one problem, however. The clock was moving towards team meeting time and I had four drips in me.

'How am I going to get out of this place, sir?'

I needed to get out and I convinced the doctors to let me out, though I had some difficulty in actually making my fast exit. We completely bluffed it. The chiefs at the clinic wanted payment for saving my bacon.

'Aye Irish Athletics will sort that. Aye, dead on!'

Away we went in a taxi, never to be seen or heard from again.

I was back in the hotel at quarter to six. The whole room fell silent when I walked in. All the staff, who had been fearing the worst, were stunned.

'How are yiz going there?'

I didn't let them dwell on my incident for a second.

'Right, we have to get this team going here.'

THE RIO OLYMPICS was in the distance, but the European Championships were in view and Ciara Mageean won a bronze in the 1,500 metres in Amsterdam.

I was in the mixed zone there and it was so exciting. Ciara's story struck a chord. She was a one-time world-class Junior, who came back into the groove after a spell out injured. Even getting back competing was a massive achievement for her.

She was a camogie player from Portaferry in County Down who became one of the best athletes in the world. In Zurich in 2014, she was among the top 1,500 metres runners. That excited me and Amsterdam in 2016 excited me even more.

An anti-doping woman came and wanted to take Ciara away immediately for a test. Because of my experience, I knew that I needed her to do as much media as she could in the immediate aftermath of the race - and, of course, enjoy her medal. Otherwise, the time is gone and, crucially, the story is gone. I needed her to stay in the moment.

An Irish coach came in and started panicking because the anti-doping woman was looking for Ciaran, but I was able to slow everything down. I killed it stone dead.

I knew my rules.

I sent Ciara for a warm down.

'This woman will be grand.'

The fella with me was learning that you didn't have to be completely reactive to officials prodding and pushing around. There are timelines to work within, and so long as you do that everything is fine.

We got the story out, and then Ciara went for the test.

Sommer Lecky is a product of the talent ID system that is primary schools athletics at Finn Valley. She won the World Under-20 silver medal in 2018.

IT'S ALWAYS DANGEROUS to get too excited once you experience a lightbulb moment with an athlete.

It was different for me with Mark English.

And it was different with Sommer Lecky in June of 2016.

Even though I watched Sommer evolve and develop over a period of time at Finn Valley, there was something in the air on a soaking wet weekend at Santry in 2016. At just 16 years of age, Sommer went out and won the National Senior high jump title. She took a centimetre off her previous best. That was remarkable enough, in its own right, to personal best at 1.71 metres and win a gold in a Senior final at 16. What made that all the more special , however, was that her performance came just 24 hours after she had shattered a 32-year-old record to win the Tailteann Games gold on the very same landing mat.

When she cleared 1.79 metres, Sommer wiped out Ursula Fay's 1984 record and she was named the best athlete of the meet. She didn't switch off even after doing all she could do the first day. She came out the next day, won the National Senior Championships, got into the car and went home.

That's the thing about Sommer, there is no fuss.

SOMMER IS A product of the system that is the primary schools athletics.

I have always been big into getting the primary schools involved in what we're doing at Finn Valley. The key to the whole thing, when we started the Primary Schools Athletics competitions in 1971, lay with the teachers. If you had a teacher who was willing and prepared to roll with you, you were set.

I ran the competitions on a Sunday, and they came on a Sunday. But over a period of time, the event grew and I got more confidence. I wasn't in a begging position to get people out, so I moved it to a school day. That was a big step considering the culture some of the people in the schools were immersed in. It was a gamble, but it worked.

Even after 50 years I don't have total engagement in my own area but, in fairness, I have 90 or 95 per cent. With some, you have to batter the door down.

We would go to some schools in the area and the door wouldn't be open to us as athletics people. There is one school in particular and they would, to this day, actually leave you standing outside.

With most schools, though, we eventually broke that barrier down and the Primary Schools Championships are now an integral part of the calendar for Donegal athletics.

THE RESPONSE OF Sommer was in marked contrast to another high jump experience I had, at a school sports day when my daughter, Aine was competing.

There were only two competitors left, one of whom was Aine.

Someone had told me she was doing well so I decided I better get down to the high jump area to see what the fuss was about.

Aine was in sixth class and I assumed she'd love me to be there.

I hurried over to see it all unfolding.

I made it in time to watch the final.

'Daddy, fuck off'.

THE FIRST TIME Sommer Lecky competed at Finn Valley, she won a 60-metre sprint. That's how it goes sometimes, kids come down and, basically, try events to see what fits. Over a short time, Sommer competed in long jump, sprint and high jump and was in a group looked after by Niall Wilkinson.

Soon, Niall – from nearby Raphoe – focused on Sommer and that connection has been very important. Sommer is very lucky with the support she has received. Niall is now working solely one-to-one with her and travels all over the world, wherever Sommer is competing.

Her father, Adrian competed with a Belfast athletics club and is an unbelievable help to her, too. He has a very sensible approach to her career. He understands athletics. I remember when she won the National Senior in 2016, saying to Adrian, 'That girl is better going a centimetre at a time'. He totally got where I was coming from.

She got an injury shortly after that, but the family didn't spare the horses to get the top man in Belfast to look after her.

THE LECKYS ARE from Castlederg, an area just across the border that has given magnificent service to Finn Valley AC.

In the early days, it was commonplace for our athletes to be lifted by the police. More often than not they'd end up in Castlederg Police Station. The story had the same pattern: Off I'd go in the mornings to verify who and what they were.

A four- or five-mile journey could become a 20-mile journey, but that never stopped some of them. They remained part of Finn Valley and many of them are still there to this day. Those people showed a resilience and a character that has coursed through Finn Valley's veins since day one.

For them to get to Finn Valley was not so much a challenge, as an ordeal. Bear in mind, this was back in the 1970s and the athletes were often travelling on roads that were, literally, being blown up, in the dark of night. At a point in time, the bridge at the border crossing at Meenreagh was blown to smithereens. It left the only access via the river. Some of us from Finn Valley drove up, flashed the lights across to a handful of men at the other side, signalling that it was safe.

They waded across the river. This was in an area where the IRA, the SAS and the British Army were all active. But the people of that area and that era were cut from tough cloth and the link has stayed intact. It's a story of families and of generations passing on the baton.

On one of those border roads there was an old disused school at Meenreagh We put some weights in it and we met up there for weight sessions. It was a sort of half-way house between us from Ballybofey and the people coming from Aghyaran or Castlederg.

People walking past used to press up against the window wondering what the hell we were at.

The word had got out about us; this group of God-knows-whats in the old school and clearly up to something.

This was the 1980s in rural Ireland.

Nobody was really doing exercises at the time, let alone lifting bloody weights in a disused school. This was all new, but it was a classic case of improvising and adapting. We had to do that a lot.

I SEE SOMMER now and I think back to the formative years on the GAA pitch when the GAA allowed us to put in a lorry trailer and we used a big bale of foam as a 'landing area'.

Sommer is the best young athlete in Ireland and is capable of making major championships. She didn't go to the Europeans in 2018, which I thought was a mistake – even if only to give her experience. I was glad that she decided to do the 2019 European Indoors in Glasgow.

She won the Commonwealth Youths in 2017 and she really outlined her potential in 2018, winning a silver medal at the World Under-20 Championships in Finland. She broke the Irish Junior record to go over at 1.90 metres. Only Karyn Taranda from Belarus was better with 1.92 metres.

Sommer was so close – two centimetres – to being best in the world. She is a great competitor and deals with the competitive environment unbelievably well.

There's no bullshit with her.

One Sunday morning in 2018, I went down to the track and the conversation began about what she was doing. I was told she was staying at home and taking 'a year out'. I felt maybe she should have moved on, but that was a coach-family call.

I thought she needed to get to Loughborough because, realistically, she needs to go another five or six centimetres, which will be hard. That being said, she has the second best ever jump by an Irish athlete and she is still only 18. She has so much experience already.

I had her for the European Cup in Vaasa in 2017 and she was the best field athlete we had. It was a horrible day, with barely 10 people on the bend and she was unbelievable, going over at 1.80 metres for fourth place. Adrian and Niall flew to Helsinki and drove five hours to Vaasa to be there. That's the dedication they show, and she keeps repaying them.

Doing what she is doing, with the travel alone, is a killer sometimes, but hers is a journey that is only beginning and I'm excited to see where it will end up for her.

There was a good Donegal connection in Vaasa with Ann-Marie McGlynn sixth in the 5,000 metres. Any time I had her on an Irish team, she performed. She ran herself into the ground, and I wouldn't have expected anything less from her.

In Tallinn in 2014, she came fourth in the 3,000 metres. That was a few months after captaining Ireland to a bronze at the 2013 European Cross-Country Championships up in the Rila Mountains in Bulgaria. The push she made there to get a bronze and her display in Tallinn showed what she was capable of.

She has had a remarkable journey. After six years out of athletics, her young son, Alfie took ill in 2012 and, initially just to clear her head, Ann-Marie laced up her runners again. Alfie had a collapsed lung and a virus. In 2013, Ann-Marie won silver in the 3,000 metres at the National Indoors – on Alfie's first birthday.

It was a lovely little aside to the story of a woman who made her Irish debut at 33 years of age.

I'M ALWAYS CAUTIOUS of talking up the prospects of young athletes and that's simply because I've seen so much talent left unfulfilled.

Ian Ward from Liscooley was a case in point. Ian was a massively talented boy who made World and European Championships as a Junior athlete. He was as good as I have ever seen.

Ian was so talented he could still win even when his desire left him.

If he needed to finish sixth to make an International event, he had such a knack of sitting back and making a move and getting where he had to be. That's how good he was. He had all the physical attributes, but he just didn't have the strength of mind for Senior athletics. That being said, a measure of his talents was when he came from nowhere to claw back Pauric McKinney to win the Donegal Cross Country Championships at Finn Valley.

It was so exciting, first with the gap that he closed to get alongside McKinney and then to get the edge in a head-to-head. I could see, though, that his motivation was nearly gone.

He was living on borrowed time for about a year and a half. Ian was really good, but long before he ever stopped, I put it out on radio one day that he had lost his desire. I sent Ian to live with the Kenyans in Teddington before the European Juniors in Budapest. Ricky Simms looked after him and all he had to do was sleep, eat and train. Everything else was sorted for him.

It just didn't work for him.

He showed not enough aggression in the heat and finished second-last. Talent is talent, and is obviously the key ingredient of any athlete, but the whole mental approach is every bit as important. His brother, Simon was a key player on Irish Cross-Country teams, too. I had it set up that Simon would join the army, but the arrangement nearly fell apart when he went to Finner Camp for the interview.

I was in Gothenburg, standing under a tree at the warm-up track before the European Under-23s, when I got a call from Finner.

'Patsy... you sent us up a boy. He hasn't a clue why he wants to join the army. All he can say is, "Patsy told me to join the army".'

I needed Simon Ward to be content and to have routine. I needed him in the army.

'When I get home, that boy better be in the army'.

WE ALWAYS HAVE to be mindful of kids who will either just drop out of sport, or who will find their calling in another code.

Of the Donegal senior football team in 2018, Eoghan Ban Gallagher and the McHugh brothers, Mark and Ryan all showed great promise as teenage athletes, and Martin O'Reilly medalled at All-Irelands as a youngster. Frank McGlynn, who also won an All-Ireland with Donegal in 2012, was very talented. In a previous era, Donal Reid concentrated on athletics and won the 1992 All-Ireland football final with Donegal. John Lynch competed for us, too, but is better known as a former Tyrone footballer.

I take a quick glance at soccer reports now and some names that stand out can all be traced back to athletics at Finn Valley AC at certain points - Amy Boyle-Carr and Amber Barrett are with the Irish Senior soccer squad, Georgie Kelly won numerous Cross-Country titles and is at Dundalk, Shane McGinty, playing for Ballymena United, was in the same boat, and Johnny Dunleavy, who has carved out a successful career, albeit an injury-hit one, was a very talented young athlete.

That is a tale that transfers to National level.

Rugby, I see, as being a big draw. At Finn Valley, even the Kelly brothers, John and James have been courted by Ulster rugby. They are two of the most promising throwers around, but they've resisted the lure so far.

The demands on youngsters for training and the pressures to commit at too young of an age, I think is a big issue nowadays. Coaches are being silly and kids aren't getting a chance to develop properly.

*My grandson, Luke saying goodbye before I headed
off for the 2016 Olympic Games in Rio.*

THOMAS BARR DIDN'T arrive in Brazil as an athlete who was going to get to an Olympic final.

Over the period of time we were there, from the training camp in Uberlandia until the races began, he came into really great form. Uberlandia worked well for us. It was funny, but I felt a little connection to the place. For some reason, I knew that Eoin Hand took an Irish squad to Uberlandia in 1982 to open the stadium. John Minnock, who spent some time at Finn Harps, was in that Irish squad. Indeed, his grandchildren were competing at home with Finn Valley AC as I arrived in Uberlandia.

It's funny how you latch onto things sometimes.

In Uberlandia, while we were on the pre-visit, we went to the civic offices and this man, who was originally from County Meath, came over to say hello. He was a former Columban priest who had since married a Brazilian woman. I had a lengthy conversation with him and clocked that he could be useful.

He went off into the day and the OCI boys who were with me dismissed my suggestion that he could prove to be a key link in the area. When we arrived back in Rio for the pre-Olympic camp, a year later, sure enough, our friend from Meath was very proactive and, indeed, had been totally engaged by the OCI. We were lucky to have him on board.

BARR WAS SERIOUSLY at ease with himself and he engaged unbelievably well in camp. His stature was rising day-by-day. Kevin Ankram, the Performance Director, did a massive one-to-one job with Thomas in Rio. There was a sense that he was building towards something and you could see that he was capable of performing.

But we couldn't have imagined what was in store.

We could never have thought he was final material and we had to keep reminding ourselves that he had been troubled by an injury in the build-up. Surely, we thought, that would affect him when it came to the crunch.

Thomas handled it all so well.

He was so good in his 400 metres hurdles semi-final. He ran 48.39 seconds, smashing his own Irish record and was the first Irishman in 84 years to reach an Olympic sprint final. At that stage, I had to control the hype and the excitement.

I was telling him not to be on Facebook, not to be saying thanks to everyone who was messaging him.

'Just stay in control.'

He remained controlled before the final. He wasn't a boy who felt that he had made it simply by getting to the final. Thomas Barr wasn't just happy to be standing on the start line of the Estádio Olímpico João Havelange. He didn't want to become an Olympic finalist.

He wanted to become an Olympic medallist.

My own mind wandered back to Sydney.

To Sonia.

To 2000.

To *that* silver medal.

Thomas had a reputation for coming on strong at the end of races. You always know that he'll eat it up. He won gold at the 2015 World Student Games in Gwangju on the basis of doing just that.

The start line is always full of tension, but the thermometer went up a few notches that day in Rio. Javier Culson from Puerto Rico, who won bronze at the 2012 Olympics, was disqualified for a false start. The athletes exhaled again and attempted to get back in the zone. As this was happening, we gathered at the finish line.

Thomas took 0.42 seconds off his Irish record as he clocked 48.93 seconds. But it wasn't enough.

Yasmani Copello won the bronze. Thomas was 0.05 seconds behind.

Inches.

Centimetres.

So close. But, at the same time, so far.

All the other Irish athletes, physios and support teams, who had all gathered in the stadium to make their presence felt for him, were all jumping up and down about a great performance.

I just sat there on a little step with my head in my hands.

Emma Gallivan, one of the physiotherapists, came over to me, 'Jesus, Patsy, that was a great performance'.

My reaction said it all.

'A great performance, aye... but he's missed a medal.'

He was so close we begin to agonise over the little moments in the race. A couple of the hurdles... could he have got over better?

In his interview afterwards, he mentioned 'stuttering' into one of the last hurdles. He put a brave face on it, but I knew, deep down, he was gutted. Someone did the maths on it and came up with a statistic that his time would have won him a medal at the last three Olympic Games. He was a couple of inches from an Olympic medal, but in Ireland we celebrate being inches from a medal the same as others would celebrate a gold.

That's an annoyance for me.

I felt that people would have a medal around his neck for the next World Championships in London, but I also knew that wouldn't work. The reaction was pretty much the same as it had been with Sonia in Sydney. I had been lifted by Sonia's response but, in Rio, I stayed disappointed with Thomas.

THE 3,000 METRES steeplechase is a real bitch of a race: 28 barriers to clear and seven water jumps.

Sara Louise Treacy was in contention for a fastest losers' spot – she was ninth at the time – when she was knocked down in her heat. Sara Louise went down along with Ethiopian Etenesh Diro and Jamaica's Aisha Praught. They had two-and-a-half laps to run, but the incident impinged them big time.

I was in two minds about appealing, but I got back to the warm-up area and indicated to Kyle Alexander, the physio, what needed to happen.

'D'you know what, sir? I need to fight this.'

After a race, there is a 30 minutes window to lodge an appeal, so you need to be on the move very quickly in these scenarios. We went to the appeals room. I saw that it could work, but it was against the odds to get a girl into the final who hadn't finished the race.

I grabbed an Irish coach, Richard Rogers and took him with me.

'C'mon, sir. You'll learn something today'.

We took the Ethiopian and Jamaican girls with us and I got Richard to keep the two of them quiet 'til I did my thing. I knew the two officials at the appeals meeting, Chris Cohen from England and Brian Roe from Australia, but we still had the case to fight.

The Ethiopian was getting excited next to us as I wrote the appeal. An hour later, the magical 'q' – for qualified – appeared next to all three athletes.

I SENT A very early morning WhatsApp message to every Irish athlete on the morning of Wednesday, June 15, 2016.

'There is an issue that is going to be massive with Pat Hickey. I don't want it mentioned.'

A story broke in the media that Pat Hickey, the Olympic Council of Ireland President, was arrested in his hotel room at the Barra de Tijuca hotel. That came after hundreds of Irish tickets were confiscated.

Pat would end up in jail in Brazil for a brief period. On release, he had to remain in Rio for a few months after the Games, pending a hearing.

Initially, he had been taken to a Rio hospital after falling ill after being taken by the police. It wasn't yet dawn and there I was messaging the athletes and team support members. I didn't want it discussed at all.

You see, the whole thing wasn't relevant to us at all.

We were probably unaware of just how big the story was back in Ireland.

We had to remain completely focussed on the job at hand, but it was obvious that something massive was going down.

One day, what seemed like the local army landed into the Olympic Village to take away one of the OCI officials and raid an office, but we didn't really engage with what had gone on until we came back home to Ireland.

Pat was later cleared of the allegations.

Rio was a much different experience to my previous Olympics Games. There were no crowds, but even at that Rio was a strange experience.

I remember going down by Santa Teresa, a neighbourhood that is quite literally two different worlds: On one side of the motorway, you have this mountain of favelas – shacks, for all intents and purposes - which people live in, and on the other you have a very rich, prosperous neighbourhood. You had to wonder about the divided state of living and how a stretch of tarmac can prove so divisive.

In one area, Rochina, raw sewage just ran down the middle of a whole group of houses. It gave a shuddering reminder about what some of the world has to deal with. The poverty was that obvious in Rio.

There is always a headline hanging over every Olympic Games.

For Rio, Zika fitted the bill.

Brazil was said to be under threat of a Zika epidemic. The virus is mosquito-borne and we were bombarded by all sorts of facts and figures to scare us. Golfers Rory McIlroy and Shane Lowry pulled out. I was disappointed with that and I felt that Zika provided them with an easy way out.

Zika was no issue. We had sprays and all sorts of protective things. We rarely had to use them. Rio, in terms of facilities and organisation, was grand.

On one of the days off, I went down to the Copacabana Beach – just to say that I was there, more than anything. I wandered across the golden sands of the Copacabana, Christ The Redeemer casting its presence. The Sugarloaf Mountain was beyond a little in the distance, and I thought of Donegal.

This wouldn't compare with some of the beaches in Donegal.

It was impressive, but it was nothing to Ballymastocker Bay in Portsalon. That view from Knockalla, looking down on Portsalon, across miles upon endless miles of the Donegal coast, is one that Donegal people possibly take for granted. For me, not even the fabled Copacabana compared.

ON THE DAY of the men's 50 kilometres walk I had my phone stolen. The battery was dead, so I plugged it in to charge in a tent at the finish line. Thinking I was being clever, I covered it with towels but, when I came back the phone was gone.

That was the only time at over 60 Internationals that something like that happened to me. It still annoys me, but I got reconnected to the world again for the race. Rob finished sixth with his massive performance in difficult conditions. In the wicked heat he gave it a good shot and Brendan Boyce was 19th; another indicator that he was one for the future.

Rio was good for us in terms of performances, and people advancing. Once that was happening, nothing else really mattered. One of the big highlights at the Games was rower, Sinead Jennings who reached the final of the Lightweight Women's Double Sculls. I had a connection with the Jennings family going back to London 2012.

Sinead was an exceptional athlete. Going back to 2001, she won a world gold medal in Lucerne and she competed at a top level in cycling - and actually came close to qualifying for the 2008 Olympic Games. Sinead making the final was massive, but a downside of it was that people started to become unrealistic and began to talk nonsense about her medalling.

Getting to the final was outstanding.

She went way beyond her ranking and did so well to get to the final.

I was lying in a wee scullery in the Olympic Village. I was sharing with the hockey lads and was in this tiny room watching Charlie Collins do a live broadcast from the Jennings house for *Donegal Sport Hub*.

There was me in Rio, and I could watch the build-up, the reaction and everything in between that was happening in Hawthorn Heights in Letterkenny. The thought struck me about how far technology had come since my early days putting coins into a telephone in Seoul in 1992 to hear the result of the All-Ireland final

I was able to message people… "I see you're out at the Jennings house."

24

My family have been the key people in every aspect of my life. My biggest supporters and the people who really made it all possible.

THERE WERE NO interviews for the Irish Manager's job after the Rio Olympics, and I just kept going.

In the early summer of 2017 an advertisement for the Senior team manager job went out. I teased it out and I applied. They wanted me to do an interview via Skype, but I was at a function in Kee's Hotel and couldn't do a Skype call. I did a teleconference call instead.

A few days later, I was in the garden with Luke, my grandson when Paul McNamara, the new Performance Director at Athletics Ireland, phoned.

I knew Paul well; I had him in Amsterdam at the European Championships as a coach and we had a good relationship. He offered me the job for the next term, ending at the Olympic Games in Tokyo 2020.

'Right, I'll take it'.

Another Olympic cycle and I was back at the pedals again.

That was me, back in the job, as easy as that. It was a case of, 'decision made, head down for Tokyo'.

THE WRITING HAD been starting to appear on the wall in Belgrade at the 2017 European Indoors. Our highlight, if it was that, was John Travers reaching the final of the men's 1,500 metres.

I had to fight a case for John after a recall gun was fired and he stopped. John and a Spanish athlete, Marc Alcala had stopped. The race went on and the results were posted, without the two of them.

Someone had screwed up, but the organisers weren't prepared to accept it. I was on their toes about it. I had my 30 minutes to lodge the appeal at the Technical Information Centre. The Spaniards were in fighting their case, too.

The stadium was closing down, people were turning off lights and locking doors. We could hear keys turn and the doors bolting around the place, while I was still there waiting for the Jury of Appeal to come to a decision.

There were times when I appealed things just for the sake of it, but this was one time I knew we were right. At the same Championships, I tried to fight for Thomas Cotter, who was disqualified from a 3,000 metres heat for stepping on the inside of the track. I appealed it, knowing rightly it was never going to succeed.

As I was going down to the appeal, I met Fintan Reilly, who was from the same club as Cotter. He and I both knew the appeal was going to be thrown in the bin. I went in and caused a stir anyway. I had to stand by my man.

Belgrade showed how different things had changed in my 25 years with Irish teams.

In Seoul, there was the famous fax and the erroneous result for Deirdre Gallagher ending up in the National media. But in Belgrade, I was able to tweet to the world for two hours about the John Travers appeal. People were getting a step-by-step guide.

"Currently in TIC (Technical Information Centre) re 1500 basis of protest is recall gun clearly fired Irish athlete stopped and request to be added to the final."

"Still with this man fighting for John Travers to be in that final 1,500 tomorrow with his Spanish athlete.

"It's kinda hard to understand why it would take so long to what to me is such an obvious decision re 1500. I heard the recall no question."

Eventually the Jury of Appeal submitted their decision. The two athletes 'were significantly affected by the incident as all others continued to race. Therefore, the Jury of Appeal has decided to advance them to the next round'.

My final tweet expressed my satisfaction. . .

"I am now one happy manager John Travers to advance to 1500 final."

BY AND LARGE, though, Belgrade was depressing. Ireland didn't impact at all. John Travers finished 11th in his final, and that was the only thing of note.

All I had in my mind were thoughts about London.

During the World Championships in London, I was different. I wasn't as energetic. I wasn't as enthused. I had a negative head on me all the time.

In London, I spoke about the culture, the fact that we needed to get tougher, that we needed to improve our structures. I even came out at one stage and said how poor the Championships were for us. I did an interview and just laid it on the line.

"It is a brutal game at this level, and I believe it's getting more competitive all the time. People at home really need to understand this is a properly global game, 200 countries-plus, and that standard is getting more brutally tough all the time.

"It's a very tough business. So just getting here is definitely an achievement. Moving from heats, to semi-finals, or especially finals is another achievement beyond that.

"And you think back to say Sonia O'Sullivan's time. An individual performance would often gloss over the overall performance. The general public would key into that lead, but the general story beyond that wasn't always great.

"Social media has changed things dramatically as well. It's becoming a more opinionated game, and it's not all knowledgeable opinion."

Thomas Barr arrived in London with a lot of pressure from Rio, but he was unable to replicate the same heights again. A norovirus was doing the rounds and Thomas contracted it. He had to pull out of the 400 metres hurdle semi-final. We had to relocate our athletes away from the Guoman Tower Hotel and those who arrived later, like the walkers, had to get housed elsewhere.

Brendan Boyce was the big disappointment in London – down to pure and utter bad luck. Beforehand, he had been going so well. His fourth-place finish at the European Cup in Podebrady indicated to us all that he was ready to move onto the world stage.

By that stage, Brendan had transferred to Finn Valley AC. It had first been mentioned pre-World Championships in 2015. He came to me about it in the foyer of the hotel in Beijing. I told him the deadline was looming, but nothing materialised out of it.

At that stage, I advised him to consider going to Milford AC, in his hometown. My thinking was that he was going to the Olympic Games and that would've given the Milford club a huge boost.

He came back to me again before London and he made the move this time. He was flying and we expected him to deliver something special in London.

We were thinking top eight, maybe even pushing for the podium, but a week before the Championship... BANG!

He was tapering off in his training and tore his hamstring. Everyone around him wanted him to stay in Ireland and not travel to the Championships. I overruled and decided to give him the opportunity. He deserved, at least, a chance.

We took him down to a park beside Tower Bridge and tried him, but it was obvious that he was in pain. He just wasn't able. Realistically, it was never going to work, but I felt he was owed that moment before withdrawing. Brendan was devastated. That race in London had been his absolute, sole focus. He was so dedicated but the whole world crashed in on top of him.

LONDON WAS JUSTIFICATION for stepping down. I could see myself getting negative.

Athletics Ireland will always try and put a positive spin and the spin wasn't long coming in London. They used the marathon performances to try and show that it had been a good Championships.

With the greatest respect, none of the athletes seriously impacted.

I didn't even think about the decision to step down. I was walking around the track at Finn Valley in July when John Foley, the Athletics Ireland CEO, rang me.

I had no thoughts about pulling the pin. I was annoyed about certain things, but I never thought about giving up. I got up that morning as the Irish Athletics team manager and had no notion that I would confirm my departure to Athletics Ireland by dinner time. Subconsciously, however, I did want to get out.

That being said, my departure was never planned. I certainly hadn't really thought about it until that phone call.

'Right sir, I'll do London and that'll be it.'

I had said it.

There was no animosity or arguments on the phone call. It was all quite amicable. That probably said a lot, though.

The excitement was gone for me. I began to dread the travelling. It got to the point, I'd be in bad form a week out from my departure. I got remorseful about it all. It was time to go.

I told Rosaleen and she was annoyed. She told me to reconsider. Others did, too, but I was done.

I had promised Rosaleen, on the Bible and on our children's lives, that I was done and dusted before. Several times, actually. But this time, I really was serious. I was gone and, strangely, they were more annoyed than I was.

In London, I told the media that it was my last Championships and I was going to leave it at that as far as an announcement was concerned.

I didn't expect Athletics Ireland to do anything.

Sure enough, there wasn't a word.

Nothing.

After 25 years and 68 Internationals as manager, I didn't get a word anywhere from Athletics Ireland; not even an email to thank me for my services. I had pulled them out of the fire at times and I worked hard. I was good at the job and was recognised as such, but I got no acknowledgement on stepping down.

That hurt.

I carried the can at a major level for a quarter of a century, but absolutely nobody from the inner sanctum even acknowledged that I was gone. That was probably a result of my attitude. I spoke my mind and that didn't suit some officials.

The journalists on the beat related to me and I was always frank and up front with them. I was on the same page as them and never gave them any old claptrap. I didn't toe a line and always called it as it was. Or, at least, how I saw it.

I HAD A talk with Pierce O'Callaghan, who kept the statistics of my tenure, but I still had to be coerced into preparing a statement. There was nothing coming from Athletics Ireland.

A statement was released by Finn Valley AC on October 26, 2017.

The day of my 70th birthday.

"Patsy McGonagle today announced that he is stepping down as team manager to the Irish Athletics team, 25 years after first managing the team at the World Junior Championships in Seoul, South Korea.

"During the quarter of a century at the helm of the National team, the Donegal man oversaw unprecedented success including Irish athletes winning 2 Olympic medals, 9 World Championship medals and 27 European Championships medals.

"A graduate of St Mary's College of Physical Education in London in 1972, the Ballybofey man was one of the early pioneers of full time PE teachers in Ireland.

"It was from this base that saw McGonagle selected to manage the National team on a record 68 occasions, including 4 Olympic Games, 6 World and 6 European Athletics Championships.

"These experiences saw him manage Irish teams on 4 continents and in 28 countries.

"To give his time at the helm some context, only one man, Jack Charlton has managed the Irish football team on more occasions while similarly only one man, Eddie O'Sullivan has managed the Irish rugby team more regularly.

"Although McGonagle was recently re-offered the post by Athletics Ireland until Tokyo 2020, after careful consideration he felt the time was right to step aside and allow new blood to take over the duties.

"'It was a huge honour for me, especially being from rural Ireland in Donegal, to have been appointed to manage the National team on so many occasions,' said McGonagle.

"'I was always so proud to wear the Irish tracksuit and to fly the Irish flag abroad at major athletics events and I am forever indebted to the Irish athletes

I managed who put in so much effort to represent their country with such distinction abroad at the highest levels.

"'I have so many highlights – the Olympic medals won by Sonia O'Sullivan in Sydney 2000 & Rob Heffernan in London 2012 and the World & European Championships championship medals also won by Olive Loughnane, David Gillick, Derval O'Rourke, James Nolan, and more recently from Mark English from my own county and Ciara Mageean.

"'I never tired of seeing the Irish flag raised for a medal ceremony and hearing Amhrán na bhFiann being played in stadiums around the world.'"

The statement continued from there… and what it meant was that I was gone…in 552 words.

It was rather sad that Finn Valley Athletic Club had to release the statement. That reflected poorly on Athletics Ireland.

I was glad that I put out my own statement because I needed to clarify the situation. Before London, I wondered a lot about it, but after those Championships I was convinced that I made the right decision.

London, I felt, became a celebration of mediocrity and I was just anxious to get home. A lot of people told me to hang in there, but I just knew it wasn't going to generate the same excitement anymore.

I was going to start challenging athletes to the point where there'd be a breakdown.

The whole culture needed a kick up the backside.

LONDON, HOWEVER, WAS a special experience in spite of the negativity.

We had 30 children from Finn Valley who volunteered to work as kit carriers. It was a great experience for them and their parents got in, too. It was an unbelievable connection for them, being able to get out into the warm-up area and be up close to the world's best athletes.

They were wide-eyed looking at Usain Bolt and company.

Rosaleen later remarked that everything was right about stepping down in London. It was only when I reflected on her words that I realised she was spot on. Stepping down in London meant the wheel had come full circle. Some 69 years beforehand, my father was in the same city, at the Olympic Games.

I was chuffed to have managed Ireland at the 2012 Olympic Games in London, using my old college – where'd I'd cut my teeth in so many ways – as a base. London was where it started for me. If I hadn't gone to St Mary's, I would never have arrived where I did. I took the opportunity.

I was at ease in London and loved the environment. In 2012, I never thought I'd have hung around for Rio, let alone London a second time. But I made it to London again.

I had my wife, Rosaleen, my son Conor and two of my grandchildren, Michael and Caitlin – not to mention a whole crew from Finn Valley – accredited for the 2017 World Championships, my final major Championships as the Irish Manager. I spent so much time away from my family over the years, it was only right that I had some of them by my side for my swansong.

ON THE SATURDAY evening, the final evening of the Championships, a photograph was taken of me with two of my best friends, Pierce O'Callaghan and Stephen Maguire.

Pierce was the Director of Operations for the Championships, and Stephen was coach of a British team that had unreal success. And I was the Manager of the Irish team for the sixth time at the World Championships.

Pierce, Stephen and I regarded ourselves as the Athletics Ireland Rejects.

The Rejects didn't turn out too badly.

Epilogue

I WAS ALWAYS called 'Patrick' by my mother.

I'm not quite sure where 'Patsy' came out of. It was just one of those quirks of Irish life, I guess, where your name could be altered a little. Regardless of who it was, a mother was always annoyed when her child was called something other than what he or she should be. After all, she'd gone to the trouble of Christening her child, and could reasonably expect other folk to get it right.

Anyone who rang the house and asked to speak to 'Patsy' got a short shrift from my mother.

'Naw, naw... there's no Patsy here.'

A certain age group of people in Ballybofey still call me Patrick.

I had long since been re-Christened as Patsy when I was named the Irish team manager for the 1992 World Junior Championships in Seoul. It might have seemed strange but, while I got a massive vote in '92 for that job, I didn't get a big vote from my 'own' people in Donegal. Around the country, people had taken notice, but if I had gone to a convention and there were 15 Donegal delegates, I might only have got the Finn Valley vote on occasion.

I wasn't going to get the other votes, but I knew that anyway. I was an in-your-face guy when it came to Finn Valley and probably wasn't cute enough in the early days, when I caused rows that I didn't need to cause.

Even now at over 70 years of age, I do my own thing.

The Donegal Athletics Board have a Hall of Fame for people who have made lasting contributions to Donegal athletics. I doubt that honour will come my way, but that doesn't bother me.

I knew I was 'different' and was content with that. I knew where I was going myself – and that was good enough for me.

There were tough times, of course, and it wasn't all plain sailing. Far from it, in fact. I put myself in a position in my community, and also in LyIT. I had a blinkered attitude, but that worked for me.

The army was different. I embraced the working relationship there, the discipline. The camaraderie and the people concentrated my mind.

Through it all, Rosaleen was a rock of support and backed me every inch of the way, around every bend and over every hurdle. Take one year in the 1990s when I was getting ready to go to Japan for a road relay.

How am I going to tell this woman that I'm for Japan?

I waited until about two days before I was set to go. The plans were in place, the team was ready, but nobody in my own house knew I was going. As Rosaleen was walking past the washing machine on the Wednesday evening, I just blurted it.

'I'm for Japan on Friday.'

I just threw it out as if I was going to Strabane.

I WAS WIRED about athletics. Totally and utterly wired.

I was the athlete when I was in England, but when I came to Ireland, I was the athlete and the admin man. I wasn't at the birth of any of my children but, then again, that was the norm for men of my era.

Niall was born in February of 1972 and, the day he was born, I drove up past Letterkenny Hospital on the way to Cranford for a race. By the time I came back down the road that evening, Niall had entered the world. I was based in London and had to fly back that night. I had come back for the Ulster Championships in Cranford, rather than the birth.

As I recall that, I'm not quite sure what to make of me!

The whole family rowed in behind what I was doing, all the way. Even now, Rosaleen's family are vital cogs on the Finn Valley wheel. Rosaleen's sisters, Susan and Bridgeen came into the club as athletes – they ran with me in Glenties and travelled in Sharma's van! – and are with me to this day.

Rosaleen really bought into it and she was seriously supportive of every move I ever made. I walked about the house, but I wasn't in the house. I always joke that Rosaleen reared the kids, but that was true to a point. My life was my family and athletics. The two worlds ran parallel.

I was difficult to live with. I was never concentrating on a lightbulb that went out or a shower that was broken. But I ended up with a very tight-knit family, a nice house and home, in a beautiful location, overlooking the valley and the community that I've given my life to.

My family were absolutely and utterly key. I couldn't have done any of that without their support.

The three boys have all won Irish medals: Conor in the high jump, Niall in the javelin and Brendan on Cross-Country teams. They were all involved. They were just lumped into the car and we ended up wherever there was athletics.

Niall had a talent for soccer and got a scholarship to the University of Mobile, Alabama. He was so good at soccer I almost got into a sticky spot while managing the Letterkenny Institute of Technology in Castlebar at one tournament. I brought Niall to play with the LyIT team that weekend. The problem was Niall was still at secondary school. He played a blinder at left-back and nearly got picked for the International Universities squad.

I had to think quick and say that he was unavailable. I just mumbled an excuse and hoped it would go away. God knows how I'd have got around that one. The morning Niall went off to Alabama, there was no big going away parade. It sounds terrible now, but we just sent him on a lorry with John O'Loughlin from Killygordon, who was driving to Dublin that morning.

It was just, 'Get the breakfast into you… and away you go'.

It was sad because Alabama seemed so far away, and Niall was only 17. He was excited and, unlike me, he never once got homesick during his seven years in the States. Phone charges were a big issue for long-distance calls, but it was possible to reverse the charges. We were living in Sessiaghoneill, near a phone box, opposite the chapel.

Niall could reverse charge a call from America to the phone box, but this arrangement got even better thanks to the ingenuity of two local boys. The boys figured that they could take a lead out from the phone box, and into the car. We had the car parked on the street and we spent hours talking to Niall in Alabama, via the phone box.

The boys got so good at that, that I got the parents of other athletes who were based in America to come up to the phone box to make contact. It was just another example of cutting some corners, but getting the job done.

I HAVE ALWAYS been very proud of my family and particularly of my children.

I never placed emphasis on studying with any of them. I took an interest, alright, but I never pushed it. Every one of them have turned out well.

Brendan went to UCD and worked all over Europe while he was doing a PhD before ending up in Vienna. He left Austria and eventually ended up living in Plovdiv, Bulgaria, where he is married to Borianna, a native of Plovdiv. They have three children – Meabh, Brenos and Aoibhne - who are all very talented in classical music, playing the harp, cello and violin.

Brendan was always very keen to learn languages and he became fluent in Bulgarian. He has actually written two books in Bulgarian and in one of them he explores how a nucleus of Celtic people settled in Bulgaria before moving westward. They spoke a language, which is now defunct, and his research shows that there are still 200 of their words in existence, which are so alike to words in Celtic languages.

His texts were somewhat controversial in Bulgaria. During the communist period, all references to the Celtic element in Balkan culture were erased from text books and the Slavic connection was emphasised.

Conor went to St Columba's and the Royal & Prior before going to the IT in Letterkenny.

He got into journalism at a young age and started working for the *Derry Journal* – in their office in Letterkenny – when he was 17. As the newspaper game in Donegal changed and evolved, he worked for the *Donegal People's Press* and the *Donegal Democrat*, as well as the *Journal*, when they all ended up under the one umbrella.

Conor has been really influential in the development of the Finn Valley

Centre and he's now managing the bar and restaurant. He is married to Maria Doherty from Convoy and is assisting aspects of club development at Finn Valley. No escape. Their son, Michael has an All-Ireland athletics medal in the hammer and plays soccer locally. Their daughter, Caitlin helps at Finn Valley and is seriously into her dancing. Both of them are doing well at school.

Niall grew up a Finn Harps maniac. The team used to leave from Jackson's Hotel to go to games and Niall, at times, could jump on the bus and be away from six o'clock in the morning to watch Harps. Other times, he mightn't have been back home until midnight.

Niall, who is married to Rachel, with whom he has a daughter, Rosie, coached a Finn Harps youth team for a couple of seasons and was successful for a period managing the LyIT soccer teams.

He put wild effort into it. I don't think Harps ever appreciated the lengths he went to. He was very professional and proactive. He brought in Strength and Conditioning people and was taking it to a new level. Rosaleen used to cook the meals for the whole team after games and they had the various supports at the Finn Valley Centre to use, but Harps as a club didn't bother too much about him. Nor, I feel, did they understand what he was attempting to do.

Aine attended the University of Bedford and, prior to that, Luton University. As she was qualifying to become a teacher she worked in Irish bars at the same time and was very frugal.

She is now living in Barton-le-Clay, a lovely little English village in Bedfordshire. She's married to Damian Gill, originally from Longford, and they have three children, Conor, Dannan and Scarlett. A highlight for me now are their visits home and the odd trip across that we take.

Aoife was accepted to study primary school education in Liverpool, but she's a home-bird at heart. She studied Special Needs education in Derry and later did a degree in Community Development at LyIT. I nearly wanted to do that course myself. I 'helped' her with one part of it and I went stone mad one day when she 'only' got a B+ in some assignment or the other.

I felt I had lived community development for years, at many levels.

'That lecturer knows fuck all about community development!'

Aoife is a Special Needs Assistant at Deele College and is married to Paul Mailey, from Convoy. They have two children, Luke and Finn. I spend a lot of time with Luke, wandering around and exploring. I take him on board, I take time to answer him and figure out what's going on in his wee head.

I make serious time for my grandchildren; to relate to them, to study them, to sit with them and have the craic with them. I suppose you could say that it's time I didn't have – or, more accurately, make – for my own children.

I always wondered what impact my lifestyle would have on the family, but all of them turned out extremely well. Every one of them has an attitude that I love. None of them have bought into what I perceive to be a silly world and they have retained the values they grew up with.

In tandem with a mad, busy life I was still able to influence my children. I was big into respect; that they would respect other people, that they wouldn't be cheeky and would have manners. Old world values.

Interestingly, much like me with my own father's Olympic story, what I have done was never a topic of conversation in the house, but I could sense their pride.

I always knew that there was a great pride and an unbelievable awareness from home about me and the Olympic Games. It was made a big deal when I went away, particularly to the Olympics.

We have retained a very strong unit at home. We are a very tight family. It's something so many people in the world take for granted. All through my journey, no matter where I was in the world – be it Stranorlar or Sydney, Ballybofey or Beijing – I carried my family with me.

I carried their support and their pride all the way.

I ALWAYS SEEMED to put athletics first, no matter what.

Late in 2014, I went to hospital in Sligo for some tests. There was a National programme rolled out offering free check-ups.

A week or two later, I ended up in a hospital in Galway staring into the eyeballs of a Mr Joyce, who informed me that I had bowel cancer and would need to undergo surgery. I had training at half-seven that evening in Finn Valley, so I needed to get back up the road again.

Even bowel cancer could wait.

Mr Joyce told me to come back in the New Year, but that wasn't going to work for me.

'Jesus, sir, what about Christmas?'

I wanted to get the operation done quickly, because of the cancer, yes, but my main motivation for the urgency wasn't actually my health. People around me would have worried more.

I told nobody outside my family, and they were warned not to breathe a word.

I didn't want to show any weakness.

'Tell them fuck all. I won't be through the Gap to Donegal Town... and they'll have me dead!

'Did you hear... Patsy's fucked!'

I didn't want that nonsense getting up. I didn't even tell my closest confidantes in the club. I kept it in-house.

My thinking was that I needed it to have as little impact on the club as possible.

I told a couple of people in the club that I wouldn't be about for the St Stephen's Day 5 kilometres. The Sunday before Christmas, I had a Christmas dinner with my family in a room at the Finn Valley Centre. The next morning, Rosaleen, Niall and Conor brought me to Galway.

As we were driving down, on a soaking wet morning, the Donegal Cancer Bus passed us. The cancer bus takes patients from all over Donegal down to Galway for treatment. It is a great service that I had serious regard for.

But my first thought was, *Fuck, I could end up on that bus. Imagine, on a balls of a day like this... having to get a bus to Galway for treatment?*

I made a comment in the car about how lucky we were to be driving down.

I had no anxiety until the anaesthetist arrived. I was in a room next to the theatre and could see all the set up for me. All the machines, the tools, everything just lying there ready for me.

My mind spun a bit.

I mightn't come out of here at all.

That was the first time I thought about it, but it wasn't long before I was knocked for six and was being wheeled in for the operation. I was away for about six or seven hours. Once I got myself together again, I sent Rosaleen, Niall and Conor back home again.

In the middle of that night, the heat became unbearable in the ward. I began to worry about the impact the operation would have on me, my body… my life. And what about the athletics?

It's time to get out of here!

I was struggling. Big time. Day-by-day, though, I could tell that the doctors were happy with my progress. Everything was looking good. Still, not many people knew I was in and I was engaging with everyone as if I was in the middle of Ballybofey.

People to this day swear they saw me at the St Stephen's Day 5k. I posted away at pictures on social media, congratulated various people. There were men who were insisting that I was on the track.

'Aye, sure I seen him… but I wasn't chatting to him..'

I spent the New Year in intensive care, but I was getting restless. When I heard a nurse pass a comment about Mr Joyce, my consultant, being off the next day, that was my opportunity. I rang home and got Aine, my daughter and her husband, Damien to come down and collect me.

In the morning, a nurse came around to check on me.

'What has Mr Joyce said about you?'

'Ah, he says I can get home today.'

'Jeez, you're a lucky man.'

I wasn't well, but I got up the road. It was a struggle to even get out of the bed, never mind come up the road. If that had been someone else on that bed, I'd have eaten them for even considering getting out and about again.

At one point, I remember feeling how I could empathise with people who were so sick that they just wanted to die. I could relate to someone feeling so sick, so weak, so helpless. I was far from that stage myself, but the whole situation allowed me to look at things through new lenses.

Once I got a little bit stronger – and it was only a few days after I came home – I got Rosaleen to drive me down to Finn Valley. She parked the car up at the fence beside the track and there I was, dictating out the window. I remember Peadar McGranaghan doing the exact same after he had a hip replacement.

Within a couple of weeks, I was back encouraging athletes from the side of the track at Finn Valley. It was as if nothing had happened at all. I had a notion where I had to stay on top of things and always be on the ball, regardless of what was happening.

The fact that I was the Irish team manager was another motivation – perhaps, on reflection, my biggest motivation – for not telling anyone.

It took a month or so for the word to get out, but I fobbed it off.

'Aye, I had an aul thing, but nothing major.'

OR, THERE WAS the time, for the 2005 World University Games in Izmir, in Turkey, where I travelled with my whole left leg in a plaster and a protective brace.

I fell on it a couple of months beforehand one night at Finn Valley. Of course, I rattled on as if nothing was wrong, hobbling about and trailing my leg, in agony, behind me. At a European Cup in Leiria, Portugal before we went to Izmir, one of the Irish medics looked at my knee. It was swollen badly.

'You could get a clot from that.'

Back in Ireland, I got it seen to at a clinic in Galway. The World University Games were coming soon and, in spite of my ailment, I needed clarification about travelling to Izmir. The doctor couldn't have been clearer.

'I never came across the likes of this. All I can do is advise you and my advice is not to go. It would be dangerous.'

I listened carefully to his advice, and then ignored every word of it.

The heat was wicked in Izmir. The 35 degrees and my plaster didn't agree too well, but I kept going. I didn't have much choice. I got used to it and we had a really successful Championships in Izmir: Ailis McSweeney won silver in the 100 metres; Derval O'Rourke won bronze in the 100 metres hurdles; Paul Hession took bronze in the 200 metres; Jolene Byrne was the 5000 metres bronze medallist; and the women's 4x100 metres team (Ailis, Derval, Anna Boyle and Emily Maher) came home with a bronze, too.

I WAS LUCKY to have the people around me at Finn Valley AC that I did. Right from day one, that is true.

Neil Martin went the journey with me. He came on board as a young boy from Glenfin when I was teaching in Glenties. He was from a big GAA family and area, but he went down the athletics route and stuck with it. He won his first Cross-Country title, an Ulster Novice title, running with Glenfin

Athletic Club, in 1971. He ran in his bare feet in Omagh and won the race.

Neil was a very talented athlete and had numerous scholarship offers from America. He was on side day-on-day as an athlete, then as a Masters athlete and he became very proactive in the journey of Finn Valley Athletic Club.

Neil has been loyal and been at my shoulder all the way as an athlete and an administrator.

My son, Conor was absolutely key in terms of the development of the Finn Valley Centre and that is something that needs to be acknowledged. Of course, he had my support and I had developed things to a point, but Conor took the baton and went the extra mile.

Two men from down the Valley came into the club through the involvement of their children. Peadar McGranaghan and Patsy McGinley are the current Finn Valley AC Presidents and were solid, loyal men. They had the courage to go with me and were so, so important to me all the way.

They spoke their mind and they were respected. They were total in their support.

We have some fantastic coaches and people in Finn Valley.

Mark Connolly from west Tyrone, just over the border in Aghyaran, is a lead coach and another who started off as an athlete. He brings great enthusiasm and energy. The Derry City & Strabane Council are lucky to have him as an Athletics Development Officer. He's so passionate about the sport.

Dermot McGranaghan also came in as a young athlete and now has a job with Athletics Ireland, but remains so vital to the club and is driven in his approach to athletics. He is already making an impact in his new National position.

Kieran Carlin has been central in so many ways. He came in as a young athlete, who became an International. He really developed the sport in terms of social media coverage in the early days of Facebook. Indeed, Kieran is still a competitive Masters athlete.

We have the likes of Rosemary Finn, Paula Beales, Patrick Galvin, Anne Slevin, Sinead Kenny, Mary O'Callaghan, Paula Jansen, Sharon Bradley, John Kelly, Niall Wilkinson, Paul Wilkinson, Dermot McGranaghan, Ciara Kearns and Shauna Carlin in a variety of coaching roles in Finn Valley.

They are all playing a massive part in keeping the conveyor belt moving.

Previous major contributions were given by the likes of Bernie Alcorn, Christine Feely and Sean Carlin.

Bernie O'Callaghan folded the club in Killybegs and threw his lot in with me. Bernie was there with me at the start in Glenties and has become a life-long friend. Our lives have crossed paths for 50 years and he's now with me at Finn Valley.

WITH TOKYO 2020, the next Olympics in mind, the outlook isn't great. As of the end of 2018, there are five athletes ranked in the top 50 - Thomas Barr, Brendan Boyce, Ciara Mageean, Sommer Lecky and Leon Reid.

If Thomas Barr gets to a final, we'll be doing well.

We'll have a better gauge with Doha in the 2019 World Championships, but I don't foresee any major breakthroughs or standouts.

Athletics Ireland are more proactive now than they were for so long. To their credit, they're spinning out really positive stuff and, of course, that is brilliant to see. They're standing up for the sport in a way and painting it in a positive light.

But, for me, the jury is out.

When Sonia O'Sullivan went, we thought that Irish athletics would be in the doldrums. We thought the sport would be off the back page, but along came David Gillick and Derval O'Rourke.

You couldn't see that coming at all.

Then Olive

Then Rob.

Thomas Barr, and Ciara Mageann.

Now, I have the same thoughts and worries as we had when Sonia crossed the finish line. I hope I'm wrong, but I just can't see where it's going to happen.

Winning a battle on Facebook isn't what counts. If I were in now, I'd still be driving the line about professional, full-time coaches. There are some positive moves in that direction, but could we spend even a little to organise regionalised event squads? Not one-off stuff. It needs to be led and supported by the National body. Why not have regional event coaches working with a National lead?

When you scrape at it, what happened in 2018 at Senior level other than one medal from Thomas Barr? At underage, Ireland got a couple of hits at underage, with the relay team and Sommer Lecky at the World Juniors. That was it.

There's more money coming in from the Sports Council to coaching, but Irish athletics is still a long way off where it should be. Rob Heffernan should be given a leadership role. His experience, his manner, his attitude and the way he can deliver, should all be used by Athletics Ireland.

Rob had a go at Athletics Ireland in his book and some noses are obviously out of joint, but the sport is bigger than anyone's ego. Athletics is still a minority sport in many ways. You have the big guns of soccer, GAA and rugby, but there is better awareness of athletics now.

Athletics is a lonely game.

In athletics no one claps you on the back. You're in the real world all the time. There is no place to hide. In football for example, the whole place engages. In our environment at Finn Valley, that exists, but that's not everywhere. You have to be motivated by the sport and by your own ambitions

There is a softness that has crept in and it is disconcerting for someone like me.

Consider that, in 50 years, I have never cancelled a training session.

Never.

Not one hour, not one day.

It has become a point of discussion at Finn Valley in the winter months to wind me up.

'Ask Patsy if training's off!'

ONE NIGHT OF a really bad wind, things were getting dangerous outside, so I took the athletes inside to the hall. Around and around we went. At least they went home having trained and a vital point underlined.

I remember six or seven inches of snow one year and I battered on with training. I see it now where schools close in bad weather and people are guessing because of a weather forecast. Everyone uses 'health and safety' as something to hide behind.

Life isn't going to be a bed of roses and you have to deal with good and bad, weather included. That's a get-out clause that is a symptom of the

Ireland of 2019. It is a world I wouldn't survive in nowadays.

This world couldn't deal with what I was like in my youth.

And the youthful me certainly couldn't deal with the attitudes and excuses that are so prevalent now.

ONCE I GOT the taste of International management with the Juniors in '92, I wanted to be in it all the time.

I wasn't just the Olympic team manager. I was also the fella who ran the local school sports. I could get off a plane on a Tuesday in Dublin, drive like hell and be on the ground with the nine-year-old athletes at Finn Valley that evening - and would be totally and absolutely excited about it.

Even when I was away, I still ran the show at home.

There are a whole lot of whys:

'Why do it?'

'Why continue to do it?'

'Why get excited about it?'

'Why come back from a medal-winning International and get back to the kids?'

There is a bit of uniqueness in my story, I suppose, and the opportunities I had won't arise for a grassroots athletics man ever again most likely

I was pushed to the limit sometimes coming back from International business.

The opening of the swimming pool – the swimming pool that I'd worked my backside off for – was a case in point. I was in Rio for the pre-visit ahead of the 2016 Olympics and the opening of the swimming pool was the day I flew back. The pool was being officially opened at three o'clock in the afternoon, but at eleven in the morning I was still in London waiting on a flight that was delayed because of fog.

I got to Dublin for 12, but I had no car.

I rang Conor in a blind panic.

'Send someone to drive as hard as you can towards Dublin.'

I ran like hell and jumped into a taxi. We met a Donegal car in Ardee. I jumped into the car, drove like a lunatic and made it with half-an-hour to spare. Rosaleen had my suit, shirt and tie waiting in the changing rooms at

Finn Valley. At the exact time it was supposed to open, I was putting on my shirt and 20 minutes later, there I was giving out this speech about the pool.

I WORRY FOR the future of athletics.

I'm against the Parkruns, especially in their current format. The experience of clubs in England is that Parkruns are destroying clubs. People with no allegiance to anyone just turn up and run for free.

There are a lot of positives in the Parkruns but it is not in any way an add-on or a positive for local clubs.

Plainly, the runs are to the detriment of athletics clubs. I sent a message to all of our groups at Finn Valley to have nothing to do with them as soon as they launched in Donegal. Eventually, Parkruns will beat athletics clubs.

Gerry O'Doherty from Letterkenny, for example, is the secretary of Essex Athletics and he runs a club there. The athletics club can't get people to turn out for athletics as they take the Parkrun option. They are actually struggling to put teams out.

It hasn't begun to impact like that in Donegal yet, but there is always a danger and it will be a problem for the running of athletics. I do appreciate the opportunity they give to health, mental health and the social aspect, but there clearly is no obvious advantage to the athletics clubs.

This view needs to be studied in the context I make it, as the world and its mother is seriously in support of and excited about the Parkrun development. I would have preferred an approach that was linked, and led by the athletic clubs.

I HAD SERIOUS pride at being manager of the Irish team. I'll take that pride to the grave.

I got an unbelievable response from home no matter where in the world I went as Irish manager. The Donegal media always showed a great interest in my role.

Subconsciously, I was driven by the fact that my father had gone to the Olympics in '48, even if there wasn't much chat about it in the house. I don't ever remember a conversation about him going to the Olympics, but I knew he did and was very aware of that.

Nothing will replace the first time I led Ireland at the Olympic Games in Sydney: the achievement of getting there, the uniqueness, and the magic.

All in, I managed Ireland 68 times, but if you take into account the smaller meets, the various trips across Europe – 'friendlies', as they'd be known in other sports – that number would be well in excess of 80. I wore the Irish badge with real honour every single time and the feeling never dimmed once.

There were difficult times, but the fact that I was the Irish manager was never lost on me.

The Olympic Games were everything to me.

The litmus test of everyone in athletics is the Olympic Games. Everyone relates to the Olympics; the iconic event.

I ran so far to get to the Olympics.

It took so much courage to just go out the door and run in the 1960s when I started off. It was normal when I was at school in Derry, but in Ballybofey it marked me out as being different. It was the same when I came back from London – where groups of runners used to always be out jogging in the parks – and started running in Glenties.

People couldn't get their heads around me.

It always seemed as if I was the one runner in a world where nobody else ran.

PATSY MCGONAGLE
RECORD AS IRISH ATHLETICS TEAM MANAGER
1992-2017

4 Olympic Games
Sydney 2000, Beijing 2008, London 2012, Rio 2016

6 IAAF World Championships
Osaka 2007, Berlin 2009, Daegu 2011, Moscow 2013, Beijing 2015, London 2017

6 European Championships
Munich 2002, Gothenburg 2006, Barcelona 2010, Helsinki 2012, Zurich 2014, Amsterdam 2016

3 World Indoor Championships
Valencia 2008, Doha 2010, Istanbul 2012

5 European Indoor Championships
Birmingham 2007, Torino 2009, Paris 2011, Gothenburg 2013, Belgrade 2017

5 IAAF World Cross Country Championships
Limerick 1979, Belfast 1999, Dublin 2002, Brussels 2004, Edinburgh 2008

4 European Cross Country Championships
Edinburgh 2003, Heringsdorf 2004, Tilburg 2005, Dublin 2009

3 IAAF World Race Walking Cup
Saransk 2012, Taicaing 2014, Rome 2016

5 European Race Walking Cup
Leamington 2007, Olhao 2011, Dudince 2013, Podebrady 2017

17 European Team Championships/European Cup
Dublin 1994, Dublin 1997, Lahti 1999, Bydgoszcz 2000, Vaasa 2001, Tallinn 2002, Aarhus 2003, Banská Bystrica 2006, Vaasa 2007, Tallinn 2008, Leiria 2009, Budapest 2010, Izmir 2011, Dublin 2013, Tallinn 2014, Heraklion 2015, Vaasa 2017

2 World Junior Championships
Seoul 1992, Lisbon 1994

1 European Junior Championships
Nyíregyháza 1995

1 European U23 Championships
Gothenburg 1999

3 World University Games
Beijing 2001, Daegu 2003, Izmir 2005

1 World University Cross Country Championships
Luton 1998

1 World Military Cross Country Championships (CISM)
Curragh 1995

1 Celtic Cup
Falkirk 2007

PATSY MCGONAGLE
MANAGEMENT MEDALS WON BY IRISH ATHLETES

2 Olympic Medallists
Sonia O'Sullivan (silver), Robert Heffernan (bronze)

9 World Championship Medallists
Olive Loughnane (gold), Robert Heffernan (gold)
Antoine Burke (silver), Team Ireland (bronze - Sonia O'Sullivan 7th, Ann Keenan-Buckley 10th, Rosemary Ryan 18th (19th), Maria McCambridge 50th (62nd), Valerie Vaughan 64th, Maureen Harrington 92nd)

27 European Championship Medallists
David Gillick (gold), Sonia O'Sullivan (two silver), Derval O'Rourke (two silver), James Nolan (two silver), Mark English (silver), Team Ireland (silver - Sonia O'Sullivan 4th, Rosemary Ryan 13th, Ann Kennan Buckley 27th, Catherina McKiernan 34th, Marie Davenport 52nd), Derval O'Rourke (two bronze), Robert Heffernan (bronze), Mark English (bronze), Ciara Mageean (bronze), Roisin McGettigan (bronze), Mary Cullen (bronze), Ciarán Ó Lionáird (bronze), Fionnuala Britton (bronze), Kate Veale (bronze), Team Ireland (bronze – Alex Wright 6th, Robert Heffernan 13th, Cian McManamon 26th)

11 World University Games medallists
Gareth Turnbull (silver), Paul Hession (two silver), Ailis McSweeney (silver), Jolene Byrne (bronze), Derval O'Rourke (bronze), Team Ireland (bronze - Derval O'Rourke, Anna Boyle, Ailis McSweeney, Emily Maher)

IRISH ATHLETICS OLYMPIC TEAM MANAGERS

1924	Major General William Murphy	1976	Ronnie Long
1928	Dr Robert Rowlette	1980	Liam Hennessy
1932	Harry Cannon	1984	PL Curran
1948	Jack Palmer and	1988	Chris Wall
	Charlie Rothwell	1992	Paddy Marley
1952	Billy Morton	1996	Nick Davis
1956	Lord Killanin	2000	Patsy McGonagle
1960	Louis Vandendries	2004	Michael Quinlan
1964	Louis Vandendries	2008	Patsy McGonagle
1968	Brendan Foreman	2012	Patsy McGonagle
1972	Eddie Spillane	2016	Patsy McGonagle

IRISH TEAM MANAGERS AT
IAAF WORLD ATHLETICS CHAMPIONSHIPS

1983	Bobbie Begley	2003	Michael McKeon
1987	Ronnie Long	2005	Georgina Drumm
1991	Chris Wall	2007	Patsy McGonagle
1993	Fr. Liam Kelleher	2009	Patsy McGonagle
1995	Chris Wall	2011	Patsy McGonagle
1997	Nick Davis	2013	Patsy McGonagle
1999	Michael Quinlan	2015	Patsy McGonagle
2001	Paddy Marley	2017	Patsy McGonagle

IRISH TEAM MANAGERS AT
EUROPEAN ATHLETICS CHAMPIONSHIPS

1954	Billy Morton	1990	Bobbie Begley
1958	Frank Cahill	1994	Michael Quinlan
1962	Frank Cahill	1998	Paddy Marley
1966	Frank Duffy	2002	Patsy McGonagle
1969	Jimmy Kelly	2006	Patsy McGonagle
1971	Dermot McDermott	2010	Patsy McGonagle
1974	Ronnie Long	2012	Patsy McGonagle
1978	Dermot McDermott	2014	Patsy McGonagle
1982	Dermot McDermott	2016	Patsy McGonagle
1986	Paul O'Connor	2018	Paul McNamara

IRISH TEAM MANAGERS AT
IAAF WORLD INDOOR CHAMPIONSHIPS

1987	Ronnie Long	2004	Michael Quinlan
1989	Ronnie Long	2006	Paddy Marley
1991	Sean Naughton	2008	Patsy McGonagle
1993	Liam Hennessy	2010	Patsy McGonagle
1995	Bobbie Begley	2012	Patsy McGonagle
1997	Liam Hennessy	2014	Kevin Ankrom
1999	Liam Hennessy	2016	Kevin Ankrom
2001	Georgina Drumm	2018	Paul McNamara
2003	Paddy Marley